JOHN LAW

As a young Scottish financier, John Law was brilliant, unusually handsome, and daring. For killing his man in a duel over a woman he was forced to flee to Amsterdam where he became a close student of Dutch trade and banking practices, then the most advanced in the world. Returning to the British Isles in 1700, by special arrangement with the Crown, he failed in his attempt to convince the British Parliament of the need for a national bank and in frustration departed for France. In Paris he was soon known to many of the foremost figures of French finance, and with the economy critically shaky he was able to persuade Philippe II, duc d' Orleans, Regent for the child king Louis XV, to back his extraordinary scheme for issuing unsecured paper money. Under it anyone could get rich quick, including Law and the Regent, who did.

Law founded his own royal bank and soon controlled all of France's improving finances. To back up the resulting orgy of uncurbed speculation, he advertised the fabled riches to be found in the French

(continued on back flap)

(continued from front flap)

colonies of the Mississippi Valley, particularly Louisiana, described as a land filled with mountains of gold and silver, and precious gems to be picked up from the river shores. In 1720 the "Mississippi Bubble" burst, ruining thousands of investors. Law's whole monetary system quickly collapsed and he fled to Venice where, after supporting himself ably for nine years with his mathematical knowledge of gambling, he died unattended and unmourned.

This biography of the father of paper currency portrays the life of a financial genius which was as fantastic as his successes, along with the defects in his System which brought about his downfall.

5-28-75

John Law

THE FATHER
OF PAPER MONEY

ROBERT MINTON

ASSOCIATION PRESS / NEW YORK

JOHN LAW

Copyright © 1975 by Robert Minton

Published by Association Press, 291 Broadway, New York, N.Y. 10007

International Standard Book Number: 0-8096-1904-0
Library of Congress Catalog Card Number: 75-15734

Library of Congress Cataloging in Publication Data

Minton, Robert, 1918–
John Law, the father of paper money.

Bibliography: p. 279
Includes index.
1. Law, John, 1671–1729.   2. Capitalists and financiers—Biography.   3. Paper Money—France—History.
I. Title.
HG172.L3M55   332'.092'4 [B]   75-15734
ISBN 0-8096-1904-0

PRINTED IN THE UNITED STATES OF AMERICA

1882180

for GAM

Acknowledgments

My wife, Lal, a teacher of French and a student of French civilization, introduced me to France and French history. This eventually led to John Law, whom we came upon in the bookcase of an apartment in Paris loaned to us by our good friend Alfred DeF. Keys. Thereafter Lal often accompanied me to the Bibliothèque Nationale and other libraries in Paris, London, Edinburgh, Aix-en-Provence, taking notes and guiding me to useful sources. Her insight and comments on the manuscript were invaluable.

M. Le Comte Louis Law de Lauriston and Mme. La Comtesse were kind enough to receive us at their lovely chateau, Chantepie par Couterne in Normandy, and provided useful documentation of Law's descendants.

Encouragement to persevere in this study came from many colleagues at Boston University following publication of my article on John Law in the Boston University *Journal*. I should particularly like to thank Professor Kurt Ackermann, Professor Sidney Burrell, Professor Nancy Roelker, and Professor Karel Holbik. Howard Gotlieb, director of Special Collections at Mugar Library, read the manuscript and made valuable suggestions.

M. Henry de Montferrand was kind enough to obtain a reproduction of a painting of John Law which hangs in the Versailles Museum. I owe a special thanks to Margaret Amaral for typing the manuscript with such assiduity and patience. Others who helped in one way or another in the completion of this work include Ralph and Betty Woodward, Aleksander Leyfell, and Max Gartenberg. William Minto, of the National Library in Edinburgh, gave us a private tour of Lauriston Castle, of which he was curator at the time.

R. M.

Concord, Mass.

Contents

14. Manon Lescaut   144
15. A Portfolio Is Worth a Mass   152

THE CRASH

16. Winter of Discontent   163
17. Crime in the Streets   176
18. Inflating the Bubble   183
19. Fatal Edict   195
20. *La Peste*   207

THE END

21. A Splintered Carriage   217
22. Liquidating the System   226
23. In Exile Once More   234
24. The Beau's Return   245
25. Death in Venice   256

     Epilogue   265

     Appendix: John Law's Legacies   269
     Selected Bibliography   279
     Index   283

Introduction

In France the grade-school textbooks generally carry a paragraph on John Law that the children easily remember. He created so much stock speculation in the rue Quincampoix, the story goes, that a hunchback made a fortune by renting out his back as a desk for traders signing contracts. In New Orleans, Law is remembered for founding the city and for instigating the Mississippi Bubble, which burst in 1720 and ruined hundreds of thousands in France. It is seldom remembered that John Law was a financial genius and a monetary theorist of the first magnitude, that he was the most popular man in Europe in 1719, that he was two centuries in advance of his time in his ideas about money, and that having risen to be the most powerful man in the government of the Duke of Orleans, he tried to use his power to correct the evils that were violently addressed half a century later by the French Revolution. His virtues have been overshadowed by the catastrophic collapse of the currency he created, and his name has become unjustly associated with crackpot schemes, doubtful adventures and financial charlatanism. In his own country of Scotland he is almost completely forgotten.

The reader may require a brief sketch of the condition of Europe in the early 18th century. In 1715 France was the richest and most powerful country in Europe—and almost bankrupt! The French

lacked a sound financial system such as their chief rivals the Dutch
and English had evolved. For two centuries a revolution in international commerce had been going on, owing to the flood of gold
and especially silver from Latin American mines. Bullion was
turned into coins, and coins became the medium of exchange that
allowed Europe to leave behind the commercial limitations of the
Middle Ages with its cumbersome bartering of goods and services
that had isolated even Mediterranean Europe from the Levant and
Eastern Roman Empire.

However, navigation alone was not sufficient to create dynamic
new trade routes. It was the combination of the precious metals
plus oceangoing fleets that made the Renaissance possible. France
profited less than others from the new conditions because of her
enormous internal wealth. Smaller countries relying on foreign trade
were forced to pay more attention to the subtleties of finance arising
out of a vast new source of wealth. Money required more sophisticated management than the French realized.

To mediate in the exchange of money the new profession of
banking arose, starting in Italy, where those handling coins worked
at benches—*banco* is Italian for "bench." The English word
"counter" is a reminder that modern commerce required transactions involving the counting of coins on a high table. The enormous convenience of exchanging coins as against exchanging the
goods themselves (a pig for a cask of wine for example) was thus
ensured by experts who assayed the specie, stored large quantities
for the convenience of customers, and eventually loaned this idle
money to merchants in need of it. Goldsmiths and others who
had accumulated money in commerce which they were willing to
lend out were the bankers of the 17th century. They operated in-
dependently and there was no national system of finance until the
Dutch Republic's Bank of Amsterdam began to provide the capital
for an enormous colonial development in Indonesia plus a smaller
effort in North America.

When the English made peace with the Dutch and actually installed the Dutch stadholder William of Orange on their throne,
they imported from Amsterdam the idea of a national bank and

created the Bank of England to centralize large-scale government borrowing. This eliminated the disadvantage of borrowing from separate private bankers at usurious interest rates and gave the English Government a financial stability totally lacking in France. The significance of the Bank of England in Britain's rise to world dominance through the creation of the British Empire and the successive defeats of France under Louis XIV, Louis XV and Napoleon Bonaparte was such that without the bank the course of world history would probably have been quite different. By centralizing government borrowing in one institution, England was able to establish the credit necessary to carry on its expansion and to defend its interests with military force. "British credit," the historian R. R. Palmer has written, "as much as anything else defeated not only Louis XIV but also Napoleon."

Credit is another word for faith in the future. It was John Law's astute observation that France had failed to take advantage of the possibilities offered by a sound central credit system operating through a central bank. Incredibly, the French Government in the last days of Louis XIV was virtually without a sou. Law was convinced that the French Government under the rapidly sinking Louis XIV was ready to adopt some kind of central banking system such as those of its rivals Holland and England, but distinguished from them by having a bank of issue from which large amounts of banknotes would be distributed as legal tender. At that time only merchants and men of wealth exchanged commercial bills and receipts as a form of currency; circulation was limited to a small community of people who knew and trusted one another. By generalizing the circulation of paper money, Law hoped quickly to tap the dormant commercial energy of Europe's largest country.

In the spring of 1714 he left The Hague to settle in Paris and materialize plans he had been discussing and refining in great detail in persuasive pamphlets and memoranda written during a ten-year period. Law's vision was to stimulate a rapid recovery by means of radical innovations which called for the widest distribution of paper currency yet attempted in European experience.

JOHN LAW

THE PROMISE

France with her rich resources
seemed on the brink of ruin . . .
France cried out for a great
statesman to give her relief.

(*Cambridge Modern History*)

1

Gold Out of Paper

When you got within 20 miles of Paris and the wind was blowing your way, you could smell the city. To John Law, riding in a carriage on the muddy road from the Netherlands border this ought to have evoked memories of his youth in Edinburgh, where the cry of *gardy loo!* warned pedestrians that a chamber pot was being emptied into the street from a window high above. *Gardy loo* was a corruption of the French *gardez l'eau*, meaning "watch out for water." Open sewage was the price paid for urbanization in the modern world.

A city like Paris, with its 600,000 inhabitants, was already the exciting and invigorating center of commerce, culture and entertainment that drew thousands of visitors from the provinces and from abroad. What, after all, was the filth of the city compared to the filth and misery of the countryside? "A great ravaged hospital without sustenance," Fénelon, the Archbishop of Cambrai called it. Paris, Europe's leading capital, ignored this human tragedy.

John Law was coming to Paris in the spring of 1714 to change all that. "I shall," he said, "make gold out of paper." He had been saying this as early as 1702. He had publicly proposed in 1705 to the Scottish Parliament that it establish a land bank and issue paper money, but had aroused no interest. Now, at the age of forty-three, he wished to create in France for the first time the institution that is taken for granted in our twentieth century—a central bank that would issue paper money to create credit and stimulate production and commerce. He promised to make of France "the retreat of the happy and the refuge of the unfortunate," a phrase that seems more appropriate to an open colonial America than to the closed dictatorship of Louis XIV. But such hyperbole was at the very roots of his character. His was an Alexandrian mentality that literally encompassed the whole world as its field of economic operations. Later, his promise was "to surprise Europe by the changes my bank will bring in favor of France—changes more profound than have resulted from the discovery of the Indies or the introduction of credit."

Law was not completely unknown in Paris. He had been there off and on since his youth when as a Scot he had been welcome because of the traditional friendship between the French court and the House of Stuart. He had visited the Old Pretender, then living in exile at St. Germain-en-Laye. Once Law had addressed memorandums to Mme. de Maintenon, suggesting that he be allowed to organize a bank for France. He had discussed his ideas with the Marquis de Chamillard when he was finance minister. The Duke of Orleans knew Law and understood his theories about money and banking and thought well of them. Orleans was a powerful man and destined to be the all-powerful Regent. Saint-Simon, the great court memorialist, spoke kindly of Law, a rare compliment from that waspish raconteur. For the powerful Prince of Conti, Law had written a treatise on money in 1707. As a well-to-do foreigner who traveled widely, Law had made influential acquaintances abroad and they kept his name alive. Also he had been much in and out of Paris during the past year. "Jean Lass" many called him because of the difficulty of saying his name in French.

Victor Amadeus II, the Duke of Savoy, had been deeply impressed by Law's cogently written memorandum to him on banks, and Law had wished to establish the Bank of Turin for him. It was the duke's suggestion that France provided the best opportunity for such a scheme, because it had an absolute government with the power to deal with opponents and to ride out lapses in public confidence.

John Law waited two years before following this advice. He could afford to wait. He had become a wealthy man in the banking centers of the Continent by trading in securities and by foreign exchange speculation, for he had mastered those complexities in his twenties when he was forced to live abroad. Along with a fortune he had acquired a sophistication and polish that made him welcome in the highest circles. That he was an exile, wanted in England, gave him an air of romance and mystery that he knew well how to exploit.

Starting out in London as a rakish ladies' man, handsome, six feet tall, called "Beau" Law, he had later settled down with an attractive English aristocrat, Lady Catherine Knollys, who was of the same family as Anne Boleyn. Lady Catherine had been married to a Frenchman but had left him abruptly in 1702 to run off with the persuasive and compelling Law for a romantic life of travel and comfort in Genoa, Venice, Brussels, Geneva, and, more recently, The Hague. It seems likely that her mastery of French helped Law acquire fluency in the language and he developed a skill in writing French in a style without solecisms or foreign quirks, an impressive achievement in the eyes of the language-proud French that would be an enormous help in his projects. Now, with their son and daughter, the Laws were arriving in Paris in style. Seasoned travelers, they were at ease in the universe, confident, a bit haughty, the quintessential upper-class family.

Law himself was a curious combination of flamboyance and reticence. His appearance was imposing, and his haughty wife considered herself a member of the noblesse. Yet both were evasive about themselves. It was no secret that he dared not return to England lest he be hanged for having killed a rakehell named Beau Wilson in a duel over a woman in 1694. On the other hand, Lady Catherine did not conceal her illustrious ancestry. Little was said, however, of the circumstances of their lives together; there had been no divorce from her husband, a M. Seigneur, and therefore no marriage ceremony with Mr. Law.

It is possible that after so very many years of obscurity Law had reached that time in life when he longed to be somebody. Perhaps Lady Catherine felt the time had come for a settled home. His settling down in grand style arouses such speculations. His advertising of his heavy investment in government securities was calculated to establish his credibility and his sincere desire to put his financial genius, which no one disputed, at the King's disposal.

Prospects for organizing the first bank in the history of France were so encouraging that Law, after preliminary discussions with Nicolas Desmarets, the finance minister, decided to settle in Paris in as conspicuous a fashion as any rising man of affairs. He therefore purchased a house in the most fashionable new square, the Place Louis-le-Grand (now the Place Vendôme). This massive octagon of severe classical design by the famous Jules Hardouin-Mansart was a speculative building project that had not fulfilled its promise, for behind the imposing façades were vacant lots awaiting houses to be built against false fronts. The houses already completed belonged mostly to financiers and to tax farmers (the name given businessmen who bought the concession of collecting taxes). It was a veritable den of the wealthiest men in the kingdom, who lived by usury paid by the government in the shape of fantastically high interest rates on the loans necessary to fund the wars of Louis XIV. At Number 19 on the Place lived Antoine Crozat, second wealthiest man in France, who held the financially disastrous concession for plantations in Mississippi later to be taken over by Law. Number 13 belonged to Paul Poisson, a tax farmer presently to be ruined. Number 11 was the home of the son-in-law of the chief tax farmer, Luillier. There were some aristocrats, such as the Marquis de Latour-Maubourg at Number 10. Two doors away lived M. Paparel, the government treasurer, in two years to be condemned to death for misappropriation of funds . . . and then pardoned. At Number 18 lived financier Jerome Hurlaut's daughter, the wife of the former minister of finance. The record is not clear at what number the Laws' carriage stopped in 1714, because Law's name appears at one time or another on deeds to two-thirds of the lots on the Place.

A carriage swinging into that wide square from the rue St. Honoré would confront the heroic 13-foot bronze statue of Louis XIV on a horse prancing on an 18-foot marble base. Law must have admired François Girardon's bold sculpture and its successful casting in one piece, for in his tours of Europe he had become an art fancier and a tasteful collector. Above all, he would have appreciated the vision of greatness embodied in the work, ironic as it was at the time when the King had lost so much of what he had gained in war. For Law, however, Louis was still *le Grand*, and Law wished to serve the King and his country.

What inspired Law to purchase a *hôtel particulier* in this square? He had large sums invested in French *rentes* (annuities) and could have lived comfortably from his investments. But Law simply had too much energy, along with a determination to save France from financial chaos. Yet he had no real standing in the country. He was an exile, a man alone, unsettled, without a country. He was not considered altogether what the French call *sérieux*.

That Law thought of himself as a very important person Desmarets learned when Law casually asked him if he would order the customs inspectors at Rouen to forward furnishings shipped from The Hague to the Place Louis-le-Grand without inspection. This was a privilege reserved to the diplomatic corps, so Desmarets immediately turned down the request and made Law open his baggage at the Customs House in Paris. The finance minister was impressed by Law's assurance, however, and this incident did not hurt the reputation of the new arrival. When it became known that Desmarets was listening seriously to Law's proposals for starting up a bank, Law's reputation was further enhanced. Already he was known for his cool nerve while gambling. He would bet 10,000 to one that a player could not throw a certain number with six dice. But he knew the probability was 46,656 to one against the shooter.

At the same time, probably as a hedge, Law made overtures to the British ambassador, an old and convivial Scot friend, John Dalrymple, Earl of Stair. To the earl, Law suggested that he should return to England for no less a purpose than liquidating the huge

British national debt incurred during the long wars with Louis XIV. Stair obliged by writing to his superior, James Stanhope, British secretary of state, that Law "has a head fit for calculations of all kinds to an extent beyond anybody," and asked if Law might not be useful in drawing a plan for paying off the national debt. "In the matters he takes himself up with [he is] certainly the cleverest man that is." Stair concluded with a strong personal endorsement. The matter was pushed along channels all the way up to the new king, George I, but the thorough British bureaucracy did not fail to produce the record showing that Law was still under sentence of death and that relatives of the man he had killed in a duel were not amenable to the idea of a pardon. A Channel crossing at this time would be decidedly premature.

So Law persisted for more than a year in presenting his ideas to Desmarets and, at the Palais Royal, to the Duke of Orleans. He derived those ideas from the close study of existing banks in Italy and Holland, as well as in England and Scotland; his originality lay in the greater scope he proposed to give his bank. It would have branches throughout France, and paper currency would supplant coins for all but the smallest transactions. He was the first practicing monetarist who believed that an increase in the money supply *must* promote an increase in economic activity.

What is a commonplace today was a novelty in 1715. To a few men, Law's ideas were attractive because they promised a way out of an economic cul-de-sac. His arguments were made with logic, clarity, and force.

He was prepared to discuss any financial problem. On one occasion, Desmarets was considering lowering the interest rate on government bonds from 7 to 4 per cent (thus making bondholders take a cut of over 40 per cent in income) in order to ease the 3.5 billion livre national debt (the livre was equal to today's dollar in purchasing power). Law objected to imposing such a penalty on the public for Louis XIV's wars, however well off bondholders might be. He suggested that Desmarets could avoid a popular outcry by cutting the interest rate to 5 per cent and using the 2 per cent savings to redeem the bonds over a 25-year period.

At this time Law wrote *Memoire sur Les Banques,* which he delivered to Desmarets in July of 1715 at the magnificent Chateau of Marly, where the French royal court was installed that summer. Law's ideas on banking were by now becoming well known. Desmarets himself was more interested in Law's proposed bank now, especially because Law said he would stand behind it with a personal guarantee of 500,000 livres.

Louis languished at Versailles quite aware of his diminishing hold on his realm and on life itself. He struggled to cast his shadow on future events from the grave by arranging a regency for his successor, his five-year-old great-grandson. "I know how futile it is," he told Mary of Modena, wife of the exiled Pretender to the throne of England. "We do what we choose whilst we are alive, but after we are dead we have less power than ordinary individuals." He spoke of the days "when I was king."

In this summer of 1715, King Louis XIV drew up a will. His intent was to bestow his power on the Duke of Maine, his bastard son whom he had recently legitimized, by putting him in charge of the upbringing of the royal child Louis XV and also making him commander of the royal troops. This would reduce the Duke of Orleans to being Regent in name only. The Duke of Orleans, however, had other plans.

The King died on September 1, 1715. "Though the life and death of Louis XIV were alike glorious, he was not mourned as he deserved," wrote Voltaire. On September 2, Orleans, who had secured the support of the magistrates against the court of military noblemen, made a powerful speech to the Paris Parlement, requesting plenary powers that would nullify Louis's will and make the Duke of Maine little more than a glorified royal guardian. The Regency had begun.

Law had arrived in the spring of 1714, and by the fall of 1715 his immediate object was within his grasp. Call it luck, call it audacity, call it persistent petitioning, call it what one will, it was a remarkable accomplishment in such a short time, and for Law it suggested that his success was not only inevitable, but that it would henceforth come quickly. Yet even he could scarcely have dreamed that soon there would be hundreds of carriages of the rich and influential outside his house while their owners waited for a moment of his time.

How did the greatest nation then on earth reach such a desperate point that it seemed to Orleans it badly needed John Law, financial soldier of fortune, a Scot, a Protestant in a land that had forced 200,000 Protestants to leave the country? When this is understood, it may be more comprehensible how Orleans allowed Law to become the most powerful man in France.

2

A Bankrupt Kingdom

You will be a great king, but your happiness will depend upon your submission to God, and the care which you take to relieve your people. For this reason you must avoid war as much as possible. It is the ruin of the people. Do not follow the bad example I have set you. I have undertaken war too lightly, and have continued it from vanity. Do not imitate me, but be a pacific prince, and let your chief occupation be to relieve your subjects.

Those were the dying words of Louis XIV to his grandson. It is a just judgment of what Louis XIV, for all his contributions to art and culture and urban civility, wrought with his absolutism. In his last years, even nature seemed to turn against him, for during the terrible winter of 1708–09, after a disastrous drought, thousands of his subjects starved to death—and France was the world's richest country a hundred years before. Five years later, the malaise of the realm was acknowledged in the Treaty of Utrecht, which may be likened to the first of a series of cancer operations on French international supremacy. Gibraltar, Minorca, Newfoundland, Hudson Bay Territory could be ceded to the British without fatality, as a patient gives up this organ or that without giving up his life. Under Louis XIV, France reached the peak of power and prestige about 1684; thereafter the country stagnated economically.

"The history of the seventeenth century shows France rising from anarchy and poverty caused by forty years of civil and religious wars to become the most powerful and influential country in Europe," a modern commentator has said. The installation of the House of Bourbon at the end of the sixteenth century had stabilized the country by authorizing, in the Edict of Nantes (1598), the coexistence of a virtual Protestant state within a Catholic state. During the first half of the seventeenth century, two political geniuses acting as prime ministers, Richelieu and the Italian, Mazarin, checked the power of the Protestant Huguenots as well as the power of proud and independent-minded noblemen by establishing a strong central government, which has persisted in varying shapes to this day.

A bureaucracy of brilliant bourgeois administrators wielded vast influence. Major wars were avoided, while the frontiers of France were extended to approximately their present limits. Under these conditions, "modernization" could take place in the form of road and canal building, the development of industry—particularly textiles and porcelain—and the regulation of commerce. Foundations of a colonial empire were laid.

Achievement of this equilibrium required an absolute monarchy with all its cruelties, injustices, powers of arbitrary arrest, and vast indifference to the welfare of the lower orders. Worse, ironically, was an indifference to the craving for prestige and social usefulness of an aristocracy largely excluded from the management of public affairs (particularly financial matters) and from the making of decisions affecting the growth and glory of their country. Idleness among vigorous and proud men will inevitably find some political expression, and in this instance various noble factions, which could never quite put together a workable coalition, challenged the monarchy's absolutism and the ministers of the central government. For a period of five years (1648–53), a series of fruitless disorders were instigated as expressions of hostility to an arbitrary government. The sporadic violence of these rebellions was limited, yet it constituted a kind of civil war. These troubled times were given the curious name of The Fronde, which was a sling used by street urchins to hurl rocks at passing carriages. An *opera bouffe* quality characterized many of the open conflicts. Voltaire gives this description of the nature of the occasion:

The Parisians sallied into the fields dressed out with feathers and ribands, and their evolutions were a standing jest among regular soldiers. They fled on encountering two hundred men of the royal army. Everything was turned into a jest; the regiment of Corinth having been defeated by a handful of men, their defeat was known as *the first Corinthians*.

But one man failed to see the humor in it all. Louis XIV, then a boy of twelve and highly impressionable, always remembered the frightening night a mob broke into the Tuileries and demanded to see the King, who lay in his bed feigning sleep while the whispering curious gawked and departed satisfied, doubtless unaware of the historic consequences their traumatic visit was to have. The victims of Louis's anxiety were not the common people, but the nobility, whose emasculation became one of the guiding principles of his domestic policy. To insure himself against any recurrence of noble opposition, he eventually removed the center of government from Paris to the nearby and still uncelebrated suburb of Versailles.

Cunningly he expanded a gloomy old hunting lodge, a dozen miles from the capital, into what amounted to a magnificent garden apartment house. There he lodged from time to time, at tremendous expense, up to 10,000 members of the nobility from all over France. These guests were obliged to furnish themselves with the costliest and most ridiculous wardrobes in the history of costuming and to pass the hours in idle gossip, social intrigue, love affairs, card games, and ambling promenades in the meticulously groomed groves. An invitation to Versailles was a sentence of imprisonment in the most sparse and uncomfortable of quarters, and the fact that the greatest of noblemen would forsake the independence of their own chateaux for the boredom and vicious social rivalry of Versailles was the measure of Louis's success in subduing the aristocracy and guaranteeing his own absolutism.

Louis was a great manipulator of men. To prevent any untoward acquisition of aristocratic power, he made it unfashionable for the nobility to work and gave only to talented commoners like Colbert the responsibility for conducting the affairs of government. Upstarts seeking to rival the King were warned by the hideous example of Nicholas Fouquet, the superintendent of finances, who was sentenced to life imprisonment (1664–80) for daring to display too great wealth, unscrupulously amassed.

W. H. Lewis, in his book *The Splendid Century*, summarizes the nature of Versailles thus:

The enormous *chateau* of Versailles, with its ten thousand inhabitants, in which was spent six out of every ten francs collected in taxes, was something more than a mere seat of government. To the man or woman of ambition it was a lottery in which the prizes were dazzling, and in which few could resist the temptation to take a ticket. The country gentleman, sulking in enforced idleness in his manor house, did not stop to consider how long were the odds against drawing a prize; had not X, no whit better than himself, got a regiment, and little Y, the joke of the province, a court office?

While the potential rivalry (and service) of strong men was thus being dissipated, highly capable public servants made Louis's regime at first envied for its domestic progress and then feared for martial aggressiveness beyond its borders. Colbert's promotion of commerce provided funds with which to extend French conquests in the Lowlands and on its eastern frontier, where Lorraine was occupied in 1670. But war with the Dutch Republic was frustrated by the opening of the dikes and led to the foundation of European coalitions that eventually nullified most of Louis's military gains and introduced the hideous slaughter of modern warfare, the War of the Spanish Succession, last of the general European wars caused by the efforts of Louis XIV to extend French power.

The apogee had been reached in 1684. Colbert was now dead and Louvois, the efficient military administrator, was aging. Such men could not be replaced. "It is the nemesis of all autocracies that sooner or later, for lack of the vivifying breath of freedom, they cease to command the best services of the highest and the best men," wrote H. A. L. Fisher. And circumstances worked against Louis. His Catholic friend, Charles II, died in 1685, the English eventually acquired the Dutch war hero, William of Orange, for their king, and the Anglo-Dutch rivalry was turned into an unbeatable alliance.

Louis's revocation of the Edict of Nantes in 1685 ended the toleration of a Protestant sect of a million people, a decision that was as stupid as it was cruel, for it divided international forces by driving Protestant countries into an anti-Catholic alliance, and it disrupted the domestic economy by forcing 200,000 Huguenots to take their wealth and skills abroad.

There was no economic growth, and in some instances actual decline occurred in the last twenty-seven years of Louis's long reign. The population failed to increase, while the debts incurred by war rose so that they outpaced revenues by several years. The codfish fleet dropped from 300 to 18 vessels, Protestants took the hat trade to London, and in the city of Sedan 2,000 clothmakers were unemployed. Suffering was widespread enough for the Archbishop of Cambrai to ask in his *Questions for the Royal Conscience*: "Have you sought means of relieving the common people and taking from them only what the true needs of the state require you to take for their advantage?" and Pierre Jurieu in *The Sighs of Enslaved France*, commenting on taxes, wrote: "It will suffice to enable you to understand the horrible oppression of these taxes by showing (1) the immense sums that are collected, (2) the violence and abuses that are committed in levying them, (3) the bad use that is made of them, and (4) the misery to which the people are reduced."

France was still a rich country, badly mismanaged, but despite tensions still at peace with itself; civil war had been avoided and no enemy had crossed its borders. Modern times had begun and there was progress in the form of improved agricultural techniques —clover and root crops were developed to keep cattle alive in winter, garden crops were marketed in the cities, good beer was brewed because of the good barley and hops available. Technology increased productivity, particularly in the building trades, so that four men could do the work of forty in cutting stone and timber for a castle or a house. Indeed, the workers' fear of progress made it difficult to build hard roads because of the wear on cartwheels and horseshoes. But more transport was hauled by water than by land, and with the building of canals, marketing centers grew into cities and the city of cities, Paris, became the largest in Europe.

We should thank Louis XIV for Paris rather than for Versailles, whose splendor has an artificial character compared to the organic development of the city. Not wanting his government in town did not blind him to the need for expanding and beautifying Paris, and his intolerance of criticism, enforced by censorship, could not prevent a spirit of freedom from growing. A new kind of man was developing.

This Parisian *mondain* owed his style of life as much to Louis XIV as did the frustrated courtier of Versailles. The withdrawal of the court freed Paris from its worst influences, and the city was the beneficiary of the King's generosity, for he was a builder and he encouraged with ample grants of royal funds the tearing down of much of the fortified walls that ringed its limits, and the construction of shaded avenues more than twenty yards wide that later became the famous great boulevards. During the same period when Versailles was expanding, between 1667 and 1676, Paris, under Colbert's supervision, was transformed from a medieval city prepared to resist sieges into an open city welcoming new residents and travelers from all over the world.

In the middle of the eighteenth century, Voltaire wrote of Louis XIV's contribution to Paris:

The city of Paris was very far from being what it is today. The streets were unlighted, unsafe and dirty. It was necessary to find money for the constant cleaning of the streets, for lighting them every night with five thousand lamps, completely paving the whole city, building two new gates and repairing the old ones, keeping the permanent guard, both foot and mounted, to ensure the safety of the citizens. The king charged himself with everything, drawing upon funds for such necessary expenses. In 1667 he appointed a magistrate whose sole duty was to superintend the police. Most of the large cities of Europe have imitated these examples long afterwards, none has equalled them. There is no city paved like Paris, and Rome is not even illuminated.

During Louis's reign, physician and architect Claude Perrault built the Louvre colannade; André LeNôtre, director of royal gardens, laid out the Tuileries gardens; the Invalides, the Observatoire, the College des Quatre Nations (now the Institut de France), the Porte St. Denis, the Porte St. Martin, and the Gobelins factory all were built; the wooden Pont Royal was replaced by the extant one of stone, and the first grand quais on the Seine were installed. Also, the concept of open squares appeared in the Place des Victoires and the Place Louis-le-Grand, both dominated by statues of the King himself. By 1702 Paris, with its 600,000 inhabitants, was almost three times the size it was in 1610 when Henry IV was assassinated.

While Louis was reigning as an absolute monarch, watchful of any organized opposition, an opposition of another kind was developing in two Parisian institutions, the salon and the café. A spirit of freedom was growing out of the lively discussion of new ideas that preceded the writings of *les philosophes*. The period "contains the seeds not only of that general rejection of authority in the name of reason which is known as the Enlightenment, but even of the later Romantic reassertion of the claims of feeling and imagination. These conflicting intellectual and literary forces reflect the underlying tensions of the age." * Censorship made it dangerous to publish ideas that challenged the status quo. The great Fénelon, whose intellectual stature was honored by Louis, was nonetheless banished to the provinces for his penetrating critique of the regime; Jansenists, the radical Catholics of the time, were persecuted for merely writing letters considered offensive, and their headquarters at Port Royale was finally razed by royal edict in 1709.

But it was impossible to raze the lively drawing rooms of Paris, and with the vast import of coffee from Ethiopia and Yemen, the

* Jean Meuvret, *The New Cambridge Modern History* (New York: Cambridge University Press, 1951).

cafés came into being as forums of noisy discussion. As in Eastern Europe today, there was no freedom to publish in Louis XIV's France, but there was freedom of conversation. The nineteenth-century historian Jules Michelet describes the impact of the café in the following rather romantic passage:

Before the play begins, let us look at the theatre. Long before Law's System, Paris become one huge cafe. Three hundred cafes opened for conversation. . . . France never talked more, or better.

The impact [of the coffee house] was incalculable—not being weakened and neutralized by the degradation of tobacco. People took snuff, to be sure, but smoked little. The reign of the young cabaret was over, the ignoble cabaret, where the young bloods in Louis XIV's time alternated between the bottle and the tart. Fewer drunken songs shattered the night, and the gutters were less filled with drunken lords. . . . With the reign of the cafe came temperance.

Coffee, liquor of sobriety, powerfully cerebral, which unlike alcohol increases sharpness and lucidity; coffee, which suppresses the vague and heavy poetry of imagination's fumes, which seeing reality clearly evokes the sparkle and clarity of truth; anti-erotic coffee, which replaces the alibi of sex with spiritual excitation. . . .

This vast conversational movement shaping the character of the time, this excessive sociability which so quickly brings together passersby and joins them in cafes to chatter and gossip—what was its purpose, its subject matter? Minor legislative rebellions, Jansenism? Certainly, but many other things too. . . . People preferred to talk about Law, about his unusual rise to power, about the republic of speculators he was undertaking to create.

More than any man of his day in France, John Law was prepared to act on what others were only talking about over their exotic cups of coffee at café tables. The islands, India, America excited in him fantastic concepts of empire at a moment when the French colonial impulse was fading. But the immediate problem was what John F. Kennedy defined for America in 1960, to "get the country going." This was Law's immodest boast—that his bank, by creating money, paper money, would stimulate the economy, establish credit, and generate public confidence sadly lacking in a country that had revalued its coinage forty times since 1690! Whether or not Orleans, the Regent, actually believed Law's claims in the beginning, he was prepared to let Law undertake his experiment. What, after all, had Orleans to lose?

Shortly after taking office in 1715, Orleans, a brilliant but indecisive administrator, discovered the sorry condition of the finances he had to manage. As English historian H. A. L. Fisher put it: "The internal problems of France which first in the later years of Louis XIV had begun to attract the attention of the philosophical thinkers were primarily financial." The national debt was discovered to have risen to 3.5 billion livres, and the Council of Regency considered repudiation. In addition, there was an annual budget deficit of 80 million livres. Louis had been living beyond his means; his ministers had known it but dared not protest. It is to Orleans's credit that he took the pains to inform himself of the facts and set about reorganizing the administrative structure of government throughout the country. And still he had time to consult with Law and encourage him to place his proposal before a newly formed Finance Council, which heard Law's arguments for creating a national bank on October 24, less than two months after the Regency had begun.

Orleans's support of Law's bank proposition was cautious and the opposition of a dozen bankers and merchants present was vocal, only four favoring the bank. The majority of the council opposed it, and Orleans said that he must reluctantly agree to ask Law to withdraw the proposal.

The establishment of merchant-bankers, the men who had made what has been called the financial revolution, that is, the dependence of government on private money loaned at high interest, saw in Law's scheme a threat to their own enterprises. Orleans prudently retreated in their presence, but only to allow himself time to gather the strength he needed to allow Law to proceed— a period, it turned out, of only six months.

3

With a Certain Sword

John Law was born April 21, 1671, the sixth of thirteen children of William Law. The name Law was not uncommon in Scotland; in the Scots tongue it means a hill. John's grandfather, John Law of Neilston, had been a parish minister until he became suspected of Royalist sympathies shortly after the execution of Charles I in 1649. He was then deprived of the living, and had to take his family from the rectory to the anonymity of Edinburgh, where he apprenticed his two sons, John and William, as goldsmiths. There were goldsmiths of long standing in Edinburgh named Law and it is probable that there was some blood relationship between them and John Law, the rector of Neilston.

However this may be, his son William turned out to be an exceptional businessman. After twelve years as an apprentice, he joined the prestigious Goldsmiths Incorporation and was entitled to wear the scarlet cloak and cocked hat and to carry the long gold-headed cane of his calling. He was a good craftsman, but it was not as an artisan that William excelled. His great success was to come as a banker. Goldsmithing was at its zenith as a result of the outpouring from South American gold fields, and goldsmiths had become the custodians of much of the coin of the realm.

The goldsmith's receipt was an early form of paper money and was the equivalent of a modern deposit slip. Goldsmiths soon realized that the coin in their vaults could be loaned out at interest, since all the depositors would never demand their money at one time. The rule was that goldsmiths could lend three out of four coins on deposit at anywhere from 8 to 25 per cent interest. Thus, it was in his father's shop in the shadow of the Scottish Parliament that John Law learned banking principles as a lad.

He also learned something about aristocracy from his mother, Jean Campbell, William Law's second wife, a member of the powerful Argyll clan, who had brought her husband a useful dowry as well as contacts with the important families who were to become clients of his goldsmithing business.

Unlike London, Edinburgh had expanded upward in the French manner and was as crowded as any city in Europe. Manufacturing and trade were meager by English standards and kept so in part by English policy; no trade with English dependencies was permitted. Cattle, salmon, raw wool, and some cloth were the chief exports.

William Law settled down in Edinburgh to the comparatively staid life of a goldsmith. In 1683 he purchased the rather stark sixteenth-century castle called Lauriston outside Edinburgh and was well on his way to becoming one of the more prominent bourgeois of his country. In this same year, however, he became ill, and for some reason he decided to make the difficult trip to Paris for medical treatment. We know from Molière what the quality of French doctors was at this time, and it is not surprising that William Law sucumbed to some kind of stones in the gloom of a Paris December, and was buried in the graveyard of the Scots College there.

At his father's death John Law was twelve years old. He had three older sisters; an older brother had died some years before. As the oldest surviving male child, he would inherit under Scottish law all his father's fortune when he reached the age of twenty-one. Such a prospect was probably not good for his character, nor was the absence of a father at this critical age. His mother, however, was a sensible woman, who managed to keep intact the more than 55,000 pounds (Scots) in her husband's estate, a considerable sum at the time. William Law's will ran to fourteen pages and was essentially an inventory of assets and of sums owed to him by men of distinction. Hamilton, Douglas, Dundonald, Seaforth, Argyll are some of the great Scottish family names that appear. Young John Law probably rubbed elbows with members of such families, some of whom would later open doors for him in London and Paris.

The record of John Law's early years is scanty. His earliest reliable biographer, John Wood, writing late in the eighteenth century, could find no "memorials" of Law's boyhood—that is, no letters, statements, or eyewitness appraisals of the lad. What we do know of the young Law is that he was unusually intelligent and of considerable physical vigor in a time when poor health was widespread. None of his many portraits, for example, show evidence of pockmarks; on the contrary, he had no facial blemishes and was extremely handsome. Also, he was reputed to be a fine tennis player. There is no doubt that he was a deft fencer, a skill he later had reason to regret. In manhood he was six feet tall— taller than most of his companions at Eaglesham School outside Edinburgh, where he was a boarding student for several years. There are no school records of his time there, but there can be little doubt of his scholastic brilliance, and not only in mathematics. His writing style later was remarkable for its forcefulness of logic and clarity. Leaving school in his late teens, young Law came home to Edinburgh to live with his family in town; apparently the Laws never lived in Lauriston Castle.

Young as he was, Law was described as "nicely expert in all manner of debaucheries" before he left Edinburgh, and it was there he probably learned gambling, at which he later excelled. By day Law worked in the family goldsmith shop, where he had an opportunity to study the principles of banking. Had he stayed in Edinburgh, Law could have become a banker-goldsmith, but he obviously was not enamored of the family business. Like any venturesome young man, his eyes were fixed on greener fields, and so in his twentieth year John Law went off to London.

Although the Glorious Revolution of 1688 had brought about

the displacement of the lax and tyrannous House of Stuart and put that sober Dutchman, William III, and his English wife, Mary, on the throne, the cynical and worldly spirit of the Restoration had not yet died out. Already initiated in the provinces into the pleasures of the evening, Law was drawn to the better fleshpots in this thriving city of 500,000.

Had Law consorted with another crowd, he would have found plenty of opportunity to use his financial and literary talents. England in 1691 was becoming the civilized country that would show men in the eighteenth century the way to liberty and prosperity. It had passed in half a century through the successive traumas of civil war, regicide, martial law, tyranny, religious strife, and the shame of a traitorous crown, and without bloodshed had seen established the first limited monarchy and the beginning of a two-party system of parliamentary government.

John Law's London was in large measure a new city, two-thirds of it having been rebuilt since the disastrous five-day fire of 1666. Christopher Wren was responsible not only for fifty new churches, including the still uncompleted St. Paul's, but also for an improved street grid that eliminated the past inconveniences of medieval lanes and passageways. Among the conveniences the city now afforded were a large number of water hydrants linked by wooden pipes to reservoirs. A penny post had been in existence for more than a decade and allowed of up to eight deliveries a day. In 1688 the whale-oil convex lights were installed, 3,000 of them, making night tolerably safe from brigands. Coffee houses were everywhere, and they became not only centers of discussion as in France but also places where business might be carried on by merchants, and where the newspapers could be read free of charge.

John Law appears to have gambled without the success he reputedly had later, and he was a lady's man about town. However, he continued to read, study, and think about the changing nature of commerce, when "political arithmetic," as economics was first called, drew the attention of writers such as John Locke and Daniel Defoe, who elaborated on theories of earlier writers of the period, particularly William Petty and Charles Davenant. But most important was the introduction into England of the theories and methods of Dutch financiers and bankers, who followed in the train of William III and shortly laid the groundwork for the creation of the Bank of England in 1694. A fellow Scotsman of Law's, William Paterson, is credited as the founder of this institution for funding the national debt and thus eliminating the crown's dependence on private bankers in time of war. If Law knew Paterson in London, he certainly did not subscribe to his ideas; a decade later he opposed them in a speech to the Scottish Parliament.

A not unbiased raconteur said of Law's early days: "He frequented the bath at Tunbridge, and all other places of pleasure, but as his fortune was not able to support the expense of these places, he turned his head to gaming to make that carry the other." There was also a more reliable source of income. In the winter of 1692, Law arranged with his mother to convey to her his inheritance of the estates of Lauriston and Randelston, and in return she provided a sufficient allowance for him to live handsomely in fashionable St. Giles-in-the-Fields. There he kept a mistress and developed a considerable acquaintance with worldly people such as Thomas Neale, master of the mint and groom porter to His Majesty, whose duties ran from the provision of metal currency to the supervision of gambling resorts. (Neale also initiated London's first lottery, in imitation of the Italian practice.)

He became known as Beau Law, and as Jessamyn John. Through his high Scottish connections such as Argyll he moved easily in the best circles, where he impressed powerful men with his amazing understanding of finance and thrilled the ladies with his dashing manner, which bordered on arrogance. His conceit, perhaps nothing more than an awareness of his unusual powers of mind, irritated younger men, and he had few close friends his own age. He found his true friends among women and was untroubled by the hostility of youths who might have been companions but generally were rivals. The fact that he considered himself destined for great things did not sit well with the natives of London, accustomed to looking down on Scotland as a barbaric land from whence came the troublesome Stuart clan. Pride forced young Law to conceal a sense of loneliness beneath a haughty indifference to the opinions of those he knew were his inferiors. He made no effort to curb a short temper, and his physical strength added an awesomeness to his sometimes quarrelsome demeanor. Despite his frequent appearances at the pleasure spots of London, he was withdrawn, a hard man to know, forever showing people up with mathematical tricks and winning money from them at dice or cards. He knew something that others did not know, and this gave him a strange attractiveness among the bankers and stock jobbers who were just then beginning to thrive.

"Nothing becomes a man like an air of mystery," Thomas Love Peacock said, alluding to Byron. A promising career in business or government or both lay ahead for Law, so long as he kept out of trouble. But that was to be the problem.

In the spring of 1694, when he was twenty-three, John Law was having a running quarrel with Edward Wilson, familiarly known as Beau Wilson, a man of no distinction but intriguing because of his ability to live extravagantly without any visible means of support. He came from a landed family of long lineage but little substance, and he was new to London. His ostentation drew the attention of the great diarist, John Evelyn, who wrote that Wilson

lived in the garb and equipage of the richest nobleman for house, furniture, coaches, saddle horses and kept a table and all things accordingly, redeemed his father's estate and gave portions to his sisters. ... The mystery is how this young gentleman, very sober and of good fame, could live in such an expensive manner; it could not be discovered by all possible industry and entreaty of his friends to make him reveal it. It did not appear that he was kept by women, play, coining, padding or dealing in chemistry; but he would sometimes say that should he live ever so long, he had wherewith to maintain himself in the same manner. He was very civil and well natur'd, but of no great force of understanding. This was a subject of much discourse.

Gossip had it, according to Evelyn, that Wilson "was supplied by the Jews; others [said] that he had discovered the philosopher's stone that changed base metal to gold, while certain good-natured folk averred that he had robbed the Holland mail of a quantity of jewelry, an exploit for which another man had suffered death."

The answer to this mystery was provided only in 1708, by Mme. de la Mothe in the appendix of her *Memoirs of the Court of England in the Reign of Charles*, entitled "The Unknown Lady's Pacquet of Letters." According to this account, Beau Wilson was lounging on the lawn of Kensington Garden when a carriage went by several times, and shortly afterward a lady's maid approached him with an invitation from her mistress in the carriage to meet her at a rendezvous. The maid would not reveal the name of her mistress, nor could Wilson get it from the lady herself, who received him masked and remained so throughout an evening of lovemaking that ended at two o'clock in the morning.

The following day, Wilson received an offer he could hardly refuse: he was given 1,500 guineas by the lady's maid and told to live in a style befitting the lover of a great woman whose identity he was never to know. Moreover, the maid warned, should he by chance or by some secret effort find her out, he would be put to death. Wilson agreed to the bargain, but being as Evelyn said "of no great understanding," Wilson after a time yearned to know with whom he was sleeping. Loaded down with her money, acquired with so little effort, he proceeded to demand that she identify herself as the ultimate token of her passion for him. She demurred, and later she unburdened her feelings to the ever convenient maid:

Ah, my dear, what things these men are! Whilst we yet have any reserve we are importuned: 'tis a supply to conversation which without a theme languishes. Love, however omnipotent he be counted, abates much of his divinity when he comes to full enjoyment. I must either see this creature no more, or resolve to disclose myself. I cannot wisely do the latter, for Wilson seems to be too weak a vessel to trust my secret to! His good fortune has turned his brain. Is he not satisfied that I love him more than I ought, without I love him as much as I can?

The maid was sent to tell Wilson that the affair was over; she assured him that he would still be comfortably provided for. But Wilson could not let well enough alone; he smugly announced that he already knew that he had been secretly consorting with Mistress Villiers, having recently seen on this well-known lady's finger his gift of a ring as she drove in her stately carriage through Hyde Park.

Mistress Villiers was Elizabeth Villiers, mistress of King William III of England. Then thirty-seven and far from beautiful, she was a woman of great intelligence, and she well understood the jeopardy in which a scandal would put her. William of Orange had no love for Englishmen and would not be forgiving of such an infidelity. Among her acquaintances was the impressive John Law, whose mind stimulated her; he in turn enjoyed confiding his troubles to the older woman as well as bragging of his exploits at the gaming table or his fencing victories in the gymnasium. One day he told Mistress Villiers about a row he was having with this impossible Beau Wilson. Wilson's sister was living primly in the same fashionable boardinghouse where Law had set up his mistress, a Mrs. Lawrence, and this arrangement was so repellent to Miss Wilson that she demanded that Law remove the woman elsewhere. Law's response was so demonstrative that the landlady said he had in effect advertised her place as a brothel. Law found quieter quarters for Mrs. Lawrence, but Miss Wilson's priggish behavior rankled, especially since her flamboyant brother was no model of propriety. The incident became a subject of tavern gossip, and Law felt that Wilson was the one who got his sister to complain about Mrs. Lawrence. He wrote warning letters to Wilson, and the quarrel deepened into enmity.

Mistress Villiers listened to Law's side of the story and sympathized with him. In fact, she expressed a strong dislike for Wilson—without explaining the reason. Law hinted at an insult he felt had been offered him, possibly cause for a duel. Mistress Villiers remarked that poor Wilson was no match for him at swords' point. But if he should kill Wilson, what would be the consequences? Mistress Villiers assured him that her connections would protect him from any punishment.

Duelling had been condemned successively in England by James I, Sir Francis Bacon, Oliver Cromwell, Samuel Pepys, and others, so that in 1660 it was banned; yet six years later the ban was lifted and duelling became fashionable again. "All classes, in fact, were now affected by the mania for duelling, and even doctors occasionally settled their professional differences at the point of the sword." *

John Law now provoked the necessary insult and Wilson foolishly challenged him. On the morning of April 9, 1694, the two men left a tavern in suburban Bloomsbury and proceeded to the empty square, where they drew swords. Law, younger, bigger, quicker, made one pass—and Wilson fell, mortally wounded. With his dying breath, he instructed his seconds to destroy all his papers, but when they searched his lodgings all they could find was a remedy for toothache. And so Mistress Villiers' secret was preserved—at least according to the only account in existence—and she became Countess Orkney.

The record of the sequel leaves no doubt of the seriousness of Law's offense. He was not one to take reckless chances, either at the gaming table or in the field, and he had reckoned on the legal sanction of duelling plus all his high connections to rid himself of a vexatious but hardly menacing man. But his calculations were insufficient. What he did not know was that Wilson's family, though neither wealthy nor powerful, was nonetheless highly enough esteemed to put enormous pressure on the judicial apparatus to bring this Scot, this foreigner (Scotland was still independent of England), to trial for murder.

Law was jailed within a day, and nine days after Wilson died, April 18, he was brought to the bar to hear the crown's indictment: "[John Law] of his malice aforethought and assault premeditated made an assault upon Edward Wilson with a certain sword made of iron and steel of the value of five shillings with which he inflicted one mortal wound of the breadth of two inches and depth of five inches, of which mortal wound the said Edward Wilson then and there instantly died."

* Robert Baldick, *The Duel: A History of Duelling* (New York: Clarkson N. Potter, Inc., 1966).

His letters to Wilson were produced in evidence; one said "there was a design of evil against him." The jury in the Old Bailey Courthouse was instructed by the seventy-five-year-old magistrate, Sir Salathiel Lovell, to regard the case as murder in view of the running quarrel preceding it, and after brief deliberation they returned a verdict of guilty, and John Law was sentenced to be hanged.

What followed is more understandable to lawyers than to laymen. Law was shortly reprieved—*but not released.* The stay of execution was due, Law later wrote, to the intercession of noble Scots, possibly including his mother's relative, the great Duke of Argyll, later to be Marlborough's powerful rival. Or perhaps Mistress Villiers exerted some influence in his behalf. Yet whatever forces were working on the King for Law, they were met by counterforces. The family of the deceased was determined to have an eye for an eye.

Edward Wilson's brother, Robert, invoked an ancient legal precedent which allowed the relative of a murder victim to appeal an acquittal or royal pardon. This primitive custom in effect made the court a party to suspension of the rule of law, whereby a settlement was made in blood after the manner of tribal feuds; the hapless defendant *had* to be executed if the relative so wished.

This civil action was begun in Westminster Hall on June 22, and never completed because Law's expert counsel engaged in such a dazzling display of irrelevant objections that the court had to study them during the summer and early autumn, while Law was studying the fine art of escaping prison. He had not learned his lessons well enough to conceal his purpose, which was to file away the bars of his cell window. Caught in the act, he next appeared in irons at the King's Bench, to hear that his counsel's legalistic arguments against the hearings of the suit were overruled and that the Wilson argument in favor of execution would be heard in January.

Hearing an imagined death knell must have concentrated John Law's attention more completely on his determination to escape, which he did shortly after New Year's 1695—supplied by friends with files, money, drugs for subduing the guards, and a carriage waiting thirty feet below his window to take him to a channel port. In the course of the escape he only sprained his ankle, a testimony to his agility.

His escape, though, created a death warrant with which he had to reckon for a generation. The kingdom was henceforth closed to him until he could obtain a royal pardon that would not be contested by the Wilson family. He was now a notorious felon in England. The London *Gazette,* a four-page weekly, carried this advertisement in its first issue of 1695:

Captain John Lawe, a Scotchman, lately a Prisoner in the King's Bench for Murther, aged 26, a very tall black lean Man, well-shaped, about Six foot high, large Pockholes in his Face, big High-Nosed, speaks broad and low, made his Escape from the said Prison. Whoever secures him so he may be delivered at the said Prison shall have £50 paid immediately by the Marshal of the King's Bench.

The inaccuracy of description raises questions as to its seriousness. Law did not spell his name with an *e,* though such a spelling was common enough; he was not a captain; he was twenty-five; he had no large pockholes that anyone subsequently remarked; he did have a large high nose, and his voice was pleasing. Certainly, £50 would not have tempted his powerful friends to betray him. Instead, they helped him aboard a boat to Holland, where he began a new and quite different life from the one he had led and almost lost in England.

4

The Regent

During his months in jail, John Law had had time to reflect on the error of his ways. The life of a beau (the term meant dandy or coxcomb) had proven unprofitable and less filled with pleasure than appearances promised. And he realized that his true interest lay in banking and finance. Moreover, when he reached Holland, he found a more serious, hard-working society in which to mingle.

Law applied himself vigorously to the study of just how this small country had made itself so rich that it rivaled England and France in power and excelled them in trade. He was able to use his connections to obtain a minor post at the British Embassy in The Hague, where according to his earliest biographer, John Wood, he worked with the poet and diplomat, Matthew Prior. He had plenty of time to visit Amsterdam to observe the workings of its two great institutions, the venerable Bank of Amsterdam, founded in 1609, and the great East India Company. The bank was the model for the Bank of England, which had just been organized with the help of Dutch experts brought to London by William III, who ironically remained Law's sovereign, since he ruled both England and Holland. The Bank of Amsterdam had grown rich through its expertise in foreign exchange, by then so internationalized that there was a manual listing 500 gold and 340 silver coins circulating in the world. Their value fluctuated, and their weights varied because of clipping or just plain wear. The bank stabilized these monies by assaying them for a depositor and giving him a credit in guilders, which remained fixed in value; the credit could be transferred to the account of anyone to whom the merchant owed money, and this guilder credit was preferable to specie. No paper money was issued by the bank. Yet Law saw these credits as a form of money, a substitute for cumbersome and unreliable coins. He also learned the business known as *agiotage*, speculating in foreign exchange, and he began to make some money to supplement his modest allowance from Edinburgh.

The East India Company was another source of fascination to him. Dutch ships dominated North Sea trading and that was remarkable enough, but the fact that they also dominated the South Seas convinced Law that there was a future in global trade. How had the Dutch managed to build so many ships? Where had the capital come from? Law discovered that the Bank of Amsterdam, a government bank owned by the city, had loaned the East India Company the money in the form of guilder credits without collateral, certain that the company's reputation for success and prudent management was sufficient guarantee, a judgment that was quite sound. But in opening a credit account against the good name of the company and not against coins on deposit, the bank had in effect issued money to pay for ships, whose builders would receive a transfer from the company's account into theirs. The bank, he concluded, was *creating* money. Here was a new and more sophisticated operation than that of the little goldsmiths' loans he had observed his father making in Edinburgh. He also learned that the bank owned 50 per cent of the company. This was no arms-length transaction.

Fascinated, he began to read existing treatises on money, banking, and trade. It was easy to find all the English books he wanted in Holland, the largest printing center in Europe. He read and thought and wrote out his own ideas, lived obscurely for several years, and began making excursions about Europe; the road system now made carriage travel practical if not always comfortable. Traces of him are few, but it is known that he visited France more than once, a curious, aloof, superior, and somewhat lonely young man who had much to say about his ideas and very little to say about his background or personal life. During this period, 1695–1703, Louis XIV was at war, first against the Grand Alliance of Austria, Holland, and England together with Spain, Sweden, and Savoy until the Treaty of Ryswick in 1697, and then after 1700 against the same grouping minus Spain and Savoy, who switched sides in the War of the Spanish Succession.

John Law avoided involvement in these conflicts. They revolted him, and besides he was torn by sympathy for Louis XIV's friend, the deposed English monarch and fellow Scot, James II. It is interesting to note that as a young man he had no hesitancy in mingling in the highest society, and it is not surprising that there in Paris in 1701 he met the woman to whom he was devoted for the rest of his life, Lady Catherine Knollys Seigneur, a direct descendant of the father of Anne Boleyn, Henry VIII's second wife. She provided the solution to his loneliness and warmly encouraged his advances, despite her marriage to a Frenchman, about whom nothing is known. Lady Catherine was the sister of the titular Earl of Banbury, and her mother was the daughter of an Irish peer, Lord Sherard. The title of Lady was gratuitously assumed. Her brother, by coincidence, was in King's Bench Prison while Law was there, on the same charge of having killed a man—his wife's brother-in-law—in a duel. One writer suggests the possibility that Law might have been led to Lady Catherine by her brother. However that may be, the two found each other quite irresistible. Here they were, two expatriates from Britain who had broken free from the restraints of their own society, each with a problem: she had married the wrong man and Law badly wanted a companion. He could support her and offer her a life of movement on the Continent. In the world of finance, her love of display and of hospitality could be helpful. Law was struck by her peculiar attractiveness: below the eye on her left cheek was a birthmark, referred to by Saint-Simon as *une tache de vin*, a wine stain! Together, Lady Catherine and John Law made a strikingly handsome young couple. There was no time for her to seek a divorce in an ecclesiastic court, and they simply went away, confident that they were each doing the right thing and that a glorious future lay ahead.

Their first three years together were spent in Venice and Genoa, where Law made considerable money in foreign exchange dealings. Lady Catherine had her first baby, a boy christened John. Then in 1703 they decided it was time to return to Edinburgh, where Law hoped to put into practice some of the new financial ideas he had learned, and at the same time to see if he could obtain a pardon from the new sovereign, Queen Anne, a pardon that would allow him to return to London. He was safe in Edinburgh, for it was still outside English jurisdiction.

Now thirty-four and thoroughly confident of his ideas, John Law sat down and composed his remarkable treatise, *Money and Trade Considered with a Proposal for Supplying the Nation with Money*. This well-written but rather specialized document will be examined in more detail later. For now, it is enough to say that it created no particular stir then and was just one more of the hundreds of current theoretical pamphlets on "political arithmetic." Law read it to the Scottish Parliament in 1705, because it addressed itself not only to monetary theory but to the specific problems of impoverished Scotland. His proposal was to create a trade commission empowered to issue notes backed by land, bearing 3 per cent interest and passing for legal tender. The commission's writ was broad and vague and it was seen that this would be a new and powerful body made up of liberal-minded men in favor of union with England. Law was supported by the Duke of Argyll, and his proposal led to a debate that brought on a duel between two members of the Parliament. This body was not ready for Law's innovations and was convinced by the authority of William Paterson's opposition; he was the founder of the Bank of England, and since he opposed Law's proposition, it was dead.

In putting himself forward publicly, Law had it in mind to impress powerful people with his usefulness and so to have his death sentence annulled by Queen Anne, to whom he addressed his second petition for pardon with the words: " 'Tis the part of every subject to save the ease and honour of the government and the good and prosperity of the country." Only Law would have thought it everyone's duty to promote national prosperity, an idea that took more than two centuries to become a commonplace. The petition was rejected, and with union between Scotland and England becoming a certainty, Law feared eventual arrest in Edinburgh once that city became subject to English statutes. In 1706 he left Scotland with his family, Lady Catherine having had a second child, a girl named Catherine, and he never returned to his native land even after he came back to England some fifteen years later.

It is interesting to speculate on what Law would have become had he been pardoned at this time. A career in finance and even politics might have allowed him to climb to heights of power and influence in Scotland or England, but he would certainly never have held in his hands the economic reins of the nation as he held them in France.

Law had reached Edinburgh in 1703. By then, Scotland had been in desperate financial condition for several years because of a bad national investment overseas, the Darien Venture. This catastrophe strangely foreshadowed Law's own subsequent involvement in the New World. The Company of Scotland Trading to Africa and the Indies had been authorized by the Scottish Parliament to enrich that poor country through colonial trade. Under the leadership of William Paterson, a Scot who had made his fame in London by helping to found the Bank of England, a fleet set out in 1698 for Central America, financed by half the capital of Scotland, raised among enthusiastic burghers and landowners.

"Trade will increase trade and money will beget money," Paterson promised. A settlement known as Caledonia on the Isthmus of Panama was contested by the Spanish, to whom those settlers surviving the miserable life in tropical swampland surrendered within six months. All the investment of £400,000 was wiped out and only 300 of 2,000 who left Scotland returned. "The Darien Venture was perhaps the worst disaster in Scotland's history." *

While still suffering from the consequences of this misadventure, Scotland had been drawn into negotiations for union with England. It was an unsettled time, when men were casting about for solutions to the problem of national poverty in a world in which some countries without rich natural resources were able to prosper. In such an atmosphere, John Law determined to put himself at the service of his country by drafting a blueprint for its prosperity.

Law had accumulated sufficient means on the Continent to support himself and his family comfortably in Scotland while he wrote his *Money and Trade Considered with a Proposal for Supplying the Nation with Money*. This treatise was printed in 1705 by Andrew Anderson, and its preparation had undoubtedly occupied much of his time during the fall of 1704. Its 120 pages bear the stamp of careful reasoning and the examples he used to illustrate his theories were drawn both from reading and from experience in the business world. Such a work required habits of sobriety and reflection uncharacteristic of his earlier days in London.

Law's intentions are set out in a foreword:

There are several proposals offer'd to remedy the difficulties the nation is under from the great scarcity of money.

That a right judgment may be made which will be most safe, advantageous and practicable, it seems necessary 1. that the nature of money be inquired into, and why silver was used as money preferable to other goods. 2. That trade be considered and how far money affects trade. 3. That the measures which have been used for preserving and increasing money, and these now proposed be examined.

His tract is a primer in economics. He explains the law of supply and demand: "Water is of great use, yet of little value,

* John Prebble, *Lion in the North* (New York: Coward, McCann & Geoghegan, Inc., 1971).

because the quantity of water is much greater than the demand for it." The disadvantages of barter and the advantages of money are described. Money must circulate, and if men work on credit, the credit too must circulate and that makes credit a form of money. To increase money you need a bank, not a silver mine, for by the law of supply and demand the more silver there is, the less it will be worth.

Law works up to a proposal for a forty-man commission to be named by Parliament to issue paper notes backed by land, which unlike metal is a fixed quantity. He ridicules the rival scheme for a land bank offered by the colorful obstetrician Dr. Hugh Chamberlen, who accused Law of stealing his ideas. "There were banks in Europe long before the doctor's proposal, and books have been writ on the subject before and since," said Law. Law's authorship did not appear in the book, but he made no secret of it, and it struck some important people, such as the young Duke of Argyll, with sufficient force that they asked the Scottish Parliament to consider its proposals.

Law redrafted his book into shorter form and it was set on a table in Parliament Hall, beneath the curious hammer-beam ceiling from which stalactite-like golden pendentives are suspended. There was a change from the original proposal. The notes that the Commission of Trade would be empowered to issue were to be backed not by land but by the national productive capacity. Possibly, Law feared the rivalry of the older and more respected Chamberlen, and to eliminate confusion between the two proposals he pushed his own thinking into the revolutionary realm of fiat money, paper currency supported only by the strength of the economy, which is what most modern currency really is. (The danger of fiat money is that governments are often tempted to print an excess of it rather than to impose unpopular taxation.) It was an inflammatory proposal.

Two members became so engaged in debate over paper money that one challenged the other to a duel, which was fortunately broken up by the authorities. William Paterson himself had also proposed a trade commission in 1700 to stimulate economic growth in Scotland. In restating this idea, he urged a policy of

due improvement and culture of the produce of our native land . . . the only imaginable ways of increase of money in any country are these two: either to dig in mines of our own, or get it from our neighbors. And the most proper mines we can be furnished from is a due improvement of our manufactures. The only way to procure it from our neighbors is by an overbalance of trade. By this method cash would increase in our hands. . . .

Although Law should settle an imaginary credit on tallies or notes, it would not have the desired effect, in respect that everyone would hoard up their cash, until the value of money was necessarily raised. . . .

This imaginary credit would not be received in payment, though Law should establish the same and order their currency.

Such an imaginary project will end in a considerable loss to the possessors of these notes. . . . An instance of this was evident in the English Exchequer notes at the time of their scarcity of money.*

Paterson was supported by the Earl of Marchmont and the Duke of Hamilton. His own reputation was so high he was later called upon to combine the public accounts of Scotland and England after union had been voted in 1707. But his fame was eventually eclipsed by Law's, and as a result *Paterson's Proposals and Reasons for Constituting a Council of Trade in Scotland*, published in 1700, was attributed to Law until Saxe Bannister pointed out the error in 1858.

The controversy that Law aroused in Scotland was of brief duration, and he had nothing to gain from pressing his ideas on his ungrateful countrymen, especially since his two appeals to Queen Anne for a pardon during his stay had been denied. For what then loomed was the unification of Scotland with England.

---

* Quoted from Saxe Bannister, *William Paterson* (Edinburgh, 1858). Bannister was not objective about Law, whom he calls the author of Lawism. Paterson, he said, saved Scotland from Lawism, and England during the South Sea Bubble fell victim to Lawism.

The gap between his aspiration and reality was such that he again took to his heels, in 1706. For union meant that the statutes of England would apply in Scotland, and London's agents would be able to arrest Law and hang him. The bitterness he felt in remaining a condemned man is concealed by his energetic achievements abroad. But he was a reluctant exile. When he became famous, Edinburgh's merchants obsequiously sent the keys of the city to his Paris office via private messenger. Although he hired the messenger on the spot, he took six months to send his thanks back home—and his letter was written in French.

With Lady Catherine, son John, and a new baby girl, Catherine, Law set off for Brussels, the first of many cities he lived in during the next ten years, years about which we know very little that happened in John Law's life. From a few documents and memoirs that are not fully reliable, it is possible to find traces of Law here and there. In 1707 he presented an adaptation of his *Money and Trade Considered* to the French finance minister, Chamillard, and discussed it with Desmarets, destined to replace Chamillard during the terrible famine year of 1709. Probably in 1708 Law presented a *Memorandum on the Use of Money* to the powerful Prince of Conti, who passed it on to the King's grandson, the Duke of Burgundy.

Little is known of Law's moves for several years, except for glimpses of him in Florence, Rome, and Genoa. Then in 1711 he appears in Turin, where he made the strongest impression on Duke Victor Amadeus of Savoy, brother-in-law of Orleans—he was married to Louis XIV's niece, Anne-Marie. Law presented in great detail a proposal for the Bank of Turin, which would issue paper money backed up to 75 per cent by reserves and would also engage in trade of real and personal property. These so-called Piedmont papers have impressed scholars with the soundness of Law's ideas and the stringent safeguards he demanded to avoid failure and counterfeiting. The duke would have supported Law but for the opposition of local bankers, with whom in this small, provincial country the duke had to live. That Law was a foreigner would have been less disturbing to them than that he would suddenly be in control of a new and powerful financial center in Savoy. It would require a different sort of man than Victor Amadeus to support Law in what would be a struggle for the "money market" of that time; it would require a man of almost unlimited power, willing to oppose the huge class of newly rich and seemingly indispensable private bankers who had emerged all over Europe with the commercial revolution. Such a potentate would have to be prepared to protect Law economically against the wealth that these powerful men would use in manipulations against him, and if need be this foolhardy ruler must be prepared to put at Law's disposal police protection to save him from the fury of would-be destroyers.

Such a man, of course, was Louis XIV, and Victor Amadeus had him in mind as Law's patron. But Louis by that time had lost his capacity for initiating anything but schemes to preserve the status quo.

The man Law was looking for, though he did not realize it at first, was Philip, Duke of Orleans, who came to rule France for eight years in the name of the boy king Louis XV. Orleans was described by his lifelong friend Saint-Simon as the descendant of Henry IV who most resembled him. But historians have seldom taken the Regency as more than an excuse to give digests of exaggerated accounts of Orleans's famous *soupers* in the Palais Royal—evenings of supposed orgiastic revelry, which included his own alcoholic daughter, the Duchess of Berry. In fact, Orleans was unusually lusty (though no more so than his uncle, the King) and given to moods of self-indulgence that allowed malicious contemporaries to portray him as a lightweight and worse. It is true that he coined the word *roué* to describe his companions of the bottle and the bed, and it is true that his language did not always measure up to what was expected from a prince of the blood. When one of the court doctors suggested politely that he take it easy, Orleans said, *"Va te faire foutre, toi et ta medecine! Je ne le veux pas, moi."*

Such anecdotal material makes for better reading than do accounts of Orleans's skillful diplomacy, which gave France eight years of peace and international goodwill. Orleans was moody, bizarre, and unstable. He was also a hard-working and often sound administrator, a man who did his homework, as we say, one who loved life and all its pleasures and beauties, and a man who had the willingness to listen to John Law and the imagination and daring to support him in darker moments.

That Orleans was not *more* eccentric than he was is remarkable, given his parents. His father, also Philip, Duke of Orleans, was Louis XIV's younger brother by two years, and as such he was feared from birth as a rival to Louis by Cardinal Mazarin, who ruled France during Louis XIV's minority. To distract Philip from any thoughts of intrigue, Mazarin arranged to have him conditioned to become a homosexual of such wanton femininity that his interest in politics would never be seriously developed. As a child he was dressed in skirts, and at puberty he was put together with perverts. He was short, fat, and in every way outrageous— painted, powdered, beribboned, braceleted, mincing on high heels among favorites, a despised and untrustworthy member of the court, but by no means a nonentity. He was called Monsieur. His first wife, Henriette of England, sister of Charles II, died suddenly, and it was widely believed Monsieur had had her poisoned.

His second wife, mother of the Regent, called Madame, was the remarkable Elisabeth-Charlotte (Liselotte) of Bavaria, Princess of the Palatinate, earthy, Teutonic, and a gifted observer. She was a sort of foreign correspondent, forever writing letters to her Aunt Sophie, the electress of Hanover, in which she described the court of Versailles in far from flattering terms. When Orleans was born in 1674, his horoscope was cast and she wrote of her own infant: "He will be Pope. But I'm very much afraid he will be more like the Anti-Christ!" The King's wife, Mme. de Maintenon, known popularly as "the old fairy," was to Liselotte *la vielle ordure*, the old garbage.

Monsieur and Madame led separate lives, avoided hostilities, and pampered young Philip, a brilliant, talented, and handsome boy whose qualities were not esteemed by the King because they

so outshone those of his cousin, heir to the throne, the insipid
Dauphin, a royal cipher. Philip was deeply wounded by his uncle's coldness, for he was attracted like most people by Louis's
grandeur and charm, and he shared his taste for art and the theater. Monsieur openly criticized his brother for his attitude toward
Philip, and violent scenes took place, at times in front of the boy.
He hated these shouting matches of which he was the cause, and
so the court and all its artificiality became painful to him, particularly the petty wrangling over *préséance*, the order or rank at
ceremonies, the obsequious fawning, and the odious gossip. As a
child he yearned to be free of the limitations, but not the privileges, his royal blood imposed.

The Orleans family seat was the Palais Royal in the center of
Paris. This location offered the young scion the chance to meet
ordinary people. He began at fifteen by siring a child by one of
his maids. His taste improved rapidly, since the Opera was next
door and there were many dancers happy to grace his bed. His
love of venery was not discouraged by his tutor, the Abbé Dubois, whose gods, according to Saint-Simon, were "avarice, de-
bauchery and ambition." Women kept Philip from getting bored,
a condition to which he was prone from birth, his mother noted.

"I wish he preferred people of quality to actors, painters and
doctors," she wrote. "When he's with them he knows how to converse, but when he's with people of quality he looks blank, broods
and bites his nails."

In short, Philip was a putative rebel against the stultification
imposed on the nobility during the last twenty uncreative years
of Louis XIV's reign. He submitted with chagrin to a marriage
forced on him by the King with Mlle. Blois, an illegitimate daughter of Louis's by Mme. de Montespan. Louis's promotion of his
bastards at the behest of Mme. de Maintenon who had raised
them as her own was resented by the princes of the blood, and
eventually two factions grew up, one led by Orleans, the other
by his bastard cousin, the Duke of Maine.

Bored as he was, Orleans played his role at court, wrote an
opera, put on amusing masquerades, and insisted on his rank.

With his enormous wealth, he built one of the great private art collections of all time, eventually owning 485 Italian canvases and many French, Dutch, Spanish, and English works. He paid 170,000 livres for Poussin's *Seven Sacraments*. Working with a prominent chemist, Homberg, he set up a laboratory and conducted alchemic experiments. He read philosophy and explained Leibniz, with whom he, as an atheist, disagreed, to Madame his mother. She did not understand but approved his serious study. At Mass he read Rabelais while ostensibly reading a prayerbook.

In more frivolous moments, Orleans sought contact with Satan, spending fruitless nights in the quarries of Vanves and Vaugirard on ceremonies supposed to bring the devil to life. He also consulted sorcerers from time to time and had his fortune told in cards or crystal balls.

Orleans sought military advancement, for he showed talent in campaigns in Flanders and Savoy, but the King would not have it. Through Dubois, he learned diplomacy in Madrid and acquired an admiration for the English that was to have beneficial results when he came to power. But essentially his gifts were wasted in his maturing years and he became frustrated. In despair, at times he drank. "Once he starts drinking wine," his mother wrote, "he gets completely drunk and no longer knows what he's saying or doing."

Orleans was disposed to like John Law on several grounds. Law was a man of spirit, an adventurer of sorts who admired women, gambling, and beautiful works of art; he was English and he was Scottish; he was intelligent, and he believed passionately in something besides the prerogatives of rank, which sapped so much of the energy of the French courtiers. This promise of the better tomorrow Law offered evoked sympathy from a dabbler in alchemy and a caller-up of evil spirits. But before he could make possible what Law had so long planned and pleaded for, Orleans had to survive the intrigues against him. These were brought about by a series of ghastly coincidences—the successive deaths of the Dauphin on April 17, 1711, the Duchess of Burgundy on February 12, 1712, and then her husband, the new Dauphin, a week later, leaving their two-year-old son to inherit the throne. Orleans, who by law and custom would be the Regent, was openly said to have poisoned the Duke and Duchess of Burgundy in order to rule France. Crowds in the street whispered "murderer" when he passed. There was no evidence, and even motive was discounted, since Orleans was not considered a man of state with ambitions to rule, and no scholars have ever believed Orleans was in any way implicated in what were natural deaths, possibly from meningitis.

But Orleans was still engaging in laboratory experiments, not in chemistry but in pneumatics, which required elaborate and sinister looking equipment, and it was natural that superstitious servants and others ignorant of his purposes would draw evil conclusions. It had not been forgotten that as a youth he had tried to call up evil spirits, and this episode was expanded in gossip to link him to the odious Black Priests. Saint-Simon's suggestion that the Duke of Maine helped to cast suspicion on his rival, Orleans, has not been corroborated, and a defender of Maine, W. H. Lewis, takes pains to show how much damage Saint-Simon has done Maine's historical reputation by hinting that *he* was somehow responsible for the royal deaths.

During the four years before the King died, the court was filled with tension, animosities, and gossip that could only deepen Orleans's distrust of Versailles and all its inhabitants. Obtusely, the King, perhaps yielding to Mme. de Maintenon, increased his support of his bastard children, particularly the Duke of Maine. Five days before he died, Louis melodramatically wrote a codicil to his will. The codicil, to be read only after he died, was sealed with seven seals and guarded by three men in a vault with three locks in the Palace of Justice. Hypocrite to the end, he assured Orleans that he ought to find nothing in the will to make him unhappy. The codicil, of course, gave the real power of a Regency to the Duke of Maine.

Orleans now displayed the energy and force that comes to some men under intense pressure. His own wife, Maine's sister, was not unhappy at the prospect before her brother. Having several days to prepare himself, Orleans determined to nullify the King's will at once. A suggestion brought to Saint-Simon that troops raid the Palace of Justice and destroy the infamous codicil was rejected as the possible idea of an *agent provocateur* of Maine.

But the use of troops would have another advantage. For the next twenty-four hours, soldiers were very much in evidence, as messengers from the Palais Royal brought the word to members of Parlement that Orleans had ordered a reading of the will the next morning, September 2, while the dead King was hardly cold. An air of crisis was deliberately provoked by Orleans, who had the tremendous advantage of his own followers' working in the heart of the capital. He left no doubt in the minds of the members that he would demand absolute authority as Regent and that nothing in the will or its codicil would be allowed to stand in his way. The display of force around the Palace of Justice and on the bridges over the Seine awed the magisterial *noblesse de la robe*, who did not live by the sword, as did their rivals the *noblesse de l'epée*. They feared above all a civil war between two half-brothers. The word went out that they must support Orleans in his claims.

The fact was that if Orleans was unpopular he was respected, while the Duke of Maine was not taken seriously by noblemen, who resented Louis's legalization of a bastard son. But in their turn, the members of Parlement expected something from Orleans for their fealty. And they got it. It was understood that he would grant them the return of their lost right of remonstrance, the right to petition the King, the right, in short, to question his edicts instead of merely validating them unquestioningly. Henceforth, the Parlements of France, like the English Parliament, were to have power—they thought.

By dawn, the Palace of Justice was already busy with preparations. Crowds, drawn by the sight of uniformed horsemen, pressed to watch the arrival of the noble parliamentarians. Inside, the Duke of Maine, naively displaying the buoyancy of one about to assume great office, was bowing and smiling left and right, while the Regent remained somber, aloof, and menacing, reinforcing with his masterful presence the sense of domination he had been building.

The love of ceremony and drama worked in his favor. Here in one ornate chamber were assembled the leading magistrates of France, noble, proud, expectant, uneasy. For generations reduced to a nullity, they were confused by the sudden importance bestowed on them into thinking that in Orleans they beheld a servant and not a master. Wasting no time and setting the tone for the occasion, Orleans had arranged to have the will read at once by the Parlement's counselor, a man with a fine voice and diction. As the terms of the will became apparent, the longsmoldering hatred for the late King was rekindled. The will was a clumsy and insulting document that sought to impose a bastard in the place of a rightful heir. Maine could sense the rising indignation. Orleans listened impassively, then immediately stepped to the lectern. The forty-one-year-old Regent, of medium height and somewhat overweight, looked like a ruler and acted it with solemnity and self-assurance. He spoke extemporaneously in a calm and measured voice. The single point he wished to make was one of legitimacy. Before him sat men whose privileges derived from their blood lines. The *noblesse de robe* were lawyers by calling, and to an extent they had escaped the enfeeblement that the King had deliberately brought about in the *noblesse de l'epée*, the courtier class descended from the warriors of feudal times. What shocked Parlement was Louis's presumption in abrogating the law to bestow a grant of enormous power on a man born out of wedlock. Maine was a symbol of illegitimacy and a threat to the stability of the kingdom. Skillfully, Orleans played upon this one note, protesting "the prejudice done to his birthright," Saint-Simon recorded and, "to his attachment to the person of the king [Louis XV], to his love and fidelity for the Nation, such as would not let him accept it [the will] and still save his honor."

His statement was brief and overwhelming. He was granted virtually all that he sought—all the rights of Regency, the right to choose his own council, and the right to cast the deciding vote in case of a tie. Taking over the proceedings, he forbade Maine to speak out of turn. When Maine did speak, however, attempting still to claim what the King's will intended for him, Orleans lost his patience and engaged Maine in a violent debate that broke down into a personal quarrel, with name-calling and an attempt to settle old scores. This embarrassing and unedifying scene was brought to a close by adjournment. Guards stood by to prevent any trouble. In an afternoon session, Maine feebly protested that the King's codicil had been ignored and that the Parlement then suppressed it, and Maine peevishly said he could not under the circumstances command the King's guard but could only be responsible for the royal education. To his astonishment, the Parlement immediately accepted this proposal.

Orleans thus emerged after years of humiliation and virtual disgrace as a man of almost absolute power, determined to rule responsibly and to recover for France the prosperity that had been senselessly frittered away by Louis XIV. Shortly after taking office, he began conferring with John Law. On October 24, Law came to the Regency Council with his proposal to create the first bank in French history.

THE BANK

The internal problems of France
which first in the later years
of Louis XIV had begun to attract
the attention of philosophical
thinkers were primarily financial.
H. A. L. Fisher

5

The First French Bank

It is difficult in the twentieth century not to think of banks as large public establishments serving masses of people in a variety of ways. The fact that France, despite recent setbacks the most powerful nation on earth, was without a single bank shows the optional nature of this institution in the eighteenth century. If merchant-bankers who made money in trade were prepared to fulfill the banking needs of society and of the government, why establish John Law's monopoly bank to do the same thing? In England, for example, the Bank of England was a kind of cooperative, formed by men of wealth who were also the rulers of their country, absolutism having been replaced by oligarchy.

The Bank of England, founded in 1694, utilized private capital to perform public services. In France it was still risky to lend the king money, and any deficit incurred by the French government was construed as the king's personal liability. But in England, crown and Parliament floated huge war loans in the 1690's at guaranteed interest rates. The moneyed classes invested with confidence in a government they helped to control. The king's deficit was transformed into a national debt.*

* *Norton History of Modern Europe*, rev. ed. in 1 vol. Edited by Felix Gilbert (New York: W. W. Norton & Co., 1971).

But the Bank of England was not like a bank today in an American city. It had no branches and served the public only indirectly; it was as awesome as our own Federal Reserve. It served the government by pooling wealth and lending it to the King at nonusurious rates; since the King was controlled by Parliament, his borrowing was considered in the national interest. Those who put their capital at loan were, in a sense, lending their money to themselves. This is the sales psychology of our own war bonds or government savings bonds.

France was still an absolute monarchy, and Parlement was not a legislature but a promulgator of the King's edicts. The King conveniently carried on his banking privately through subordinates. Everyone was taken care of under this system, except the people and therefore the nation. Bankers, ministers, kings did not go hungry. "After me the deluge" could have been said by Louis XIV as well as by Louis XV. France was facing financial ruin: Law offered Orleans a cure.

Law was not proposing a Bank of France on the London model; he wanted a first national bank such as there is now in nearly every village, serving not just the King and his government, but all the people. If need be, all would be forced to join in the enterprise through the use of paper money. Without knowing it, he was trying to bypass the French Revolution, Napoleon, Napoleon III, and the Third Republic and to enter the twentieth century. It was as if someone had invented a rocket and proposed to send a man into outer space without a space suit.

Though based on diaries, Saint-Simon's memoirs were written in the 1740's. What he says about Law was written in full knowledge of the terrible difficulties people suffered later, so his analysis of Law's proposed bank may be an observation of hindsight. It is nonetheless valid, and it is worth quoting the two drawbacks Saint-Simon claims to have warned the Regent about:

First, to govern the bank with enough foresight and wisdom not to make more bills than they ought in order to be always above their resources and so be able to boldly face all contingencies and pay coin to every one who might ask it for the bills they brought; second, that what was excellent in a republic or in a monarchy where finance is wholly popular as it is in England, became dangerous in an absolute monarchy like that of France, where the necessities of war ill-under-taken and ill-sustained, the rapacity of ministers, favourites, mistresses, the luxury, extravagant expenditures, and prodigality of a king might soon exhaust a bank, ruin the holders of bills and overthrow the kingdom.

This was a good description of what actually happened, except that the monarchy was not overthrown until two generations later.

What the Regent's reaction was we do not know. We can only assume that what seemed a danger to St. Simon looked to Or-leans like an opportunity. He temporized, seeing how threatened Bernard, Crozat, the Paris brothers, and other bankers felt by a scheme that would have relegated them to a secondary role, if indeed to any financial role at all so far as the government was concerned. For the moment, though, the private bankers held the purse strings and Orleans needed them a while longer.

His new finance minister, successor to Desmarets, with whom Law had been dealing, was the Duke of Noailles, a man deter-mined to make the existing system work by reforming it. The policies he adopted were harsh and aimed at the French upper classes, who from the end of the Middle Ages had been largely exempted from taxation in exchange for their support of a strong central government. However justified Noailles was in cracking down on the rich and the corrupt, the result was that he created a climate in which John Law's experiment was considered less objectionable than it had been in the fall.

Noailles did three things: He devalued the coinage by 50 per cent, he cut the interest rate on state bonds from 7 to 4 per cent (a move Law had advised Desmarets not to make), and he or-ganized a *visa*, a fiscal investigation of accounts public and pri-vate, going back for a generation. Among those hit hard were the private bankers, who were terrified at finding servants, neigh-bors, and relatives denouncing those who had concealed their wealth and held back on the slight taxes they owed. Tax farmers were a particular target, since they paid far less for the privilege of collecting taxes than they should have. Under this system, after buying the right to hound the multitude for their taxes, the farmers kept whatever they could collect. There was cheating on bond issues. The private bankers underwriting a 32 million livre issue kept 24 million and gave the government 8! One was so frightened by the prospect of being hauled into the special court Noailles had created that he voluntarily handed the government 9 million livres.

Others avoided difficulties through bribery. Although fines amounting to 200 million were assessed, less than half of these were collected. One story typical of the time was that a war contractor, fined over a million livres, was told by a count he would get the fine annulled for him for 300,000. "Too late," said the contractor. "Your wife has arranged it for me for only a hundred and fifty." The arrangements were most often made at the Palais Royal, where the Regent listened sympathetically to pleas for mercy made by nobility on behalf of rich scoundrels. Not that Orleans took bribes for himself, but by his favors he kept the support of important people. Later, he used John Law for exactly the same purpose.

In all, 4,400 men were prosecuted and many were so cruelly punished that the mobs of ordinary people—who at first threw mud at offenders sitting in the pillory with signs on them like "Robber of the people"—finally sickened of degrading episodes, such as lynching threats and refusal to clothe victims during cold weather. After a certain number were condemned to be galley slaves, the Chamber of Justice, as it was called, was suspended in March 1717. By that time, Law's bank was in operation and the mood of Paris was changing from anger to hope.

Noailles is not reckoned as a notable minister, but he did bring to an end some of the abuses tolerated or ignored by Louis XIV. Perkins calls his measures "a partial bankruptcy," in that the government's indebtedness was reduced arbitrarily, but it was to some extent fraudulent indebtedness. Government expenses were reduced, too—the closing down of Versailles alone saved an enormous sum—and the Regent's peace policy eliminated the terrible drain of war.

After his setback in October 1715, Law frequented the Palais Royal and cultivated the Abbé Dubois, now one of the Regent's chief lieutenants. (Madame had begged Orleans on September 2 to have nothing further to do with this unscrupulous man who had educated him!) Orleans maintained contact with Law directly and indirectly during the winter of 1716, trying to arrive at a stratagem that would make Law's bank acceptable in the hostile climate created by the private bankers. Apparently, Orleans saw no way to create a national or state bank at this time. His position was not yet strong enough for that, even though he seriously wanted such an institution. So Law resourcefully suggested that he be allowed to charter a private bank, which would issue stock to the public like any of the many stock companies of the day. Thus the government would not be sponsoring the project, although the Regent was prepared to be its patron. Law himself would be the majority shareholder, and he sweetened the proposition by offering personally to give half a million livres to charity if the bank failed—a sort of money-back offer. What made this approach appealing was the possibility for private gain it offered to important men. Dubois, for one, received 30,000 ecus worth of shares (an ecu was worth 6 livres). No doubt others received certificates in due course. The Regent smoothed Law's path by more or less demanding of members of the Finance Council that they not stand in the way of chartering this new enterprise. Only Saint-Simon held out. The private bankers, harried by the tax prosecutions, were in no position to object to what was seemingly only another new business. They would gladly have played dog in the manger, but they were now wary of Orleans because of the investigation.

Accordingly on May 1, 1716, the Finance Council approved the bank charter as read by Noailles, and the following day the Regency Council also passed it with Saint-Simon's one dissenting vote. A royal edict announced to the nation the creation by letters patent of the *Banque Générale*, a private company with a nominal capital of 6 million livres. Subscribers to shares could pay three-fourths of the cost in government bonds at their face value, though these bonds were worth only a third or even sometimes a fourth of par.

The *Banque Générale* was to be located at first on the ground floor of Law's comfortable home in the Place Louis-le-Grand. Deposits of coin would be accepted and paper money would be exchangeable at any time for specie, so that the public, mostly businessmen, would be provided with a new convenience at no risk. (Law would shortly make paper more attractive than the coins of that time.) Something like modern checks could be used to make transfers between individual accounts. In short, Law's bank differed little from a bank that might be chartered today, except that it was a bank of issue, thinly capitalized, and completely unregulated. Its success or failure depended almost totally on its manager's genius—plus its patron's support. Well might Saint-Simon draw back from approving what could become a license to steal.

Law, however, had not come to France just to make money for himself or to take personal advantage of his financial wizardry. He was there to put into practice a substantially sound theory of money and banking that he had been working on for more than a dozen years. He knew at this point exactly what he was doing.

The origin of banks can be traced to the resumption of trade between Europe and other parts of the world in the fifteenth century, beginning with the Italian commerce in the Mediterranean with the Levantine ports of the Near East and with North Africa. Then came the discovery of America, with its vast influx of gold and later silver. An enormous increase in commerce followed. Those who take the monetarist view hold that the money supply stimulated this new economic activity. Anyway, the variety of gold and silver coins of varying value brought into being a class of men willing to handle their exchange, and they carried on their business at work benches (*banco* being the Ital-

ian word for bench; in English it became a *counter*) in Italian
port cities. In England and Scotland, this service was performed
by goldsmiths. In the seventeenth century, money had become
sufficiently plentiful to justify institutionalizing these commercial
services in banks in Italy, Holland, Germany, Sweden, and England. They handled deposits for safekeeping, foreign exchange,
and loans on bills of exchange by discounting them. Discounting
allowed a merchant to collect what he was owed before the due
date and he paid the bank 4, 5, or 6 per cent for this privilege.
Banks also made large loans to governments, sometimes to their
sorrow. The great Fugger enterprise of Augsburg collapsed when
the Emperor, Charles V, failed to pay back what the Bavarians
had loaned him to make war against the Valois and the Turks.

France managed without banks. Her wealth was more agrar-
ian than commercial, and she participated less than other countries in the development of overseas trade and colonies. She was
not a maritime power. Her people were more given to hoarding
than to entrusting their money to others. And her rulers had
allowed the country's administration to decline into a system of
universal corruption that encouraged the rapacity of men who
made fortunes supplying the government with the needs of the
armies. The war profiteers, who had the capital, sustained Louis
XIV. Nothing in such a makeshift fiscal arrangement promoted
significant economic development.

Law had the genius to perceive that a bank could be the ener-
gizing force of economic expansion by virtue of its capability of
creating money. The ships that set sail for America from Italy
or Holland or England were financed by loans that far exceeded
existing funds. Shipping companies were granted *credit* because
of the enormous profits of a single voyage—200 per cent and
up. This credit was a form of money. It appeared not as paper
currency, not as bank notes at first, but as commercial paper,
the bills of exchange just described. Money was specie—some
gold but usually silver coins. As Law saw it, money could also
take the form of paper bills. He, of course, was not the first to
suggest that something other than metal could serve as a medium

of exchange in modern times. He had read widely in the considerable literature of monetary theory. The premise he started from is stated in a brief preface to his *Money and Trade Considered*:

There are several proposals offered to remedy the difficulties the nation is under from the great scarcity of money.

That a right judgment may be made, which will be most safe, advantageous and practicable, it seems necessary: 1. That the nature of money be inquired into, and why silver was used as money preferable to other goods. 2. That trade be considered, and how far money affects trade. 3. That the measures have been used for preserving and increasing money, and these now be examined.

Money developed because of the inconvenience of barter. The more sophisticated the economy, the more troublesome it became to evaluate exchanges of grain for cattle, wine for land, and so on. Trade languished. "There was little trade and few artsmen. The people depended on the landed-men," Law complained. He was describing feudalism, the bad results of which he had seen in Scotland. Economic efficiency was one of the objectives he sought from money. Silver coins, he points out, became the universal money, not only because of their convenience of handling but because they were a standard by which goods could be valued.

He supports his arguments by many examples drawn from his business experience.

If a piece of wine was to be delivered at Glasgow by AB Merchant there, to the order of CD Merchant in Aberdeen: and the value to be delivered in oats at Aberdeen by CD to the Order of AB, the wine could not be valued by the quantity of oats it was worth at Glasgow, nor the oats by the quantity of wine they were worth at Aberdeen. Wine or oats might differ in quality, or be more or less valuable at the one place than at the other. The way to have known what quantity of oats was equal to the wine, was by the quantity of silver each was worth at the places they were to be delivered.

In praising silver, Law is building his argument for introducing paper as a more convenient form of money. The results of silver circulating were these: "the poor and idle were employed, more of the land was laboured, the product increased, manufactures and trade improved, the landed-men lived better, and the people with less dependence on them."

There is some narrow vision here. All economic progress in this view is apparently determined by one development, money. But what of technology? It was during a barter economy that metal was extracted from ore, for example, and the improvement in sailing vessels preceded the discovery of Latin American ore, from whence came the silver and gold of modern times. Furthermore, this ore could have been obtained in such quantities only through the German mining technology of the sixteenth century, and it could have been converted on such a scale only because of the newly discovered mercury amalgam process of refining. Law is writing a tract, not an objective scholarly research paper. Hence, "Domestick trade depends on the money. A greater quantity employes more people than a lesser quantity. . . . An addition to the money adds to the value of the country." As Earl Hamilton has pointed out, Law's theory depended on a disequilibrium in an economy, on shortages, and on unemployment or underemployment. In such circumstances, we know that an increase in money or credits, as is said in Europe, will stimulate production. The Marshall Plan is the great modern example.

To put it another way, John Law was living in a time of deflation, which had fallen on Europe after two centuries of great inflation. Prices on the average had doubled or trebled up to 1700; wine had risen from eight shillings for twelve gallons to ninety-six, parchment from three shillings a dozen to eighteen, candles from one to five shillings a dozen. Then had come a depression. Law sought to end it through a policy of government intervention by means of a bank chartered to issue paper money as a new form of credit. For this reason, he has been called "the father of inflation" and the first man to advocate government direction of a nation's economy rather than just the government's own finances.

He was so far ahead of his time in this respect that he became the only man capable of carrying out what he advocated.

Given the rightness of his arguments favoring an increase in the money supply of a country, how is it accomplished? "The use of *banks* has been the best method yet practised for the increase of money," wrote Law, and he cites the examples of Italy, Sweden, Holland, and England. "So far as they lend they add to the money." They lend out more than they have on deposit, through a book-keeping system that was the forerunner of our modern method, whereby a loan is a credit entry in your bank account. Law was aware of the danger of a run on a bank, when everyone asks for his deposit at the same time, but well-secured loans would eventually be repaid to the bank and would provide the wherewithal to satisfy depositors. While true in theory, the conditions that cause a bank run are likely also to make it difficult, if not impossible, to liquidate loans. In the end, Law recognized the risk of failure, but claimed the benefits of increasing the money supply were worth it.

The history of banking in the United States seems to bear Law out, for it is a history of difficulty, repudiation of paper money (the famous Continentals issued during the American Revolution), and disastrous bank failures down the years. Banks still fail today, but because of Federal Deposit Insurance instituted by the New Deal, depositors no longer suffer.

If the increase of *silver* was good enough for prior generations, why was Law insisting on its replacement for all but small change by *paper*? Because, useful as silver had been in the past, its value had been falling because of an enormous supply that had been brought to Europe from South America and Mexico. Between 1540 and 1590, the annual import of silver shot up from a million and a half ounces to 10 million. In the first 140 years of Spanish exploitation of Mexico, Bolivia, and Peru, 18,000 tons of gold and silver reached Europe. As the supply of bullion rose, its value fluctuated. What kind of money is it that varies in its intrinsic value?

Law gives many examples of the inflation in the price of land and goods over the centuries. He fails to mention the crisis that

arose from the wearing out and the clipping of coins, which reduced confidence in their face value. (He would appreciate the
recent coining of our own quarter, now made of silver sides on a
copper alloy, which is plainly visible by looking at the edges.) What
is needed, held Law, is a new form of money that has no intrinsic
value whatsover, namely paper! He talks of *coining* notes. The advantages of paper over coin are obvious—it is easier to carry,
cheaper to transport, cheaper to store, cheaper to produce, and
less likely to be counterfeited. The last is dubious, and Law was
at great pains to design a note that would be difficult to counterfeit. The *Banque Générale* bore his signature, for example. The
penalty for counterfeiting in France was death.

This was spelled out in Law's *Mémoire sur Les Banques*, July
1715:

[The director] will be allowed his own presses to print and package
the notes, and a stamping machine to apply the bank's seal, declaring
that it will be a crime of *lèse-Majesté* to counterfeit its notes as it is
to make false coin, to counterfeit the signatures, seals or the plates on
which the notes are engraved, or to have knowledge of these crimes
without revealing the criminal. A reward of a thousand livres will be
provided to those discovering [the counterfeiting] and criminals who
reveal their accomplices will be pardoned.

Would mere paper be acceptable to the public? Law cites the
preference of goldsmiths' notes in England over gold or silver coins.
"Money is not the value *for* which goods are exchanged, but the
value *by* which they are exchanged. The use of money is to buy
goods, and silver while money is of no other use." Why take up
space with a lot of metal that has no other purpose than to be paid
out, when you can carry a fortune in paper in your purse? The
one danger Law does not seem to have anticipated is bank robberies. None in fact occurred in his day, because the few banks
there were in the world were heavily guarded.

Granted that goldsmiths' notes and other forms of paper were
acceptable to merchants who knew one another in the small world
of commerce, would paper money pass for currency on a wider

scale? In Venice, a city Law knew well, paper passed easily among its 1,500 merchants. Law believed, and proved, it would pass among millions. In this he was not bringing France up to date; he was advancing it beyond any existing practice, and he knew it and foresaw correctly its benefits. Orleans, who had consulted fortune tellers much of his life, believed in Law's predictions, and was prepared to back Law with his name, and soon with his money—or rather, with the King's money.

Meanwhile, money was still something of a problem even to the rich John Law, who had brought to Paris a personal fortune of 1,600,000 livres; he took a month to sell enough shares to allow him to open for business. Of the 6 million livres capital promised, only a fourth had to be paid in cash. But he did not wait for this million and a half. He actually started with 375,000 livres! When it is seen what developed from this paltry sum, it must be admitted that John Law had audacity as well as convictions. Just how much of his own money he put up is not known, but he held a majority of the shares in the bank. But, as Balzac remarked, a man's best capital is his energy.

6

Billets de Monnaie

During May 1716, Law became a French subject and began printing paper money in preparation for the bank's opening early in
June. This event was greeted with skepticism, since few people in
France knew what a bank was and paper money seemed like some
sort of a joke. The suspicion of paper money continued in France
into the middle of the nineteenth century, and Eugene Daire, an
economic historian who wrote an important study of Law's system,
said in 1843 that paper would never be successfully circulated in
his country.

Actually, paper money had already had a long history, appearing
first in China in 177 B.C. It was introduced into Europe by the
Arabs in the sixth century A.D., and Kublai Khan used paper money
in the thirteenth century. During the Renaissance, Italian deposit
receipts for coins circulated as money. According to Norman
Angell, "the first bank notes properly speaking which were known
in England were the acknowledgements made to private depositors
by the old goldsmiths."

France itself had experienced a form of paper money called
billets de monnaie, notes bearing 8 per cent interest that appeared
briefly during the War of the Spanish Succession between 1703
and 1707. There were 180 million in circulation in 1706, but a

year later they had lost 63 per cent of their value, so anyone remembering them would have little confidence in pieces of paper signed by John Law.

Indeed, the bank was publicly ridiculed at first, as well it might be, given its lack of substance. The Regent perceived the difficulty. Unlike Lenin, who when asked for money by a comrade of little importance at a party meeting told him he would do better than that, he would let him take his arm and walk around the hall with him, the Regent put his money directly behind Law by depositing a million livres in specie in his bank. Delivery of the coins was not made in the dark of night, but in broad daylight with some fanfare. Law and Orleans had in common an innate sense of public relations. This gesture caused others to imitate it, and soon deposits mounted.

The paper money drawn against the specie began to circulate, with the constant reiterated assurance from Law that while coins might be clipped or devalued, his bills would not lose value. Furthermore, Law reduced his discount rate in a few months, attracting a thriving loan business. In a small way what Law had predicted became evident: paper money meant easier credit and signs appeared that business was picking up around Paris. Even abroad, interest was sufficient for foreigners to obtain modest amounts of his paper money for their business affairs in France. Expansion required that the bank premises be moved to the Hôtel de Mesmes in the rue St. Avoix in the financial district.

At Law's urging, the Regent took a giant step on October 7, 1716, four months after the bank had opened. He instructed the powerful provincial governors, known as *intendants*, that they must henceforth pay their tax revenue to Paris in notes of the *Banque Générale*. This forced the circulation of paper throughout the nation, and the bank quickly took on a quasigovernmental character, despite the objections of some *intendants*. By April 10, 1717, the government issued a decree that allowed the taxpayers themselves to pay their taxes in paper.

This rapid increase in circulating paper, with its stimulating effect on commerce, made John Law a widely known public figure.

His name, after all, was on the money, a privilege until then reserved to princes, whose faces had been stamped on coins from
early classical times. It says something of Orleans's shrewdness
and lack of vainglory that he forbore from the temptation to have
his portrait engraved on the bank's money, even after the bank
was nationalized. Our own currency seems to require the reassur-
ing profile of a president stamped on coins or printed full face on
bills.* Law's notes resembled the modern British five pound note,
being white and relatively unadorned, more like a true commercial
note or bill promising payment in specie, printed with black ink and
signed boldly by the bank's manager.

Whatever satisfaction such attention as he drew gave to Law, it
was also a source of constant uneasiness to him in the early days
of the bank. Recently Peter L. Bernstein, in a useful little book, *A
Primer on Money, Banking and Gold*, described the basic uncertainty that faces any banker:

> The public and the banker sit on opposite sides of the desk or look
> at each other from opposite sides of the teller's window in a figurative
> as well as a literal sense. We are all interested in getting money out of
> the bank either because we are depositors and will demand our money
> when we need it, or because we hope to borrow from or sell securities
> to a bank in order to replenish our own cash resources. The banker
> wants us to leave as much money as possible with him, even though
> he lives in a constant state of uncertainty as to our intentions. . . .

> Thus the banking business is a constant struggle between the necessity
> to be liquid to meet net withdrawals and the desire to have money lent
> out and invested so that it will earn interest to show the bank a profit.

As public confidence in Law's bank grew, so too grew individual
malice among the fraternity of private bankers, envious of Law's
sudden success. They could easily have ruined him by undermining
faith in the convertibility of the bank notes, but instead they clum-
sily made a frontal assault through two agents who arrived suddenly one day with 5 million livres in paper money and demanded

---

* Recall the lines of the English poet, Arthur Hugh Clough: "No graven
images may be worshipped except the currency."

specie for it, as was their right. A genuine run will wreck a bank because of the anxiety caused by the sight of a long line of people waiting uncertainly to be paid. In this case, Law quietly assured them he could obtain the necessary coin in twenty-four hours, which he was able to do with the Regent's assistance. A timely delivery of coin from the royal treasury enabled Law to meet this obligation, which only strengthened his reputation for probity.

Throughout 1717 the bank prospered, and there is little noteworthy to say about a bank that prospers. Banking is not in the normal course of events an exciting business, though it may be fascinating to bankers themselves. Had Law been content merely to manage a successful bank, he would no more be remembered in history than any of the thousands of men who have creditably handled the world's money. But Law was more than a banker; he was a banker under attack, not from the normal economic and whimsical factors described by Bernstein, but by powerful personalities who were threatened by his growing influence and jealous of his ascent. His praiseworthy desire to revive a moribund commerce was particularly resented by some aristocrats whose fortunes, unlike those of the bourgeois, were derived from the land. Already the seeds of the French Revolution were sprouting in this contest between the inheritors of a feudal economy and the untitled upstarts of the cities and towns, who were implementing technological change and trying to line their pockets by buying cheap and selling dear. It was the townsmen who had most need of money, and the townsmen who knew how to put it to better use than men who lived off their means and spent their lives in chateaux, riding to the hunt, worrying about *préséance*, or status. Such men had reason to worry, for nobility was a fabrication of titles whose value was what convention gave them, which could now be purchased by these very men that Law's bank was benefiting, those vulgar bourgeois brilliantly satirized by Molière.

Orleans's ambivalent attitude toward the aristocracy created a crevice through which John Law was drawing himself and others, but there were also those trying to seal it up, particularly the

Parlement of Paris, the *robins*, the *noblesse de la robe* who had validated the Regent's right to rule.

Their desires were responded to by Noailles, the finance minister who had first praised the usefulness of the *Banque Générale* because of the prosperity it generated and the increased revenues that followed. But in the modern world, as was being demonstrated in England, an increasing population could not indefinitely be made to serve the exclusive interests of families who owed their position to the fact that their ancestors had been rewarded with vast domains by a king for fighting his battles. Merchants, lawyers, and now bankers had to have their places in the sun.

In the beginning, Law was busy being a sober banker and making his new venture thrive, which it certainly did in a respectable but not a spectacular way. But he recognized the tenuousness of his enterprise in the face of pronounced and powerful opposition. And in the course of doing business with men of vast wealth, his ambition to engage in trade himself was whetted. His theoretical masterpiece had been entitled "Money and *Trade* Considered," and he could not long generate trade by printing paper money without starting up a trading company of his own.

During the spring of 1717, an opportunity arose. At this time, the financier and private banker, Antoine Crozat, one of the richest men in the world and no admirer of Law's, indicated publicly that he intended to cut his losses in the futile Mississippi colony, for which he had a royal charter. Law heard the rumor, substantiated it, and began to make plans for reorganizing this miserable venture on a scale no other man dreamed of. The beginnings of the Mississippi Bubble are to be traced to the brilliant fantasies of John Law.

7

No Life on the Mississippi

The existence of the Mississippi River was unknown * until Louis XIV's minister, Colbert, stimulated explorers in the tradition of Cartier (1491–1557) and Champlain (1567–1635) to expand the Canadian province of New France westward in search of more fur and possibly minerals. At the Gulf of Mexico, its meandering delta streams offered no promise to coasting sea captains, and they ignored it during the sixteenth and much of the seventeenth century. In June 1673, the fur trader-explorer Louis Joliet and the Jesuit Father Jacques Marquette found the river in Wisconsin and descended it in two canoes with three other men as far as the Illinois River. It was another nine years before a remarkably determined Norman, René-Robert Cavelier, Sieur de la Salle, set out from Montreal in November 1681. On April 9, 1682, he erected a column bearing the arms of France at one of the mouths of the Mississippi. Following this momentous discovery, France claimed as her own the new territory of Louisiana, extending as far west as the Rocky Mountains. But exploitation was slow and ineffective.

La Salle, an autocrat characterized by Francis Parkman as a "tower of adamant," was murdered on the frontier in 1689 by some of his disgruntled followers, and Louisiana lay undeveloped

* DeSoto crossed it above the confluence of the Arkansas River in 1594.

for a decade until a colony was hastily established in 1699 by Pierre Le Moyne, Sieur d'Iberville, one of the remarkable Le Moyne brothers of Montreal. He approached the Mississippi Delta from the Gulf of Mexico. The immediate motive for the settlement was to validate French claims against the encroaching English, who were threatening to move up the Mississippi with both English and Huguenot colonists.

But why should anyone at this time have suddenly thought of developing a hitherto neglected semitropical marshy land, which flooded uncontrollably each spring and whose climate was pestilential and inhospitable? Because it was thought to be an area rich in mines. "Inscrutable history shows that the chronicle of an expedition is sometimes infinitely more important than the expedition itself," John Anthony Caruso wrote recently in *The Mississippi Valley Frontier*. He was referring to the account of La Salle's journeys by Father Louis Hennepin, a Franciscan friar from Paris, who wrote three popular books that stirred public imagination in France. Filled with contradictions, complete fabrications, and self-advertisement, and practically ignoring La Salle, who was not even credited with leadership of his own expeditions, Hennepin's work was belatedly exposed to ridicule. But he was a born raconteur, and the exotic tales and colorful descriptions made his works enormously popular. He said of canoes: "This boat might indeed be called a death-box . . . the least motion of the body upsets them." He described how he saved the lives of Indian children bitten by rattlesnakes. His adventures took him through frozen lakes: "Our legs were all bloody from the ice which we broke as we advanced in lakes which we forded." Too slow for their Indian guides, they were speeded up, says the good friar, when the Indians would set fire to prairies behind them "so that we had to advance or burn."

Some of Hennepin's maps were accurate, but his accounts of the lower Mississippi were misleading, because contrary to his claim, he did not go on La Salle's expedition to the Gulf of Mexico. But one lie he did not tell was that Louisiana was rich in minerals. This myth was propagated by one of La Salle's friends, Sieur de Remonville, whose *Mémoire* on Louisiana in December 1697 caused a sensation in Louis XIV's court. Not only did he state the facts that game, pelts, silk, and hemp might be had there, he added wine and *minerals* to his list of potential products from the area. Twenty years later, the notion that Louisiana, or Mississippi, as it was better known then, was another Mexico, rich in silver, was still believed, despite the fact that the colony settled by Iberville had yielded literally no return to France. John Law was able to kindle a new enthusiasm about Mississippi by blowing on the dying embers of de Remonville's hyperbole, and many an artist who had never left the banks of the Seine painted, during Law's tenure, pictures of New Orleans as if it resembled a Riviera port with mountains rising directly from the shoreline. De Remonville's was one of the most misleading real estate promotions in history,* and John Law adopted it.

The realities of Louisiana at the beginning of the eighteenth century were unremittingly harsh. Iberville's several hundred men and women from France were at first faced with camping on beaches with inadequate shelter, scorched by heat, blinded by the sun, and lacking enough fresh water. Worms began devouring their two frigates. By winter, the colony was reduced by death and desertion to 150, to which another sixty were added. During the next fifteen years or so, there were never more than 700 people in the new French Eldorado. And it was on this territory that John Law fixed his attention.

The failure to find minerals and the absence of a labor force to develop the rich delta potential for crops could end only in administrative difficulties. Iberville died in 1706. His brother, Bienville, who succeeded him as leader of the colony, was unable to impress Paris, where, conflicting reports of what was going on and a shortage of royal funds led Louis XIV to turn to the financier Antoine Crozat for help, as he had done so often during his wars. Crozat had interests in many trading ventures. In return for a fifteen-year lease, Crozat agreed to finance an expanded search for minerals further upstream in Missouri. The king was to get 25

* A cousin of Iberville named LeSuer actually mined two tons of what he thought was copper ore in Minnesota, 1701. It proved to be common clay.

per cent of the profit. Bienville was superseded by the impetuous and imperious Antoine de la Mothe-Cadillac, founder of Detroit, who arrived in 1713. In four years, Crozat sank 2 million livres in the project, and that was enough for him. Not only was he faced with financial losses, but Cadillac, in letter after letter, vilified and complained about Bienville, who had been kept on as lieutenant-governor because of his knowledge of the territory. Apparently Bienville was to blame for everything—the weather, agricultural failure, disadvantageous trading arrangements, the absence of the fabled mines—and the final insult was Bienville's refusal to marry his daughter. In exasperation, Crozat withdrew Cadillac, but his replacement, Espinay, could not dominate the tough and experienced Bienville either. Crozat, concluding that nothing would work, asked that the contract for this worthless monopoly be cancelled.

What was the government to do with the remnants of its futile colony of the Mississippi? Were things as bad as they seemed? The history of new enterprises is often salted with stories of mismanagement and undercapitalization at the start. How many suburbs of America were laid out with paved streets and utilities by an eager developer, who then could not afford to await with patience the inevitable sale of his lots and had to turn his dream over to shrewder men at a financial loss? How many small businesses have been sold at a discount to organizations with the money and the expertise to turn them into great industries? Despair over the Mississippi colony in the office of Noailles, the finance minister, worked in Law's favor.

Law listened to all the bad news, while he tabulated the existing assets and their potential. That he was no idle dreamer is evident in the fabulous subsequent history of the territory of which he was shortly to become the absolute master for a few brief years. What Crozat was giving up consisted of territory represented by the present states of Louisiana, Mississippi, Arkansas, Missouri, Illinois, Kansas, Oklahoma, Nebraska, North and South Dakota, Iowa, Wisconsin, and Minnesota. Texas and California were Spanish, and the Rocky Mountain area was still unexplored. But Crozat, for all the land in his nominal control, was losing money.

Yet in fact, his agents had set up a number of useful trading posts, one of which eventually became the city of Natchez, Mississippi and another Nashville, Tennessee. Crozat's barges at first floated down the Mississippi loaded with pelts and deerskins. Unfortunately, little cargo reached France. English and Spanish agents had infiltrated the Indian tribes and were outbidding the French. Spanish men-of-war drove Crozat's ships out of the Gulf of Mexico. His hope of importing slaves from Guinea to work the land was thwarted by the Treaty of Utrecht's provision that gave the slave trade exclusively to the English. But lead ore had been successfully mined in southeastern Missouri, giving credence to the recurring myth of mines of precious metals.

What Law brought to the project was not just a promise to do a better job with better management, but a vision of grandeur. What was needed, he said, was a vast investment of capital, a large migration of colonists, and slaves, who were to come from French Senegal. He laughed at Noailles' modest proposal of recapitalizing the company at 2 million livres. Accustomed to handling that kind of money every week, Law suggested that a minimum of 25 million livres would be required, and eventually he got an authorization for a capital of 100 million livres. Of course, Law's knowledge of America and particularly of Louisiana was based on what he was able to glean from others and from his broad acquaintance with foreign trade. He had never been to sea, and his only experience with boats was limited to three crossings of the English Channel and gondola rides in Venice. He had no intention of playing any active role in Louisiana, and never showed the slightest inclination to visit the New World. He kept his mind on the trade to be generated there by others employing the capital he would provide.

That capital would not be money drawn from his own pocket or from the *Banque Générale*; it would be raised by public subscription. It would be venture capital in a stock company, by then a common device for launching new enterprises, though it was used far more in England and Holland than in France. The government had to have its share, its objective being a return of a million livres a year, which was 4 per cent interest on 25 million. Since he had already had success in raising money for his bank by accepting depreciated state bonds at face value as payment, he proposed to do it again. Each share would be paid for with a 500 livre *billet d'état*. Then he added a new wrinkle to satisfy Noailles. Once the bonds had been turned over to the new company, he would burn them and acquit the government of the necessity of paying burden-some interest, while the company would assume this obligation in perpetuity, presumably paying 4 per cent without difficulty from the anticipated profits. There was one stipulation however: no interest would be paid to stockholders during the first year after subscribing. Instead, the company would collect the interest on the bonds it took in and use it (4 million livres) as working capital. Considering that some mutual funds today take 7 per cent of the value of the investment to cover sales costs, John Law was not being particularly unreasonable in making this condition, and his capitalization was thin, since the bonds he took in payment were worth only 40 per cent of face value.

Law was much more demanding of the government than Crozat had been: Law obtained a twenty-five year lease of the territory; Crozat's had been for fifteen years. Law's company was to keep all profits, and any minerals discovered would belong to the company; Crozat had agreed to give the King 25 per cent.

The company had the right to maintain its own navy with armed ships, sailors, and soldiers; Crozat had had to depend on the government to protect his ships, and this it had not been able to do.

It is true that the company agreed to settle 6,000 colonists and 3,000 slaves, a condition not required of Crozat, but Law was happy to meet this requirement, believing, correctly, that an ex-panding economy calls for population growth and an adequate labor force.

Law obtained tax exemption for his colonists; Crozat had tried to recreate a colony in the wilderness in the image of a French province, an obviously unattractive proposition to settlers forced to live in primitive huts.

The company had the right of eminent domain; Crozat had had no such right (not that it mattered at this time).

In short, Law demanded and got "all the prerogatives of a sovereign."

The name Law chose for this newest endeavor was *la Compagnie d'Occident* ("the Western Company") implying something larger than Mississippi or Louisiana. But the title of the older association persisted in the public mind, and everyone called it the Mississippi Company. Its legal beginning was recognized by Parlement on September 6, 1717, but it was five months before the first three ships arrived at Dauphine Island off the mouth of the Mississippi, bringing settlers and a letter from John Law entrusting the direction of the territory once again to the tenacious and experienced Bienville. This time, Bienville was to be provided with everything necessary to create a genuine colony.

One of his first moves was to establish a "capital," a trading post and village in reality, accessible to the sea, and named after the Regent. Thus the humble beginning of New Orleans.

How much this impressed the Regent is not recorded, but in the coming struggle facing John Law, Orleans put behind him all his power and prestige. And Law needed every bit of it. Hostilities were reaching a point where his life was at stake when the Parlement tried to pass a measure that would have required that he be hanged.

8

Refuge in the Palais Royal

The public at first took little notice of the Western Company, which appeared to be such a risky proposition that few subscribers could be found. Law bided his time and strengthened his relations with the Regent, who found him useful in matters more frivolous than economics. When Thomas Pitt, grandfather of the great statesman William Pitt, came to France to sell his famous diamond weighing 500 grains, the world's largest, Law, together with Saint-Simon, helped buy it as a crown jewel for the Regent in the name of the King for 2 million livres, and made arrangements for installment payments. It was a sound investment and was worth five times its price by the time of the Revolution.

Law had developed a relationship with Saint-Simon, probably the closest man to Orleans. It is difficult to assess Saint-Simon's true feelings about Law because his memoirs, though based on journals, were written between 1740 and 1750. He does criticize Law's System and its fallacies, yet he was careful not to malign Law personally. A clue to a probable conflict between his instinctive dislike of financial matters (and hence those expert in them) and his gratitude lies in his frank admission that, thanks to an arrangement the Regent made with Law, he received half a million francs in settlement of a claim his father had never been able to

collect from the government for military outlays made while defending the town of Blaye during an eighteen-month siege. The
arrangement was nothing more than a disguised bribe, for Law
had tried in vain to press upon Saint-Simon sufficient shares in the
company to make him a rich man. When the Regent more or less
told him he was a fool not to accept Law's offer, Saint-Simon himself proposed the liquidation of his father's bill, knowing that the
Regent would use shares from Law to satisfy the treasury. In other
words, the Regent acted as a "cutout" because Saint-Simon was too
delicate or too prudent (not too honest) to take anything directly
from Law. "My notes and orders [his father's] were little by little
burned up in the Regent's cabinet; and that is what paid for the
improvements I have made at La Ferté," he writes disingenuously.
La Ferté was the ducal chateau to which Saint-Simon retired after
the Regent died in 1723.

More than a year before this transaction (Saint-Simon's chronol-
ogy is far from exact), he began seeing Law every Tuesday at the
request of Orleans. "Saint-Simon was a little man of sickly appearance, with a pointed turned-up nose, of violent temper and narrow intelligence, with an antipathy to knaves and hypocrites." *
Law was tall, healthy, equable, and brilliant. That the two got on
so well is remarkable. Law must have fascinated Saint-Simon with
his ideas and his reports, for Saint-Simon later wrote:

One hour and a half, often two hours was the usual length of our con-
versations. He always took care to inform me of the favor his bank
received in France, and in foreign countries, of his proceeds, his
prospects and his conduct, of the counteraction he met with from leaders
in finance and in the magistracy, of his motives, and, above all, of his
balance sheet, in order to convince me that that he was more than in
a condition to meet all holders of bills, no matter what sums they might
demand.

I soon knew that if Law desired these regular interviews it was not that
he expected to make me an able financier; but as a man of intelligence,
and he had plenty of it, he wanted access to a servitor of the Regent

* *Oxford Companion to French Literature.* Edited by Paul Harvey and
Janet E. Heseltine (New York: Oxford University Press, 1959).

who was more than all others truly in his confidence . . . he was seeking by this frequent intercourse to win my friendship, and learn from me the intrinsic quality of those surrounding the Regent, whom he could only judge by the outside; and little by little get counsel from me on the obstacles he met with and the persons with whom he had to do. The bank being underway and flourishing, I thought it necessary to sustain it.

The Regent took such pride in Law that when Peter the Great visited Paris in the summer of 1717, arrangements were made for him to visit the bank and meet Law himself. He shared the Regent's enthusiasm for Law's new financial schemes, and years later, after Law had been expelled from France, he invited Law to set up his system in Russia, an appeal that Law declined.

Perhaps the Czar knew only the happy side of the story, for he met Law at a propitious time, when the bank was just beginning its second year. Not long after Peter went home, Law declared a six months' dividend of 7 per cent and reduced his discount rate from 6 to 4 per cent. Orleans was delighted.

The Regent, though, had other things to attend to, and he could not prevent Noailles' conniving against Law—"to set all machines at work to overthrow him," says Saint-Simon, to whom Law complained. "I have often owned my incapacity in the matter of finances; but there are things that sometimes depend on good sense more than on knowledge; and Law, with his strong Scotch accent, had the rare gift of explaining himself in so plain and clear, and intelligible a way that he could not fail to be perfectly understood and comprehended. The Duke of Orleans liked him and enjoyed him. He looked upon him and all that he did as the work of his own creation."

As an ally against Noailles, Law cultivated the Abbé Dubois, Orleans's tutor turned statesman, of unbounded ambition, dreaming of a cardinal's hat; and showered him with stock certificates. Noailles' position became tenuous. Orleans, a conciliator by nature, brought Law and the finance minister together on January 6, 1718 for supper at a country house called La Raquette. There he found Noailles irreconcilably hostile to Law, and he made his choice: Noailles had to go. "He could not part with Law and his system," Saint-Simon writes, "because of his natural love of indirect ways, and the attraction of those mines of gold which Law made him foresee all opened and worked by his operations." For Law had promised the Regent that his trading company would enrich the kingdom so that the debt would be extinguished and the population enlarged by a third.

In place of Noailles as finance minister, Law wanted Saint-Simon (according to Saint-Simon), but Saint-Simon declined the dubious position of fronting for Law. They then agreed to put before the Regent the name of Marc René D'Argenson, sixty-five, chief of police. To Saint-Simon, D'Argenson was a man "with a terrifying face, which recalled that of the three judges of hell," but he was apparently compliant and willing to let Law determine fiscal policy. Law and Saint-Simon could not have been more wrong. Within a few months after his appointment in January 1718, D'Argenson was in league against Law, of whose genius he was extremely jealous.

By spring, some 50 million livres of paper money were circulating without difficulty, and the bank was preparing to open branches in the provinces and thus extend the scope of credit throughout the nation. The achievement was modest but impressive for two years' work, and there was promise of a greater expansion throughout 1718. This was not to the liking of the traditional bankers, who saw that eventually the lending of money would be institutionalized and they would lose power, prestige, *and* money.

Since Law was promising to retire the national debt by absorbing state bonds into his Western Company, D'Argenson was persuaded to go Law one better and devalue the currency—that is, the coin; he could not affect the paper bills. And he could not see that if paper money remained stable while the purchasing power of coins slipped, paper would become more desirable. This is precisely what happened. But meanwhile, even the Regent was blinded by the way the devaluation was to be carried out: a person bringing 48 livres (each weighing 9 ounces) and 12 state bonds to a treasury office would receive 60 livres of new coin (each weighing, however, only 8 ounces). This worked out to a devaluation of one-sixth. And it supposedly got rid of those troublesome obligations, the bonds created to pay for Louis XIV's wars and extravagances at Versailles.

Since his first treatise on money, John Law had dogmatically opposed devaluation under *any* circumstances. He considered it simply cheating. "But as 'tis unjust to raise, or allay money, because then all contracts are payed with a lesser value than was contracted for; and as it has bad effects on home or foreign trade: so no nation practises it that has regard to injustice or understands the nature of trade and money." (*Money and Trade Considered*).

Strictly speaking, Law held that the only way to make a coin more valuable is by lessening the quantity of silver or gold in the world or increasing the demand for it. It was a view to which he was deeply committed until the time came for *him* to try the expedient with paper. But he apparently put up no fight against D'Argenson, perhaps foreseeing that the government's action would help the bank. Failure to oppose publicly a measure that he censured in private proved to be unwise, because the devaluation aroused the wrath of Parlement. This was the King's money, and the Regency Council had published an edict in May 1718 announcing devaluation, without so much as a by-your-leave. The Regent was requested to revoke the decree authorizing devaluation; he refused. Parlement challenged the refusal and demanded a rendering of accounts, never before available. The Regent's soldiers seized the presses printing the Parlement's resolution. A childish tug of war ensued, in which Law privately sided with the Parlement over devaluation. But such is the nature of politics that the Parlement now turned its hostility from the Regent back to Law, who was blamed for the devaluation carried out by his rival, the minister of finance.

On August 12 the Parlement issued a decree saying in part:

This court ordains that ordinances and edicts bearing creation of offices of finance and letters-patent concerning the Bank registered in this court, shall be executed. That being so, that the Bank shall be reduced to the limits and to the operations established by the letters of May 2d and 20th, 1716; and, in consequence, it is forbidden to keep or retain, directly or indirectly, any of the royal funds in the coffers of the Bank. . . .

The quasigovernmental character that made the bank a powerful tool for the Regent was to cease. If this were allowed to happen, those with all the gold would have had their successful run on the bank and Law would be finished. But to give the edict an even more explosive charge,

. . . it is likewise forbidden to all foreigners, even naturalized, to meddle directly or indirectly, or to participate under assumed names, in the handling or the administration of the royal funds, under the pains and penalties enjoined by the ordinances and declarations registered in this court.

At this time, France still remained an absolute monarchy and there were no political parties such as had arisen in England. Nonetheless, every ruler, no matter how firm his grip, has his opponents. The Regent, ruling for Louis XV, was faced with the rivalry of the Duke of Maine, whose followers in the Parlement of Paris saw in John Law an opportunity to unseat Orleans. If they could show that a foreigner was arrogating to himself rights belonging to the King, they might be able to arouse such anger that Law would be forced out and Orleans seriously embarrassed. The equivalent of the modern cry, *Nous sommes trahis!* was hurled at Law.

What had got him in trouble was Orleans's willingness to back the bank with royal funds. Here was a private enterprise guaranteed by the King's money. What an advantage this gave the Scotsman! Secret hearings were held, in which witnesses presumably revealed some of the details of the royal treasury's support of Law's bank. Emotions ran high and rumors spread that Law was to be declared guilty of treason and hanged within three hours. Law heard them and grew frightened. His success and his popularity meant nothing in the face of royalist sentiment that he had betrayed the King's trust.

It was a critical moment for the Regency, not to say for Law, whose life appeared to be at stake. Had he fled from a noose in London to dangle from one a generation later in Paris? The thought of it made him lose his self-control. He conferred at Orleans's request with Saint-Simon and others at the house of Saint-Simon, who wrote: "At this conference I saw the hitherto great firmness of Law shaken even to tears. . . . Law, more dead than alive, knew not what to say, still less what to do. His safety seemed to us the most pressing thing to secure." There was doubt that, if Law were arrested, the Regent's guards could rescue him in time. This would be a dangerous expedient and "shocking if, instead of Law, they had found a hempen cord and a corpse."

The decision was that Law must take refuge in the Palais Royal in the apartment of a friend who was away in Spain. It should be remembered that the palaces of those days were in a sense huge (and not necessarily glorified) apartment houses. Their security arrangements, however, were often more impressive than some present-day urban dwelling places.

In giving Law a place at the Palais Royal, the Regent was throwing down the gauntlet to the Parlement. Whether Orleans's personality was deceptive and he deliberately misled people into considering him vacillating and permissive, or whether he roused himself only when threatened, his behavior now was no more anticipated than when he had placed troops after Louis XIV's death to show that he meant to take power. He was not about to let the French Parlement, a court comprised of notables who inherited their offices, exercise any significant legislative authority. Encouraged by the Abbé Dubois, who had observed the English Parliament's power over the English King, Orleans accepted his advice to "Let your wisdom avert from France the dangerous project of making of the French a free people," and determined to crush its incipient legislative tendencies. James Breck Perkins' comments are apt:

The French Parlement was sure to oppose the enterprises of Law, because all new measures were distasteful to it. The conservatism often
found among lawyers was exaggerated in these courts (there were 8
Parlements of which the one in Paris was foremost); the hostility to
innovations, which was strong among the French people, was strongest
among jurists who cherished hereditary traditions, who enjoyed assured positions, and who desired the world to remain as it was. . . . The
Parlement was a respectable body, but incapable of taking any part
in the affairs of the state; the older members were learned in the law,
but wedded to the modes of thought of their youth; they had not
followed the changes of governments, or the fluctuations of politics;
many of the members were young, rich, and ignorant, and were incapable of either forming or expressing an opinion.*

To let such a body assume control of the royal treasury was
unthinkable, and Orleans set about putting these gentlemen in their
places by summoning them to a *Lit de Justice*, an extraordinary
session of the Parlement presided over by the King, whose will by
tradition must be obeyed in all matters he set before them.

Orleans ruled as more or less an absolute monarch, but he was
Regent acting for the King. Louis XV was five when his father
died. As anyone who has dealt with children knows, they are formidable creatures despite their limitations. Orleans was his uncle,
and he had a genuine affection for the boy as well as a sincere
reverence for his position as titular head of France.

Despite the fact that it meant a carriage trip from the Duke's
residence at the Palais Royal to the King's apartments in the
Tuileries (a palace then and not simply a garden as it is today,
it was burned down by a mob during the Commune in 1871),
Orleans paid the boy a visit every day, called him "Sire," and
treated him with customary deference. He was of course much
closer to his nephew than any of those fierce monarchists in the
Parlement who were so anxious to preserve the royal prerogative.
The charge that he was abusing his power in putting the King's
gold at Law's disposal opened all the wounds he had suffered at

* James B. Perkins, *France Under the Regency* (Boston: Houghton Mifflin
Co., 1901).

the hands of gossip and rumor in the past. In eventually confronting these *robins* with the boy King himself in a *Lit de Justice*, he was showing them that they could not manipulate public opinion by trying to arouse the passions of those devoted to the King. In fact, no one was more devoted to Louis XV than the Regent himself, and his effectiveness in chastising the Parlement of Paris was an emblem of this devotion.

The *Lit de Justice* was held in the Tuileries Palace, where the young King lived. August 25 was a very warm day—not so warm, however, that the nobility would dispense with their magnificent trailing robes. Guards were everywhere, to make sure that no one walked out of the session. A throne had been built for the occasion, and the entire scene was highly formal and ritualized. Though all had been arranged by Orleans, he never spoke. He let D'Argenson, who was also Keeper of the Seals, deliver the edict of the Regency Council forbidding the Parlement any control over the royal treasury or the kingdom's finances. In reply the president of the Parlement read a remonstrance. "But the scoundrel trembled," wrote a gleeful Saint-Simon. "As he uttered it, his broken voice, the constraint of his eyes, the shock and trouble visible in his whole person counteracted this last drop of venom, the libation of which he could not deny to himself and his Assembly." It was a futile gesture of defiance. The Keeper of the Seals replied, after climbing to the throne, talking to the boy, Louis XV, and descending deliberately, "The King chooses to be obeyed and obeyed upon the spot." To this there was no reply.

As the members filed from the chamber, Saint-Simon recalls the exaltation he felt. "Way was made for us to the steps. The crowd, the company, the spectacle restrained our talk and our joy. I was choking with it."

A few members brave or foolish enough to express their opposition to the Regent were arrested and detained for several months. Parlement's attempt to limit an autocratic government by holding the purse strings was over. The episode was not only an endorsement of John Law but a recognition that in modern times, whoever controls the finances controls everything.

Under the Regency, there was to be no legislative check. This was good news for John Law, but it would have been healthier in the long run if the government's accounts had not been the narrow preserve of a few rich noblemen and the various bankers. R. R. Palmer in *The World of the French Revolution* compares the British and French systems of the time:

In England, through the institution of Parliament, economic and political power coincided and the elites of wealth and government were the same people. This fact, peculiar to England, had very many important consequences. It made the government financially very strong. The Bank of England was founded in 1694 chiefly to provide a channel by which private wealth could be made available to William III in his wars against Louis XIV. Men of means would more readily lend to a government whose policies and finances they could control. The government, in sharp contrast to France, could draw on the full resources of the country. The credit of the British government, seemingly inexhaustible, became a puzzle to the rest of the world where the mechanism of credit was not so well understood. It was widely expected, during the French Revolutionary wars that England would soon collapse in a pile of worthless paper, but the truth is that British credit as much as anything else defeated not only Louis XIV but also Napoleon.

Law now had his chance to develop a daring expansion of trade, to be carried out on credit by the Western Company. There would be challenges from private quarters, but no group of men of wealth were to be a match for the combination of Law's initiatives and manipulations of credit so long as Orleans and his followers supported him. It was during the next twelve months that John Law completed the chief features of his famous "System" and rose rapidly to a position of importance second only to Orleans himself.

THE SYSTEM

Money is not the value *for* which
goods are exchanged, but the
value *by* which they are exchanged.

John Law, 1705

9

Diversifying the Western Company

Although shares of the Western Company had not yet become the hot issue they would shortly be, during 1718 the public was made acquainted with the supposed glories of Mississippi, and some unsavory moves were begun for forcing its colonization in the face of a population reluctant to emigrate from a France growing in prosperity. The propaganda had begun as a justification by the government for granting such a concession to a foreigner. So sensitive was the question of Mississippi's golden promise that when the terrible-tempered Cadillac returned from there with reports of the meagerness of Crozat's colony and its extensive financial losses, of bad weather, smuggling, cheating, lazy *coureurs des bois* from Canada who would not till the land, canards about Bienville, the one man who really knew the territory, Cadillac was warned to be silent. When he continued to denounce the Western Company, he and his son were clapped into the Bastille from September 1717 to February 1718.

There was, of course, no opposition press at the time. Statements like that of Noailles went uncontradicted: "There are solid reasons to believe that [the mines of Mississippi] are as abundant as those of Mexico." There really was lead in Illinois, and on the strength of convincing evidence, Law probably hoped that other minerals would be found, because he had the government transfer Illinois from New France to Mississippi as part of his concession. The public could read in *Nouveau Mercure* in September 1717 about the quantities of gold, silver, lead, and "a very precious rock from which natives removed certain green stones, beautiful and hard, resembling emeralds." Government memorandums described the rich soil, several crops a year, forests, wild cattle with "a fleece finer than that of European sheep." In February 1718 Cadillac might have read in the *Mercure* that Mississippi was "one of the most beautiful and fertile   countries in the world." By September there were reports of fabulous wheat crops. A letter from the colony published in the *Mercure* said that France needed only to send industrious people who like work in order to make Louisiana the most flourishing country in the world.

Undoubtedly, such reports had their inspiration in John Law's agents. We can only assume that Law distributed stock in the Western Company generously in quarters where it counted. His proposal to settlers seemed like an offer they could not refuse: free housing, land, horses, cattle, seed, barnyard animals and fowl, furniture, cooking utensils. There was almost no response.

In fact, Law recognized that there was no motive for colonization among the French, and from the beginning he sought to populate Mississippi with those who had no other choice. Salt smugglers condemned to the galley ships of the Mediterranean were transferred to the colony in 1717. In the fall of 1718, nearly 300 people detained in Bicetre Prison on charges ranging from begging to murder were sent off to America, and a royal ordinance of November 10, 1718 authorized the practice—which was not publicized. Publicity gave it out always that anyone going to Mississippi was going of his own free will and gladly.

Clearly, it was in Law's interest to deceive the public at this time. Just how much he or anyone knew about the colony is a question. It was less a *place* to him than an abstraction, a symbol of trade. Here was the beginning of that modern irresponsibility that allowed the evils of slavery, dark satanic mills, and sweat shops to support a growing class of people who never saw, or

cared to see, the source of their wealth. Law well understood the
necessity for populating the colony, and he was prepared to go to
extraordinary lengths to do so. Perhaps the suffering he indirectly
brought to the miserable dregs of humanity sent to Mississippi
was no more than they would have suffered in jail or in galleys.
But he cannot escape criticism for this cruel policy.

At the same time, he must be applauded for his memorandum,
the *Denier Royal* (Royal Revenue), issued in the spring of
1718, proposing sweeping reforms of the outrageous system of
taxation. His hatred of inefficiency and sympathy for the people are
in the finest liberal tradition, and he attempted to practice what he
preached as the opportunity arose. Even before he became minister,
he was able to save millions for the government by having useless
office holders eliminated and he made a beginning on a better tax
system, which unfortunately reverted to its old vices after he left
France.

A week or so after the humiliation of the Parlement, John Law
took the first of a series of steps to "diversify" the assets of the
Western Company. He acquired the monopoly on tobacco manu-
facture and marketing, believing that his colony would supply
large quantities of this expensive plant to France. He agreed to
pay the government 4 million livres a year for nine years for this
privilege. This was twice the previous revenue and suggested great
expectations from plantations in Louisiana. Such generous terms
helped to strengthen confidence in the Western Company, which
together with the bank was now being called the System, an apt
epithet for summing up what no one quite understood (and one
we use ourselves for the Federal Reserve). At this point, the System was just developing, but the word anticipated Law's domination of the country's economy. Its connotation was favorable to
some, but not to all. D'Argenson, despite his prominent role in
the *Lit de Justice*, where he defended Law by implication, would
have been happier without the Scotsman on the scene.

And so the minister of finance encouraged the so-called Paris
brothers, four of the private bankers who had grown rich supplying Louis XIV's armies, in their desire to create what was called

the Anti-System. These men were hard working and feared. They had been in charge of the *visa*, the investigation of tax returns under Noailles, and now they gave their stern attention to Law, a man they detested. Recently, they had bid successfully for the contract for "farming" the taxes (collecting them), agreeing to pay the government 48.5 million livres a year. Observing that Law was selling shares in a company with a meager income, they decided to sell shares in their profitable concession, and they capitalized it for the same sum as the Western Company, 100 million livres. Since the Paris brothers were a known quantity, it seemed likely that their proposition would make a handsome return for investors. The shares sold well and at par, while shares of the Western Company languished at half price despite the fabled riches of America. This worried Law. If rival companies were to absorb the capital he needed to attract to his overseas enterprises, he would have no more luck than Crozat.

The Anti-System started September 16, 1718. Law immediately prepared a counterattack. During the fall, he worked as much as five hours a day with the Regent. Despite a seizure of apoplexy on September 9, Orleans was up to these demands and he showed no aftereffects of his illness. On November 12 it was announced that a large group of colonists had embarked from La Rochelle for Louisiana. The word was put forth that another Western Company acquisition, which had to do with slavery, was in the offing. By December, arrangements were being made to transfer the slave trading Senegal Company to the Western Company at a price of 600,000 livres.

The company now had interests at home, in America, and in Africa, and Law had his eye on Asia. Ever since he had lived in the Netherlands, he had admired the East India Company of Holland. Although the East India Company of France was nothing by comparison, Law began a campaign to bring this enterprise under his control. It was unprofitable and troublesome to all concerned, but what he liked about it was its monopoly of French trade in the Far East—feeble now, but sure to grow along with the rest of the commerce of the nation, providing it had new management.

Law would settle its debts, provide adequate capital, replace its rotting ships. The plenitude of paper money would stimulate new business.

Before this new expansion of trade occurred, though, a far more serious development arose, over which scholars have long argued. Late in November, the decision was taken to nationalize the *Banque Générale*, which became on January 1 the *Banque Royale*. Was this dramatic shift in accordance with Law's wishes, or had the change been forced by Abbé Dubois? Or by the Regent himself? The interpretation that Law sought to keep his bank to himself and that more powerful men wished to wrest it from him would scarcely explain the power that Law acquired during 1719 once the government stood completely behind the bank. It may be true, though, that Dubois and the Regent saw the advantages accruing to them if the bank belonged to the King and not to the stockholders. And by paying off in specie the stockholders who had bought into the bank with bonds worth only a fourth of their value, the King's men did their friends a great favor. Recall that Dubois had received 30,000 livres in bank shares as a gift from the Regent at the very beginning, and later, Saint-Simon records, Law continued to finance the foreign minister's extravagances and his campaign for a cardinal's hat. But the biggest favors lay in the future, and by hindsight it appears probable that the Regent planned to use the Royal Bank as an unlimited resource by simply printing more money when the need arose.

Law had argued ever since he had come to France that the country needed a state bank; he organized his private bank only as an expedient to satisfy the council. After his narrow escape from the clutches of the Parlement, he saw that his background, as a foreigner and a Protestant, would always be a target for his enemies. The memory of Mazarin had left a heritage of xenophobia, and although the cruelty and stupidity of the Revocation of the Edict of Nantes moved the Regent to consider allowing the Huguenots to return, in the end he did not do so because of their aggressiveness and capacity for making political trouble at home and aligning themselves with the traditional Protestant enemy countries abroad. All in all, these circumstances were a hazard to the bank's duration as a private institution. Wrapped in a royal mantle, however, its future was secure and the King would reap great benefits. And since the people loved the young King, they would be pleased with his new bank.

And so the new year of 1719 began with the establishment of the *Banque Royale*, with Law at its head. The details were worked out without consulting D'Argenson, whose role in finances was henceforth so diminished that by the end of the year he was willing to give up his office. Branches of the Royal Bank were set up in Lyons, Rochelle, Tours, Orleans, and Amiens. There were about 120 million livres in paper money circulating. But in the next six months, new events developed that forced paper money on the public willy-nilly, and by June the King's bank had had to increase its circulation of notes to 300 million to meet the demand. These were the seeds of a coming speculation never before experienced in the history of man. During the winter of 1719, John Law found new means to encourage public confidence in his System, and particularly in shares in "Mississippi," as the Western Company was called.

10

No Innocent Pleasures

The Regency of the Duke of Orleans was now more than three years old and its effects on France were evident. It was a postwar regime, peaceful, gay, greedy, and pleasure seeking. "I don't like *innocent* pleasures," wrote Madame, the Regent's aging mother. Charm and corruption went together among the upper classes, and the masses were caught up in the spirit by the spread of easy money. The noun *libertine* has two meanings: moral laxity and spiritual freedom. The Regency was libertine in both senses. Situated in Paris in the Palais Royal and in the Palais du Luxembourg, home of the Regent's wild daughter, the Duchess of Berry, the Orleans family set the tone of the times by their luxurious living and self-confidence. The Duchess of Berry, with her 680,000 livres a year income, had 800 servants and gave dinners with menus such as this one of February 28, 1718:

First Service

    31 soups
    60 light entrees
   132 hors d'oeuvres

Second and Third Services

   132 hot platters
    60 cold platters
    72 mixed dishes

Fruits

100 baskets of fresh fruit
94 baskets of dried fruit
50 plates of iced fruit
106 compotes of stewed fruit

About 200 people, including princes and princesses of the blood, were served their meals by 200 Swiss waiters, hired for the occasion, while 132 footmen of the palace poured the wine. There was music and afterwards a masked ball, a *divertissement* that had recently been introduced in Paris. The variety of fowl included 327 chickens, turkeys, and ducks, 382 pigeons, and 370 pheasant and other game birds. The dinner was reported in the official press for two months.

In November of 1718, a young poet named François Marie Arouet staged his first success, *Oedipus*, and earned a pension from the Regent, even though he had denounced Orleans during his eleven months in the Bastille on a false accusation of writing a satire he had probably never seen. Young Arouet then changed his name to Voltaire.

Conspicuous consumption moved from Versailles to Paris, and the repression was gone; the theater was free to speak out. Fénelon's *Télémaque*, banned under Louis XIV, was published, Cardinal de Retz's *Mémoirs* was published, and Montesquieu's *Lettres persanes*, satirizing the Regency, appeared.

The Opera was always crowded, especially after the speculative craze began. Easy money made it possible for social climbers to spend their evenings at the Opera, which had been built as an adjunct to the Palais Royal the year Law was born, 1671, and which thanks to his System was enjoying enormous revenues. It was just as expensive relatively to attend a performance then as it is today, but the season was far longer—as many as 161 performances—and no subsidy was required because of the low cost of labor. In 1721 the profit for the year was 117,098 livres. Part of this came from balls given on free evenings, when a dance floor was put up over the orchestra, bleachers were erected on the side, and two string ensembles played at either end of a vast arena for dancing until dawn.

One difference between the Regency and the last days of Louis XIV was the removal to Paris of many of the upper classes, tired of chateau life and the court of Versailles. These people brought money to town, built fine houses, and patronized the arts.

The best music was now to be heard at Paris. The best theatrical performances relied on popular support, instead of on the patronage of the monarch or of some great nobleman; writers no longer measured their success by the favor they obtained at court. The Regent did much to make the capital attractive; it was his favorite residence; he preferred the excitement of new ideas to the courtly platitudes of Versailles. In this atmosphere the dazzling ideas of the Enlightenment were first conceived by Voltaire and Montesquieu. And let us not exclude Law's influence on the spirit of the 18th century. An anonymous student of Law's theories wrote in 1851: "Before approaching the material side of this great deception [the belief that it is easy to get rich] which is to be found at the cradle of the time deservedly called the century of light, it is absolutely necessary to come back to its chief author, to the doctrine, to the conviction and to the economic credo of Law.*

Law's money was a catalyst for bringing the classes together and was to draw huge numbers to the rue Quincampoix to trade shares for paper money in the conviction that their activity was actually generating wealth. It was as if everyone had read *Money and Trade Considered.*

"During the first years of the Regency, French society was carried off by a tempest of folly. Far from dying down, this bestial frenzy, shameless, hungry for scandal, intensified in 1719 and 1720 at the time of Law's System, during the recoinage and the speculation." †

Among the scandals discussed was what went on at the famous suppers (*soupers*) given privately by the Regent at the Palais

* James B. Perkins, *France Under the Regency* (Boston: Houghton Mifflin Co., 1901).
† Charles Kunstler, *La Vie Quotidienne sous la Régence* (Paris, 1960).

Royal. He would gather his intimate male friends, the *roués*, his current mistress and perhaps former ones, and late at night, with guards at the door, would enjoy a banquet, drink, sing, tell risqué stories, and . . . No eyewitness recorded the proceedings, and we are left with Saint-Simon's priggish reports. Saint-Simon, no *roué*, had no mistresses and was true to his wife. He delighted in describing the infidelities of the Regent's clique. A handsome playboy named Fargis, who was angry with a Mme. du Brossay, sent a note to Orleans listing fifty-two men she had slept with. The Regent showed the list to a particularly insolent *roué*, who looked it over and said, "You must add a fifty-third—me."

Events at the suppers, widely discussed by those not present, included: the representation of the Garden of Paradise by nude ballet dancers, who later flung themselves among the party in the dark; the numbers of whores sometimes present, and what a joke it was to have venereal disease. Orleans enjoyed himself shamelessly, but never discussed affairs of state. "Look in your glass," he told one prying woman, "and see if such a pretty face was made for politics." One gathers his little orgies, if indeed that is what they were, were not so very wicked and harmed few.

But Orleans's laxity troubled the public. He flaunted his affairs. On one occasion, he celebrated a new liaison as though it were a royal marriage. Mme. d'Averne was feted at a public ball at St. Cloud overlooking the Seine, and carriages lined the banks for miles to watch the illumination from 20,000 lanterns of varying colors that were turned on and off. Voltaire composed fulsome verses to the new Venus, who was not even very attractive. Still, she wheedled 100,000 livres and a post for her husband out of the Regent. One who watched expressed the confused feelings of the onlookers, at once enthralled and disgusted: "It is against religion to proclaim so publicly the triumph of vice."

The habits of his favorite daughter, the Duchess of Berry, to whom his attachment was so close as to create rumors suggesting incest (Voltaire hinted it), were disgraceful. Brilliant but spoiled, she slept until noon and wasted her life on men and alcohol, often drinking herself into a stupor. She did everything to excess, including smoking. "Barring avarice she was a model of every vice," said Saint-Simon. Two days after her marriage she slept with a lover. On one occasion, she appeared in the nude as a statue of Venus on a pedestal in the Palais Royal. Moralists can take comfort in her demise. Although she finally became a religious fanatic, she gave herself over less to God than to an adventurer named Rion, who dominated her with a Rasputin-like charm and controlled her to the point where he could force her to wear clothes she did not like and to stay home when she wanted to go out. She died from dissipation at the age of twenty-four, and despite her high birth, she was denied the customary funeral orations and was mourned by her father alone.

Orleans indulged his appetites, but they did not entirely satisfy him. He had so many mistresses that his mother compared him to a sultan, and she described one mistress, Mme. de Parabere, as the favorite in his harem in 1716. When he tired of a woman he would sometimes pass her on to a *roué*, particularly the Duke of Richelieu, who was perhaps the most famous womanizer of that circle, and an exquisite who paid 260 livres a yard for gold cloth for his cloak. Relationships were frivolous, sensual, and not deeply felt.

License was not a novelty among the French nobility. Louis XIV in his prime escorted his mistress into a boudoir in front of the court. Orleans was more informal and, like some American presidents, was known for his salty language and candor. When the Prince of Condé said he had missed a council meeting because he was drunk and that his servants would swear to it, Orleans said, "When I'm drunk, I go to bed." Hypocrisy was not one of the vices of the Regency. Orleans was tolerant of malicious gossip and indifferent to calumny. A recent biographer plays down his scandals as the exaggerations of enemies and not the accounts of objective observers.

But there were signs of a society not quite in control of itself, and one of them was duelling, which, though illegal, was as frequent at that time as ever in history. A duel was fought by two friends sharing a bed after an argument over which one of them was taking too much of the blankets. Two men who slapped each other while drunk and had forgotten about it the next morning were forced by friends to duel; one was killed and the other jailed. There was duelling everywhere, even next to the King's residence, the Tuileries. Women duelled. Two marquises fought with daggers and would have killed one another had not servants stopped the bloody struggle. Their dispute was over the twenty-two-year-old Prince of Soubise, called the handsomest man of the court. Madame did not think him worth the trouble. "Not bad, but he looks like a nursing calf," she said.

Even the clergy could not resist duelling. The Bishop of Puy-en-Velay got into an argument with a distinguished officer who challenged him. The bishop, a former cavalry officer, killed the poor man and then obtained pardon from the Regent.

A harmless habit then was tobacco. John Law's aim was to step up consumption, and he was on the right track. The use of tobacco was just starting, the preference being for snuff. All the court *prisait*, as they said, took tobacco into their nostrils and never wiped their noses, which made Madame remark that the ladies looked as if they had been swimming in a privy. Moustaches disappeared to accommodate the habit. Women pinched snuff from the snuff boxes of men.

John Law had decrees passed to promote the import of tobacco leaf, and there was a fine of 10,000 livres for growing it domestically. He did not stay in France long enough to see the hold tobacco was to get on his adopted country.

Gambling, by comparison with our own day, was not for the millions in Regency France, but among the upper classes it was vicious and ruinous. John Law himself was said to have won a man's estate during his stay in Scotland in his thirties, but while developing his System he had no time for cards or dice, which suddenly became the rage in 1719. A nobleman lost 100,000 livres at one sitting; the Duke de Villequier took three days to lose 43,000. These were petty sums compared with the dowry of 600,000 livres lost by the Viscount de Tavannes a few months after marrying the daughter of the receiver general of finance at Tours. However, because the winner was a woman who would not herself have been able to pay off if she had lost, pressure was brought to bear and she settled for 20,000.

Women loved gambling, some of them were inclined to cheat shamelessly. Caught cheating, Mme. de Saint-Sulpice insulted her accusers and pocketed what she had stolen. It was all part of the social scene, and one could pick up a game all over Paris. At the home of Prince Rakoczy on the Quai Malaquais, known as the Transylvania, an "Academy of Gambling" was set up. The atmosphere of this sinister place is described in the opera *Manon Lescaut*.

And there were the card sharps, who accommodated the many visitors without connections in Paris. One Army officer, who was down to his last 500 livres, bought a dozen lamps, which he set up outside his door and offered to amuse anyone who cared to enter. All they found inside was a table covered with a cloth, the officer, and his few livres. The first night he cleared more than 2,000 livres and said he owed it all to the beauty of the lights, which drew the innocents like so many moths.

A psychology of pleasure and of great expectations was developing among thousands in Paris, and John Law must have sensed the possibility of launching a far greater enterprise than his bank. He saw that men and women were throwing discretion to the winds, that society was in a turbulent mood and would be prepared to support a venture that would carry them farther along the path of hedonism than they themselves conceived possible. His System had reached that point of economic development where it was ready to burgeon. All that was required was capital. He now began planning to expand geometrically and to bring the public into his enterprises on a scale never before attempted.

11

And Now the Indies

"By the beginning of 1719 all the wheels of the System had been mounted," wrote Eugene Daire, the economic historian who published much of Law's writings in the middle of the nineteenth century. The wheels consisted of the bank, paper money, credit at low interest (4 per cent as opposed to the usurious rate of 30 per cent that obtained under Louis XIV), and a trading firm, the Western Company, to expand overseas commerce and compete more strenuously with the Dutch and English. The bank was now a royal or state bank, which was what Law had in mind from the beginning, and its operation was sound.

Reflecting with pride on the monetary edifice he had erected, Law noted in a memorandum later in the year: "The first expedient [for enriching the country] is a royal bank which increases the nation's money. There are 18 million people in France. To make so many people react [productively] requires immense sums for daily expenditures and perpetual circulation of a very large amount of money." At the end of 1718, a total of 148 million livres in paper bills had been issued.

Fewer compliments were forthcoming about the Western Company, which had not excited public interest; its shares could be had for 250, half the price at their issue. It was this segment of Law's

System that called for his attention. Key accessories had to be added to the "wheels" Daire refers to—a dazzling body, so to speak, and finally a more refined fuel to make the whole thing move rapidly had to be developed. The body was to be a new trading company, and the fuel a mixture of more paper money and more shares of stock.

Designs for these innovations were not wanting in Law's fertile intelligence. A hint of his conception appeared in a memorandum he wrote to Orleans shortly after he became Regent: "Your Highness will recall the day at Marly when you honored me by saying that my proposals were allowing you to begin to see an end to the country's commercial difficulties. I then had the honor of saying that my idea for a bank was not my best idea, that I had another worth 500 million that would cost the people nothing. I cannot believe Your Highness has forgotten this proposition, or wants to neglect it; it is worthy of your attention." After three years' time he now had the Regent's attention. Law would show him how to get something for nothing.

Carefully he explained the limitations of the Western Company, which were essentially those of scale: its capital was too meager and its scope not broad enough. True, it had acquired the tobacco monopoly and the Senegal Company's trade in slaves, but this was only a beginning of what might be possible.

A company could be formed [the *Cambridge Modern History* tells us] to which the government should grant all the commercial and financial privileges farmed by various bodies; in which the creditors of the State should receive shares in exchange for their debts, and in which the public should be induced to invest their savings. The one great organization would control the foreign commerce of France, develop the magnificent resources of her colonial empire, reorganize her fiscal system, and if necessary, exercise a controlling influence on domestic producers; by consolidation with the state bank it would unite the money and trading powers so that the stream of money should flow straight into the fields of commerce; by swallowing up all existing associations, and thus engrossing all large capitals and sources of revenue, it would enable the French nation to trade as a unit, and [Law would] "compel all subjects to find their fortunes only in the happiness and opulence of the whole kingdom." Thus would be reared a giant trust, broad-based as France, wide-reaching as the realms of commerce and finance. No foreign rival could withstand such an institution, and English and Dutch would be swept from the seas.

If this had been but a sketch for adoption in some future century, like Leonardo's flying machine, one would marvel at the prescience of its author. But Law the theoretician was also the practitioner; he was trying to be a combination of the Wright Brothers and Colonel Lindbergh in the realm of finance.

His new company, to supersede the Western Company, was designed in the winter of 1719. Its foundation was none other than the moribund French East India Company, which together with the even less profitable China Company would conduct the entire overseas world trade of France. To be sure, Law was very much aware of the small share of such trade France then had, and it was the shimmering prospect of outdistancing rivals that particularly struck the Regent and Dubois, with whom he worked assiduously on the drafting of essential papers and edicts. In September 1715, Law's memorandum, *The Reestablishment of Commerce*, had harped on the fact that tiny Holland, unable to produce a thirtieth of its own needs, had become very rich, in part at the expense of France, by developing a world trade with which it could pay for food and goods produced by the French. "The Dutch sail more than 30,000 ships all over the world. . . . They have become the factors of all the other countries." It was the Dutch model, well known to Law, that he hoped to imitate and eventually destroy.

The conglomerate he was putting together would provide increased efficiency (all conglomerates promise increased efficiency), improve profits, and through an increase in capital, expand its business. Had Law not run into difficulties elsewhere, he might eventually have succeeded in some of his overseas objectives, but the trade that he generated shortly was not in merchandise; it was in securities.

Years later, Law reflected on what he did then and concluded that he had tried to move too quickly. His triumph in seeing Parlement subdued and the conversion of his bank into a national enterprise had begun to blind him to certain human limitations, his own, and the frailty of his fellow men. He was already greatly admired. Lady Mary Wortley Montagu returned from France in 1718 with the report that she had found "an Englishman (at least a Briton) absolute in Paris." The parenthesis was a putdown of Law's Scots blood.

Two immediate steps were taken on the road to new riches for France. The Royal Bank began printing new money, and Law forced up the price of Western Company shares. The 148 millions circulating in paper were not excessive, but neither were they as inflationary as was required if the indebted upper classes were to pay off mortgages and other loans advantageously. Appetites had been whetted by the arrangement that gave the stockholders of Law's *Banque Générale* enormous profits when it was nationalized. The Regent was under pressure to make the largess more general. Just whose responsibility it was to determine the money supply in the King's bank is not clear, but in the King's name the amount of paper rose by 30 per cent during its first four months in 1719. To justify such an expansion, it was necessary to encourage a preference for paper over coin, and this was done by stipulating that no matter what devaluation might occur in the specie of the realm, the paper would remain constant. Even Law's greatest admirer, Professor Harsin, had to admit that Law intended to devalue the coin and thus force the public willy-nilly to prefer paper currency. The royal decree of April 22, 1719 says just that: "As the circulation of bank notes is more useful to His Majesty's subjects than gold or silver coin, and as they merit special protection because of the preference of metal money abroad, His Majesty intends that these notes stipulated in current money cannot be subject to the diminutions which might happen to coins, and that they are always to be paid in full."

This decree is considered by Eugene Daire as the most important in the entire history of Law's System, because it opened the flood gates of paper money. As coins came into the bank and its new branches, the demand for paper required that more of it be printed. Even though the original bills of Law's private bank were retired and no longer circulated after July 8, the amount in circulation by then was already double what the *Banque Générale* had issued. In six months, a policy of prudence had been transformed into one of generous expansion. What was all this new money for? Speculation!

In April, Law accomplished one of his most surprising gambits to make the shares of the Western Company attractive to the public. In his long experience as a speculator, he had become familiar with the occasional practice of dealing in futures—in effect betting on the rise or fall of a price on a given future date of a security, commodity, or foreign currency. ". . . A large proportion of such dealings is purely gambling, and upon this ground the suppression of futures by law has been advocated." (Palgrave's *Dictionary of Political Economy*.) The practice had not yet been introduced in France, and Law startled the financial community by offering to pay par (500) several months hence for shares of the Western Company, then selling at 300. He made a contract with each buyer and gave him a down payment of 40 per cent, putting up a total of 40,000 livres against 100,000 contracted for. As Perkins points out, the public should have reasoned that something was wrong with such an offer, since all Law had to do was buy at the lower price and sell when it rose. Why should anyone offer to pay more for a stock in the future and let the present opportunity pass? The answer is that the customer does not care if the seller is crazy, and since it was a bona fide offer, why not seize the chance to get out of a stock that was not moving?

Of course, the very irrationality of Law's gesture led people to only one conclusion: he knew something no one else knew. The financial community, then very small, was suddenly talking about the Western Company. Rumors circulated about Mississippi, which was the name that became current rather than Louisiana. It was said that there was gold and silver over there. Within a month, the stock had recovered and was selling at par early in May. It was time for launching the new venture.

Late in May, the Regency Council issued an edict authorizing the acquisition by the Western Company of the East India and China Companies. There was no financial press then, so word of mouth carried the news around Paris. Anyone owning Western Company shares suddenly found himself a rich man, because the new *Compagnie des Indes*, the Indies Company, required capital and was going to sell shares exclusively to the Western Company stockholders.

There were no prospectuses, and if there had been it is doubtful that anyone would have had time to read them in the excitement that swept through the city during the month of June. The great John Law was going to modernize French overseas commerce, and he would bring out the gold and silver and precious metal in the mountains of Mississippi. But he needed money to reorganize everything, 25 million livres to start (modest in comparison with the Western Company's nominal capital of 100 million). And in all justice, he owed it to those who had faith in him to let them in on the ground floor. Just as those who had faith in the bank had been rewarded for putting up capital in depreciated state bonds with payment in specie at face value, now those who had bought into the Western Company would be allowed to buy one 500-livre share of the Indies Company for every four Western shares they owned. Suddenly, Western Company stock was in great demand. The two kinds of stock became known shortly as *mères et filles,* mothers and daughters. To buy a daughter you needed four mothers. Issued late in May, daughters were selling at 1,000 livres, and those who sold out doubled their money in less than thirty days. By the time Law met his obligations for his futures, the Western Company shares had risen to several thousand livres per share, and the owners had to give them up for a mere 500 livres.

The boom in Mississippi shares in the summer of 1719 was not due only to Law's genius for manipulating the public by gestures that appealed to their essential greed. They had to have money, and this he had printed up for them. He had sense enough to avoid overissuing paper at this point. Ever confident in the future of all his endeavors, he gladly extended credit to his customers. One only had to put up 10 per cent and twenty months remained to pay off the balance in equal installments. It was actually a margin system, since shares could be sold at a profit within a month before any payments came due. One might net 450 livres on a payment of 50, a profit of 900 per cent. Even the grasping Fuggers in Augsburg realized only 50 per cent a year in their banking heyday in the sixteenth century. The situation Law had created was revolutionary. It promised to provide for the multitude wealth that had until now been given only to the nobility by the King. Here was the chance to realize the universal dream of instant riches. A sort of financial democracy reigned, in which equality with his master could be obtained overnight by a valet. And it was no dream. The humblest people *did* make fortunes, *did* buy chateaux, *did* live outrageously, and *did* thumb their noses at titled persons.

The caldron where this financial concoction bubbled was located in a little street in the business district of Paris on the Right Bank near Les Halles and the Hôtel de Ville, a street altogether undistinguished for anything but a few good restaurants. Its odd name, the rue Quincampoix, has remained, remembered through all the years.

12

Rue Quincampoix

There was no stock exchange, no Bourse in Paris during the Regency. The financial district as such was a warren of narrow streets, where Italian bankers and money changers had set up shop several centuries ago not far from the Hôtel de Ville (City Hall). The rue des Lombards and the rue de Venise, the busiest streets, had an ancient if not honorable past, given the ecclesiastic strictures on usury. A Lombard banker named Boccaccio had been one of the rue des Lombard's visitors, and while in Paris he found a mistress who gave birth to a child destined to be the author of *The Decameron*.

Just off the tiny rue de Venise is the rue Quincampoix. Now a miserable slum, in the eighteenth century it was an attractive street, short and narrow, with a mingling of tall houses, some handsome new private homes, and old medieval structures piled oddly atop one another. Its name derived from the original proprietor of the land, Nicholas de Kiquenpoit, and it had become the headquarters of the Drapers Guild. It was near the rue des Cinq Diamants, a center for jewelers, and pawn-broking spilled over from there into the rue Quincampoix. Loan sharks set up shop there, and as stock companies grew in number their shares and the various state bonds floated under Louis XIV were traded in cafés, restaurants, and the street itself. The activity was not great enough to attract much attention until 1719.

Then, as the market in Law's shares took hold, this little street, not much longer than a football field, became the scene of an increasingly hysterical pit of auctioneers and speculators. Here indeed paper became king. Stock certificates, sales slips, and millions of livres of currency suddenly transformed the place into an arena of competition that attracted not only thousands of Parisians but also provincials, and eventually foreigners. There were no rules or regulations in the beginning. After the tumult became almost insane and trading continued into the night, arrangements were made to fence off the rue Rambuteau at one end and the rue des Ours at the other. Guards were posted who, with a roll of drums, opened the gates at seven in the morning and closed them again at dusk, allowing the neighborhood some relief and a night's rest, and giving the "Mississippians" a chance to spend their money in a good restaurant or at the Opera. Saint-Simon describes the activity at the height of the frenzy as such "that persons rushed there all day long." People would have spent their Sundays and holidays on the rue Quincampoix had it been permitted.

The smallest space soon brought enormous prices, and almost every shop was converted into some kind of brokerage house, café or restaurant, or any sort of a public place that provided shelter on rainy or cold days where business could be conducted. A cobbler could rent the use of his bench, providing pen and paper, for 200 livres a day. Attic rooms rented for 400 a month. Superstructures were tacked together on roofs, and these found tenants. Enterprising types set up chairs for spectators to rent, as more and more curiosity seekers of the upper classes wandered over to take in the spectacle, to watch faces light up as fortunes were made. Euphoria brought fantastic tips in its wake. One man paid 200 livres for a partridge in celebration of his luck. A hunchback is said to have made 150,000 livres by renting his hump as a desk, no doubt an apocryphal story; he probably made huge tips, though, and many a trader must have paid for the right to rub his hump for good luck.

Seeing that at last his System was evoking a sensational response, John Law did not pause in his program of acquisition and expansion for the Indies Company. Now was the moment to seize every possible opportunity to do away with the vestiges of medieval commercial practice, to put down his rivals, the Paris brothers and their accursed Anti-System, to press on with colonization of Louisiana. The Royal Bank, which he still ran as though it were his own, must be moved to more fitting quarters, from the modest building in the rue Ste. Avoie, to the Hôtel Nevers in the rue de Richelieu, which was to be enlarged and decorated by Antonio Pellegrini of Rome. (His sister-in-law was Rosalba Carriera, a popular painter who became an intimate of the Law family in 1720.)

Next, the Indies Company was installed in the handsome Mazarin Palace near the Hôtel Nevers. The purchase price was said to be one million livres, further evidence of the difference John Law was making in the world of booming money and trade. This sum was more than half the amount of his entire fortune on his arrival in Paris five years before. Now he tossed such sums around almost casually. He bought six more buildings for the purpose of creating a Bourse, and had he succeeded he might have brought the entire mechanism of the System into one great financial park. In the meantime, he accepted the reality of the rue Quincampoix's makeshift facilities and took over the Hôtel de Beaufort, at 65 rue Quincampoix, as a branch office of the Royal Bank.

These real estate developments were to be expected in a city beginning to feel a sense of dynamism. What was new under the sun was the opportunity for anyone to make a killing in the stock market. The success of the mother-daughter issue deserved to be repeated, thought Law, and in July he announced that the Indies Company had acquired a nine-year monopoly on the royal mint for 50 million a year. Henceforth, Law would be in charge of the considerable manufacturing work involved in providing coins for the realm. He arranged for fifteen months' credit to pay for this new privilege, which would return a good profit— Law claimed 10 million a year, but more conservative estimates were not less than 4 million. Additional capital of 25 million was needed at this time, however, and the public was again invited to subscribe for shares at 1,000 livres, the current price of other Law stock. This offer was open to holders of either of the previous issues on a five-to-one basis; these naturally became "granddaughters" and were as eagerly sought after as the rest. At this time, Law promised to pay a 12 per cent dividend at the end of the year.

By the beginning of September, there were 380 million livres in paper bank notes circulating, ten times the amount of gold and silver in the Royal Bank's vaults. In nationalizing the bank, Law had reasoned that the King would never be so foolish as to abuse his power by printing more money than necessary and thus ruining his own credit. And who was to say at this point whether such an expansion of money could not be absorbed? The rue Quincampoix gave every evidence of an enormous enthusiasm for the System and its anticipated profits. Not only Paris but provincial cities too showed, upon subsequent examination by economists, that during this period genuine prosperity had taken hold.

For example, the debt of the city of Toulouse fell from 142,-000 to 112,000 livres. In Marseilles, commerce with Africa went up from 138,184 livres in 1716 to 914,368 in 1720. Imports likewise rose during the period at an average rate of 100 per cent a year. Law was well known and feared by Marseilles ship owners, who saw his System as collectivist and a threat to their existence. One official wrote in a report, "I hope to God he forgets about Marseilles." In Normandy prosperity reigned, large amounts of paper money circulated, real estate turned over rapidly, and mortgages were paid off.

The signs were all favorable. During August, Mississippi shares —mothers, daughters, and later granddaughters—were bid up in the rue Quincampoix from 1,000 to 2,000 to 3,000 to 4,000.

Imagine the good fortune of those who had bought shares in April for 300, or even in July for 1,000! The scramble to pay off debts filled the land with paper money, and because it was only paper and inherently untrustworthy, the best thing to do was to buy things—real estate, jewelry, clothes—to travel, go to the theater, dine out. The cautious converted their money to jewelry and deposited it abroad—or sold their paper bills to foreigners for coin, which could also be conveniently hoarded abroad. French coin was less attractive than paper at the moment, because Law had devalued it in July. Had Law been unscrupulous, he could have put a fortune aside in London or Amsterdam, and it was assumed that he had done so. In fact, his money went into French real estate and before the boom was over he had bought eleven chateaux in the countryside in addition to the considerable property he owned in Paris.

The chronicler Buvat records that on March 27, 1719, Law had recently acquired the duchy of Mercoeur from the Princess of Condé for 865,000 livres, the estate of Tancarville in Normandy once owned by Crozat who had paid 509,000 livres for it, and seven houses in the Place Vendôme and had contracted to buy for 750,000 livres the Hôtel de Soissons, though that deal never went through. Law sometimes paid too much, which may have been a way of doing someone useful to him a favor. For the land at St. Germain on the Rouen road, valued at 400,000, he paid the Marquis of Vieubourg a million livres.

John Law was used to money and elegant living, but he was not greedy; he took no step to secure for himself a great personal fortune. His interests and his passions remained in financial manipulation. He was like a creative artist, burning with a need to express himself in the terms he understood and which he had done so much to refine.

On August 27 some shares traded at 5,000! There was delirium in Paris, and some amusing stories have been preserved. Perhaps the most famous "Mississippian," as the new millionaires came to be called, was the widow Chaumont, who had come to Paris in 1717 from her home in the provincial town of Namur to collect a debt she was counting on to keep her out of the poorhouse. Alas, she was able to collect only in state bonds selling at 60 per cent discount. What to do? Knowing nothing of finance, she used the bonds to buy shares in the Western Company. Within three years, her fortune stood at 100 million livres, and she had moved to a chateau at Ivry and hung the walls with Gobelins tapestries. There on a typical day, friends feasted on an ox, two calves, six sheep, and numberless fowls, all washed down with champagne and burgundy.

Among the humble who prospered in the rue Quincampoix were a waiter (30 million), a chimney sweep (40 million), a lackey (50 million), a beggar (70 million), and a shopkeeper (127 million). "God never made men out of nothing faster," Montesquieu later commented when he satirized the System in his *Persian Letters*. A clerk made an 86 per cent profit during his lunch hour. A cook turned up at the Opera loaded with diamonds and pronounced herself as good as her astonished mistress, who was foolish enough to ask what she thought she was doing. A simple soul who had got rich quick served soup out of a handsome bowl she had bought, not knowing that it was a particular kind of chamber pot used discreetly by elegant ladies during long church services.

And the rich got richer. The Princes of Bourbon and Conti respectively made 20 million and 4.5 million livres. An Englishman named Guesche made 4 million livres and distributed 500,000 among his servants. The young King gave a servant shares valued at 25,000 livres that soon rose to 200,000.

Of course, shares fluctuated wildly. A rumor that the Spanish had ravaged Louisiana sent prices tumbling precipitously toward the end of August. The story is told of the Regent's physician, who naturally plunged in the rue Quincampoix with great hope. He was taking the rather feeble pulse of a sick man during a slide in the market and was heard to say in an agitated voice, "It's falling, it's falling!" The frightened patient groaned in despair until reassured that the doctor had just learned of bad news about his investments. "You see doctors of the Sorbonne, priests and nuns who mix in this business with everyone else. The world is enchanted by it all," Buvat noted in his journal.

The quotation of 5,000 on August 27 "was the signal Law was awaiting before he pulled off his final coup," wrote Daire. This was the assumption by the System of the national debt, then standing at a billion and a half livres. What had occurred up to now was to be but the prologue!

In the name of the King, the Regency Council announced that the Indies Company had outbid the Paris brothers, whose stock company held the contract for farming the taxes. Revenge was sweet, and the Anti-System, supposed to draw capital away from Law's enterprises, was eliminated. The Indies Company was now in control of foreign trade, tobacco marketing, and the mint; it was moving in to take over much of the finances of the government itself. Also, it would henceforth be the collector of the kingdom's taxes. Moreover, the council announced, the Indies Company was going to lend His Majesty's government a billion and a half livres, representing all the state bonds in circulation.

Why had the government decided to get out of the bond business? Because it was costing 4 per cent to pay bondholders' coupons, and John Law's company would only charge 3 per cent. It was understood that bondholders would be paid off at the face value of their bonds, and that they could then reinvest their money on the rue Quincampoix.

This *démarche* was overwhelming. The daring of John Law took away the public breath. His genius was now doubted by none. Any man who could provide a billion and a half (the term *billion* was unknown then, and the term *millionaire* was invented at this time in Paris to describe pejoratively the upstart rich) was a sort of god to be worshipped, for he would surely shower infinite riches on the multitude. What next? Law in fact had no such funds available. But he knew where he could lay hands on them. On September 13 he issued 100,000 new shares at a par value of 500. The public fell on them like pigs at a trough, because all you had to do was walk a few blocks from the Indies Company to the rue Quincampoix and sell them for 5,000. The subscription gave Law a third of his loan to the government; two more issues of 100,000 each followed on September 28 and October 2, and these were also eagerly subscribed.

A billion and a half livres of shares purchased in three weeks time? But there was nowhere near that amount of paper money in circulation. However, John Law's terms were 10 per cent down. So his company actually took in only 150 million livres in cash, and counted on receiving the balance over a period of nine months.

If all this seems dizzying today, consider the confusion of a public unacquainted with finance, for whom paper money and a profusion of stocks and bonds were a new phenomenon. There was no equivalent of *The Wall Street Journal* to straighten matters out. All one could do was talk to people in the rue Quincampoix and try to understand what was happening.

Here is how matters stood at the beginning of October 1719. There were 200,000 shares of the Western Company (mothers), 50,000 shares of the Indies Company (daughters), another 50,000 (granddaughters), and 324,000 shares of the Indies Company issued to fund the national debt, for a total of 624,000. Early in October, the price of a share of any of these stocks rose to 8,000 livres. The paper value of Law's empire at this moment amounted to 5 billion livres!

But already there was a hint of trouble in paradise. The holders of state bonds, being forced to redeem them, no longer had the security of their annual 4 per cent. They had the choice of hoarding cash, investing in Law's stock and awaiting a dividend, or becoming speculators. Law's critics later maintained that what he had done was to activate an enormous amount of dormant capital for his System, without regard to the consequences for those conservative people who had loaned their money to the government in good faith, expecting a modest but steady return. Bonds worth 5,000 livres yielded 200, year in and year out. The same amount of money after August 1719 would buy a share in the Indies Company with a face value of 500 or 1,000 livres and a promised 12 per cent dividend worth no more than 60 or 120 livres. It was true that the price of the stock was rising and a bondholder might take profits. But the situation was too confusing for many people, and they lost out in the public subscription, which was on a first-come-first-served basis, and they ended up with cash that would not buy a tenth of the stock they deserved. Everyone who might lend an ear to their complaints was too busy making money speculating, an activity abhorrent to many bondholders.

Later, Law felt it necessary to defend his treatment of bondholders, which he did with arrogance: "He who lends [to the government] stipulates that his money will not be used in any sort of business, and he wants to see it sitting on funds clearly marked. The capital dies for the lender, and he agrees never to see it again. Thus the bond money lies immobile between two men who are chained to each other." So Law wrote in a letter to the *Mercure* in February 1720. In other words, he was deliberately breaking this chain, forged freely by ignorant men, so that the nation as a whole might benefit from a more productive use of the capital.

"I admit," Law went on, "that the total transformation of the government's finances causes a real upheaval which hurts a certain group of people at the moment; that is the inconvenience attached to all change, and all the more inevitable the convenience when change is more necessary and more urgent. One would like to have the kingdom arrange things without hurting anyone. Only God could do that, and moreover He does not do it in the order of nature."

Or, you can't make an omelet without breaking eggs.

But up to this point, the only eggs broken were those of powerful people. Now a whole class, the *rentiers*, were suffering. Why did he do it? Why, when a fantastic speculation was already under way, did Law not wait to see what results it would have? No satisfactory answer has been found in view of the sorry consequences that followed. His conversion of the enormous national debt in the form of bonds into common stock was his first grave error, not because of its injustice to the bondholders, but because of its impact on the nation's credit. To carry out the project required the issue of so much paper money that a collapse was inevitable. The only rational explanation for Law's folly at this point is that he was demonstrating a theory and truly believed that he had found a way to breathe life into what he called dead capital. What he overlooked was the limited wealth of even wealthy France, which simply could not make productive use of so much money. The country would therefore have to suffer an enormous inflation of the cost of everything, including, for a short time, those shares of new stock that thousands of people were queuing up for at the Indies Company offices on the rue Vivienne.

These were happy queues. In time, there would be queues drawn by anxiety and panic, ending in tragedy for some. But in the fall of 1719, there was a *gaité Parisienne* the like of which would never recur.

13

O More Than Man!

The boom on the rue Quincampoix carried John Law to the heights of public adulation. "He was the most prominent figure in Europe," Perkins writes. According to Saint-Simon, he provoked mob scenes: "Law, besieged by suppliants and aspirants, saw his door forced, his windows entered from the garden, while some of them came tumbling down the chimney of his office."

Madame, the Regent's mother, always scribbling at her *escritoire*, wrote: "Law is so run after that he has no rest, day or night. A duchess kissed his hands before everyone, and if duchesses kiss his hands, what parts of him won't ordinary ladies salute?"

Law was a goose sitting on a golden egg. His company was issuing new stock at the absurd price of 500 livres, perhaps a tenth of its value. He was the director. It followed that he was in a position to do favors, since the public queues quickly exhausted the supply of securities for sale. That he held back a supply for private distribution cannot be doubted, but no records are available. Franklin Ford, one of the foremost scholars of this period of French history, has said that he was unable to discover, despite diligent search, who were the holders of record of the Western Company and the Indies Company stock. The records were burned in the great *visa* that followed Law's departure from France at the end of 1720. Rumor had it that as much as a third of the last issue of 300,000 shares had been given at par to Orleans alone. An even more sinister suggestion has been made that more than the official number of shares was issued, that some certificates were seen during the burning to bear the same numbers as others that had already been destroyed. Whatever the facts, Law had it in his power to make a man rich if he chose.

Carriages lined up in the Place Vendôme before Law's house, while people of the highest rank waited hours for the chance to see him. They had not come simply to praise him, but to flatter him in the hope that they would be rewarded with some of his shares at a bargain price. Women particularly fastened on him. Several ladies who had the luck to gain an audience with him in his office refused to let him go to the bathroom and obliged him to urinate in a chamber pot in their presence!

A woman deliberately caused her coach to overturn in his path, so that she could ask him for stock when he came to comfort her. Another woman set up a cry of fire outside a place where she knew him to be dining, and when he rushed out, she made an ardent plea for his favor. A slip of the tongue resulted in a lady begging him for a "conception" when she meant "concession." Law is said to have replied with a smile that this was not a propitious moment to grant her request.

Lady Catherine and the children were likewise courted. The papal nuncio attended the birthday party of seven-year-old Marie-Catherine and played dolls with her. Young John Law danced a quadrille with young Louis XV and also went hunting with him. Offers of marriage came from home and abroad to both Law children. They were politely turned down. Not so in the case of the Marquis d'Oyse, who arranged to marry his two-year-old daughter to an upstart Mississippian in search of a title.* The Marquis was to receive 20,000 livres a year until the wedding,

* "The babies of the Mississippians now cry for marquises instead of dolls," an observer remarked.

when the new husband would settle 4 million livres on him. Lady Catherine became the leading hostess of Paris, and on occasion there were as many carriages outside her house as in front of the Palais Royal.

Law, only human, was carried away by so much attention and flattery. His generosity was ostentatious, and he gave to charity as well as to deserving nobility, whom he expected to support him in any political difficulty. In fact, he now looked and played the part of an aristocrat, sitting for his portrait before Hyacinthe Rigaud, the great court painter, and Simeon Belle, whose picture of Law is now in the National Gallery, hanging in the board room together with Craggs of South Sea Bubble fame. These paintings portray a handsome man in the prime of life, haughty, rich, confident. His demeanor appears calm, but his behavior at this time was becoming more emotional and less attractive. The Regent, while continuing to admire and support his wizard of wealth, expressed to others his dislike of the new airs the Scotsman had assumed. Particularly, he was wary of any political ambitions Law might have. It was known that Law had responded favorably to a veiled request for money from the Stuart Pretender, and this indiscretion went against the new *entente* between France and England. Law was a political amateur.

He had understandably never lost his attachment to Scotland. He always received Scottish visitors and was rewarded for keeping up his connection with a gift of the keys of Edinburgh, brought to him in a gold casket together with the most fulsome homage to his genius by Robert Neilson, son of a prominent Scot. Law was so moved by the gesture that he hired the courier on the spot as his private secretary. The prominent Scottish poet, Allan Ramsay, wrote a panegyric of seventy lines in praise of Scotland's great man:

> Blest Monarch! By indulgent Heav'n carest
> Whose Crown's of such a valu'd Gem possest . . .
> So all his just Ideas fertile flow,
> And by their Course prolifick Riches grow . . .

The chearfull Peasant no more now repines,
Eas'd of his Tax, with Pleasure prunes his vines . . .
The grateful Gauls your Mem'ry will revere,
And glorious in their Annals you'll appear;
Who formed them Banks, their sinking Credit rais'd,
Whilst Your warm Fancy in Missisippi blaz'd . . .
O More than Man! . . .

However warmly Law may have reciprocated these feelings, he retained a Scot's scorn for England and predicted that France would run the British off the high seas. His egotism and boasting about the System led his fellow Scot, the Earl of Stair, British ambassador to France, to change his opinion of Law. Stair refused Law's offer to make him a fortune (although Stair's secretary reportedly made 200,000 livres) and was aghast at Law's threat to drive down the price of British East India Company shares.

Law seems to have adopted an isolationist outlook at this time, quite opposite from his former internationalism when he was prepared to hire himself out as a fiscal soldier of fortune to any country that would have him. Now, only France counted. It was the foremost country and Paris the greatest city. Xenophobia was building up in him as he beheld the wonders he was working for his adopted fatherland. This extreme nationalism was of course not uncommon, and in anyone else it would be seen as the consequence of mercantilist theory—the idea that wealth is limited and national policy should consist of gathering in as much of it as possible, particularly bullion. Law's nationalism was the zeal of a convert or the jingoism of some American immigrants.

That his object was to turn France into a model of financial soundness and efficiency is evident from the amount of time and thought he gave to the problem of tax reform. With all he had to do, he still found time to study the existing chaotic and grossly unfair system, if it can be called that, for collecting the royal revenue. Among the flaws he pointed out in his *Denier Royal* (Royal Revenue) memorandum, written in June 1719, were: failure to collect more than half of taxes imposed, the rest being siphoned off by tax farmers, who had paid for the right to collect them, and other middlemen; 40,000 officials and clerks needlessly employed in tax collecting; the burden the system imposed on business; the "infinity of privileges" exempting the clergy, nobility, and others; the terrible impact of taxation on the peasant; the hatred stirred up by the arbitrary nature of the system. In a nice turn of phrase, Law said concerning the unfairness of the salt tax, "The peasant has more animals than the nobleman has valets and salt is as necessary for one as for the other; it follows that the tax on salt is not equitable." This was written seventy years before the French Revolution—but it was not published. Law was not a pamphleteer, but he was in a position to do something about matters that troubled him. Having taken over the farming of the taxes himself, he began to eliminate some of the 40,000 needless bureaucrats, defending his action with this statement:

What will become of the 40,000 men who are today employed in the King's financial offices, who live on this and support their families by it? What will become of the rats who live in my barn if I remove the grain and take it to another and more secure place? I ask your Royal Highness's pardon for the familiarity of the comparison.

This tough-mindedness did not mean Law believed these people deserved to starve; he believed that his System would easily find more productive employment for them. The bureaucrats were hardly convinced. What Law really wanted was a single tax on national production, something like a value-added tax. But he knew, really, that such a sweeping reform could not be obtained at once, so he proceeded to attack the injustices piecemeal. There were the empty bureaucratic offices, for instance, some in existence for a century or more, many of more recent origin, when Louis XIV created them in return for ready cash. Such offices, which were hereditary, might be grand criers of funerals, wig inspectors, measurers of every commodity, tallow controllers and hay trussers, guardians of the woods and waters, and so on. These were not merely honorific positions; they entitled the holders to collect fees from the public. A fish selling for 28 pistoles (about $2.80) carried the cost of 11 pistoles ($1.10) collected by the fish inspector. To general acclaim, John Law abolished a number of these needless government jobs, with the result that the prices of commodities like wood, coal, and fish in Paris fell by a third. The office holders were vocal in their protest, and a little more than a year after Law left France, they succeeded in having their privileges restored. They were the featherbedders of their day, and the public was grateful to Law for attacking that larcenous form of taxation.

He also succeeded in eliminating the burdensome inland tariff on grain so that it could pass across provincial borders freely. Some twenty edicts bringing tax relief were issued during the second six months of 1719. These were among Law's most constructive and meritorious actions, and the forty-seven pages of memorandums on the subject are considered by Paul Harsin his best theoretical work. Had there been a way to make these tax reforms permanent, one of the chief causes of the French Revolution would have been peacefully eliminated. But the reforms were the work of a man and not of a nation, and when he departed France, his enemies sent his reforms with him, so to speak.

Modesty was not one of Law's virtues. Looking upon his work during the summer of 1719, he found it good. A utopian fantasy grew in him, and he determinedly avoided any transactions outside France unless they brought money into the country. He welcomed foreigners so long as their money stimulated French prosperity. It was estimated that there were 25,000 or 30,000 foreigners in Paris at one time during the fall of 1719. They came from almost every European country, but chiefly from England and Holland, the great mercantile powers whose people had the cash to gamble with on the rue Quincampoix. So numerous were these Protestant visitors that they occasionally exhausted the supply of meat, because they did not observe fast days and were not great fish eaters. Through such people, Law could easily have placed large sums abroad safely and secretly, but he objected to this practice because he wished to see France grow constantly richer, so that the whole world could behold what he had wrought with his System.

A striking instance of how harshly he could deal with those who transgressed his principles may be seen in his clash with Richard Cantillon, a man now judged to have been one of the great economic theorists, "the greatest economist before Adam Smith," according to Professor Arthur Monroe.* Cantillon was born in Ireland around 1680 to a family of French extraction. He was endowed with money and a brilliant intellect, and he was the equal of Law in the mastery of finance. Until 1718 he was probably much richer than Law. Not a public man, his vision hardly extended beyond his own class; in fact, his chief passion was making huge sums at the expense of others. For some years he had been in Paris, on the rue de l'Arbre Sec, quietly and without scruple pursuing a lucrative practice as a private banker. Two Paris bankers, the brothers Jean and Remi Carol, stated that he had engaged in the worst sort of usury. Cantillon was also a scholar, who read Latin and studied the Roman monetary system, and he was far more deeply versed than Law in the economic thought of Petty, Locke, Mun, and Child. His connections included the British statesman and philosopher, Bolingbroke, and wealthy men and women in England sought his advice during the boom in France. A clash with Law was inevitable, for Cantillon was not only a rival for favors but he also scoffed openly at the System and advised his friends in the summer of 1719 to sell their shares and take their profits while the going was good.

Law might have been able to put up with this, but he could not accept a man of Cantillon's influence sending to Amsterdam and London the huge sums he was making in the market created by Law. Cantillon was lending money against shares of Mississippi stock to allow the greedy to pyramid their gains. The amounts were enormous—40,000 pounds to Lord Montgomery,

* Arthur E. Monroe, *Monetary Theory Before Adam Smith* (Cambridge, Mass.: Harvard University Press, 1924).

20,000 pounds to Lady Carrington. Certain that the market must fall, he sold these mortgaged securities, which he had no right to do, with the intention of buying them back at lower prices when the time came for his debtors to remit to him. This only came out later during lawsuits in London, but John Law knew of Cantillon's foreign remittances and he called the operator to order. "If we were in England we might deal as equals and come to an understanding," Law told Cantillon. "But as we are in France, I can send you to the Bastille this evening unless you give me your word to leave the Kingdom in twenty-four hours."

Cantillon temporized and told Law that he was going to make his System succeed. This sounded reasonable to Law, who then helped this man he did not like to make a huge sum of money. Cantillon feared a trap and took his winnings back to London. There he eventually bought Law's shares when they became cheap and put pressure on all his customers who had borrowed on them at the high point. Vainly the customers sued for damages, and they had to pay him in coin that had meanwhile been revalued.

A vengeance on Law was Cantillon's *Essai sur la Nature du Commerce*, described by a modern scholar as a refutation of Law's ideas, written some time after the collapse of the System. It was not published, however, until 1755.

Cantillon outlived Law by five years, and there is no evidence they ever met again. He died a violent death May 13, 1734, at the hands of his French cook, whom he had discharged after eleven years' service. The man stabbed him in his study, burned down the house and fled to the Continent. The famous essay somehow survived, presumably because it was circulating in manuscript form. Its posthumous publication years later met with little public response, but Adam Smith, who dismissed Law in a sentence, praised Cantillon, and Mirabeau's *The Friend of Man* was strongly influenced by *Essai sur la Nature du Commerce*. The French Revolution obliterated Cantillon from memory, and while John Law's work was being studied all during the nineteenth century, Cantillon's essay was unknown until 1881, when a British scholar, W. Stanley

Jevons, rediscovered it. Rivals during their lives, Law and Cantillon still represent in their opposing views conflicting theories about money. Law's view, with reservations, is the currently acceptable one, but if metal should make a comeback as money, as it did in Greece during and after World War II, Cantillon's *Essai* might draw the attention of certain economists.

In November 1719 Law, who worked either at the Royal Bank in the rue de Richelieu or at the Indies Company in the Mazarin Palace, or received in the Place Vendôme, or consulted at the Palais Royal, decided to indulge a whim—to visit the rue Quincampoix for the first time. He had listened with pleasure to the fantastic stories of the fortunes his initiatives were making for the most ordinary people. The tempo on the little street exchange was such that there was no time to write contracts. Money and stock passed from hand to hand, and fortunes could be made in hours. A servant acting for his master took shares to be sold at 8,000, but finding the price already at 10,000 kept the difference and bought on his own account until he emerged in a few days a millionaire. Prices often rose as much as 10 per cent while people were having lunch. Some of the stories were apocryphal, but they passed as true because of the fairy tale character of the times.

There was the coachman who grew rich, bought his own coach, and then forgot and climbed up onto the driver's box. And Law's own coachman is supposed to have made a killing. Law asked him kindly to find a replacement, and the coachman appeared with two men. When Law said that he needed but one, his former employee replied, "Ah, but there is only one for you. Take your choice. I will hire the other."

With whatever coachman, Law and some friends showed up in the rue Quincampoix on November 12, 1719. The street had been closed to carriages for months, and the greatest lords had to park in neighboring side streets, with as much difficulty as anyone would have today finding a parking place off Wall Street. The traffic was so heavy that a nobleman complained it took him an hour to cross the rue des Ours. Law had a clear passage that day, and the crowd cheered as his carriage rolled up the street like the car of a hero on

Lower Broadway. Graciously, he tossed gold sovereigns from the window, a gesture later criticized as entirely too presumptuous, and one reserved to the King alone. Reportedly, some friends of Law had buckets of water poured from a building on those scrambling for coins. If Law enjoyed this dampener, it prefigured a feeling of contempt that he was to show to speculators a few months hence.

Whatever uneasiness he may have had about the unreal character of his boom at this time, Law himself seized the day and became one of the great benefactors of the kingdom. Some of this was indirect, and the Regent took the credit. According to Saint-Simon,

... four millions were paid to Bavaria, and three millions to Sweden, in settlement of old debts. Shortly after M. the Duke of Orleans gave 80,000 livres to Meuse, and 80,000 livres to Madame de Chateauthiers, ladies in waiting to Madame [his mother]. The Abbé Alari too obtained 2,000 livres pension. Various other people had augmentation of income given to them at this time. . . . He [Law] had, as it were, a finance tap in his hand, and he turned it on for every one who helped him. The Duke, the Duchess, Tesse, Madame de Verue had drawn many millions through his tap and drew still. The Abbé Dubois turned it on as he pleased.

Millions passed through Law's hands to individuals and to charitable institutions. He distributed packets of cash and also stock certificates to friends. The King, the Regent, princes, dukes, counts, and the crowd of *roués* and their mistresses all received huge gifts directly from Law. If anyone had stopped to think, the source of so much paper was the ever turning printing press. During the fall of 1719, authorization was given to issue up to the point where a billion livres were in circulation by the end of the year. Thus, all the careful control maintained by the *Banque Générale* was abandoned. In view of the killing made by those in power, an element of cynicism seems to have appeared in the System at the very height of its success.

Still, Law and the Regent could not have conceived of the devastation that lay ahead or else they would surely have held back to some degree from their excesses. They were obviously carried away by the delusions of the mob, unable or unwilling to look to the consequences. They took leave of their senses. All proportion was lost. How else would it have been possible for them to allow the Duke of Bourbon to reap a fortune of 50 million livres, which he converted from paper into real wealth (and became prime minister in the aftermath)? The Regent's failing was his desire to please, to please everyone. He had spent much of his life feeling uneasy, hated, being called a sorcerer and a murderer. Now he was beloved, because he had had the good judgment to install John Law as his minister of finance in all but name.

Why not in name? Law politely pressed Orleans on this point? How could he continue to keep a poseur like D'Argenson in office? Law in retirement, writing a history of his System, described D'Argenson as a man who pretended to "sacrifice his life to excessive *work*, he affected a schedule of *night work* for the benefit of his associates, and *spent the day sleeping at home*; at night he rode in his carriage with a candle to show the public that he had no moment without work. That is what all his financial operations came down to." What had happened was that D'Argenson had carried over his habits of night work from his days as chief of police, when it was necessary to question witnesses at night. Law pressed further. Who was responsible for the well-being of France? Why should not John Law be controller general of finance in the King's government? Even Ambassador Stair was saying that Law was already in effect the prime minister of France.

The Regent temporized. He was put off by Law's overbearing manner. But he liked the fellow, and he ought to grant him this sop to his vanity. D'Argenson could remain Keeper of the Seals. There was only one thing in the way, Orleans told Law—his religion. It might be possible to elevate a foreigner, but not a foreign Calvinist. It was not long before Law found a solution to this difficulty.

14

Manon Lescaut

If anyone had taken a sober look at the reality behind the millions
in shares and bank notes in France in 1719, what would he have
perceived? The Indies Company was no fiction. Somehow amid all
the turmoil of financial manipulation and stock jobbing John Law
was also running a bank and a large trading company that em-
braced the mint, the tax farming concession, and two recent acqui-
sitions, the African Company and the San Domingan Company.
He had the help of competent people. He even picked up a royal
port, Lorient in Brittany, which was simply handed over to him for
nothing by the Regent.

What was lacking were colonists. All the broadsides, all the
enticing pictures of a thriving Louisiana, all the stories of mines,
gems, rich crops, and the growth of New Orleans (still but an out-
post full of shanties) had drawn few volunteers to the Mississippi
paradise. Propaganda had helped to sell Indies Company stock, but
with prosperity returning to France, what purpose would be served
by becoming a pioneer in America? The place to migrate to was
Paris, not the hot delta on the Gulf of Mexico. The capital swelled,
while Louisiana remained almost empty.

Aware of the absolute need to populate his vast preserve, Law
undertook to set an example by establishing a concession of his own

in Arkansas during the spring of 1719, hiring workers from Germany to farm the rich soil. This was widely publicized and it brought immediate results. Seeing that John Law planned to create a town in Arkansas with a circumference of twenty-four miles, a number of prominent men—the secretary of state for war, Le Blanc, the Duke of Guiche, the Marquis of Asfeld, the Count d'Artagnan—obtained their own concessions in America. These small settlements were the source of continuing exaggeration about the Mississippi basin's benign climate and great fertility. It was said that there were not enough ships to carry the crowds eager to resettle thousands of miles from home.

Inquiries at the Hôtel Nevers headquarters of the Indies Company brought ready answers about the amount of money needed to get the concession going—200,000 livres—and the number of workers required—200 of all kinds including butchers, bakers, tobacco planters, and unskilled laborers. A kit of instructions was issued, explaining conditions in America, wage rates, food to be supplied, terms of employment. After three years, the employee was to get land of his own and a year's salary or a free trip home.

All of this was the grossest public deceit. The fact that Law had to recruit workers in Germany meant that he could find few French volunteers. Just as the Western Company's early settlements were increased by salt smugglers and people from prisons or the galleys, so the Indies Company looked to the one certain source of labor, those at the mercy of the government. It was not just jailbirds who were now sent abroad, but men and women about to be sentenced, and worse, unfortunates still to be arrested who were complained of for their evil habits, particularly lechery. A curious contradiction arose: the more Louisiana was acclaimed a paradise, the more widely it became known as a place in which to dump undesirables. Parents petitioned the government to send their troublesome children to the new colony. After July 1719, when the rue Quincampoix became active, such petitions poured into precinct offices, from all classes, rich and poor, imploring Orleans to send young libertines to Mississippi. The boy King was implored as the head of the French family to save the honor of the home by deporting young people who had caught the spirit of the Regency *roués*.

The police were only too happy to oblige the moralizers. The more serious the offense, the more likely a *lettre de cachet* (arbitrary warrant of arrest) would be issued. In the eyes of the police, "Louisiana seemed to serve no other function than as an internment camp for all the rascals of Paris," wrote Pierre Heinrich, an authority on the settlement of Louisiana. Embezzlers with prison records, madmen leading scandalous lives, criminals of any sort, degenerates —these were the kinds of men or women, according to the records, who were unfit for France and belonged in Louisiana! It seemed no matter that the new colony might be the worse for known men of violence, thieves, prostitutes, and social misfits, who would certainly be incapable of the necessary industry required on the frontier. What this policy did was relieve Paris of some of the embarrassment of having attracted so many wretched people, who came to share the spoils of the System. For Louisiana it was a disaster. And for those transported it was hell.

The human tragedy of the mass deportations to John Law's Mississippi later seized the imagination of the remarkable and not always admirable Abbé Prévost, whose pre-romantic novel, *Manon Lescaut*, became one of the great stories of French literature. It opens in the Norman town of Pacy:

I was surprised on entering this town to see all the inhabitants in confusion. They rushed from their houses and collected in front of the door of a cheap inn, where two covered wagons were standing. . . . I stopped for a moment to see what was causing the tumult, but got little information from the crowd, which ignored me and pushed confusedly toward the inn. Finally a soldier wearing a bandolier, his musket on his shoulder, appeared at the door and I beckoned to him.

"Pray tell me what's going on here."

"It's nothing, monsieur," he said. "Just a dozen whores me and my buddies are taking as far as Havre-de-Grace where we put them on the boat for America. There's a couple of good lookers in there, and I guess that's what's exciting the peasants."

I would have gone on after hearing this, if it had not been for the lamentations of an old woman who came out of the inn wringing her hands and crying,

"What a barbarous thing! Horrible! Pitiful!"

"What's the matter?" I asked her.

"Ah monsieur," she replied. "Go see for yourself if the scene doesn't melt your heart."

Inside, the narrator finds the prostitutes in chains, filthy, and ashamed, and he has to pay the corrupt soldiers a considerable sum to let the lover of one of them, Manon Lescaut, talk to her during the terrible journey. The lover, Chevalier des Grieux, later in the novel describes what it was like in New Orleans: "We found a miserable cabin built of boards and mud. . . . Manon seemed frightened at the sight of such a sad dwelling." Which is why she gives herself to the governor of Louisiana, a betrayal that provokes des Grieux to stab the governor, carry Manon into the wilderness, and there watch helplessly while she dies of exhaustion. A romantic but not fanciful tale; Prevost knew the Regency, and his story captures the spirit of greed and hedonism that infected all classes. Manon had started out to become a nun and had opted instead for what she hoped would be a gay and comfortable life. More weak than wicked, she yielded to the pleasures of Paris and left des Grieux for a rich tax farmer. Another rich lover, whom she robbed, had her arrested for immorality. Des Grieux became a murderer.

The novel appeared in 1731, two years after John Law had died and eleven years after the Mississippi Bubble. It was an immediate hit with the public and a target for moralists, one of whom suggested that it should be burned because of the degradation it depicted. Prevost did not tell half the story. *The Journal of the Regency*, by Jean Buvat, an assidous chronicler of Law's rise and fall, reported that on August 14, 1719, "They took 500 boys and girls from the hospitals of Bicetre and de la Salpetriere to be embarked at La Rochelle and transported to Mississippi. The girls were in wagons and the boys on foot, escorted by 32 guards." The right to do this was granted to the Western Company by the Regency Council on May 6, 1719. It was presumed that these young people, confined to institutions called hospitals (they were more like prisons), would prove to be better colonists than the scum collected at random for the French West Indies. Avoidance of the spread of venereal disease was uppermost in the minds of managers of the Indies Company. They had little concern for what happened after the young people were handed over to the semigangster company police called *archers*. Sometimes the women were attacked by peasants or highwaymen as they marched to the sea. Sometimes the food supply failed. Disease carried off some before embarkation, and there were suicides. Perhaps as many as half of those seized failed to reach Louisiana for one reason or another.

John Law visited the hospital of Bicetre in mid-September 1719, and promised to give the institution a million francs. If all such places in Paris had sent their young *voyous* (not hardened criminals but juvenile delinquents) to America, Law would have had 4,000 people right there. Probably no more than a third of this number were transported before objections from Louisiana authorities made an impression in Paris. The public character of the transportations was deliberate, and it was not to shame the delinquents that on November 10, 1719, 300 of them were paraded chained through the streets of Paris; it was an advertisement of the population growth of Mississippi. These were the workers and servants of the New World. Later, the chains were disguised on other groups under garlands of flowers. To cause a sensation, a mass wedding of 180 couples was held in the open. Another spectacle was a wedding in Notre Dame Cathedral of a colonist and an Indian maiden he had brought back to France. Later, when they returned to her territory, she murdered him.

One of the most notorious and comic injustices was done to a butcher named Quoniam, who was sleeping in a chair by the fire while his wife carried on upstairs with her lover. Something roused him, and he decided that the lover was a burglar and called the police. Instead of the police, he attracted a bunch of Law's *archers*, to whom the quick-thinking lover and Quoniam's wife denounced the poor butcher, and he was seized as a dangerous brigand who carried a knife on his belt. Only the strongest protest by his friends obtained his release from Chatelet prison before he could be sent off to America. Following this, public indignation forced the police to put the *archers* under their supervision and to restrain such casual brutality. The *archers* were not unlike Haiti's *tonton macous* —bandoliers of Mississippi, they were called. Pierre Heinrich, in *Louisiane Sous la Compagnie des Indes, 1717–1731,* notes:

Not satisfied to commit a host of uncalled for deeds to collect a few francs a head granted by the Company, these improvised policemen took advantage of the occasion to enrich themselves by brigandage, robbing their captives or releasing them for ransom. Their outrages, rather enlarged by public imagination, led to frequent riots, in which a goodly number of them were killed or wounded by a furious mob.

Saint-Simon recorded his impressions of them in moving words:

In order to people these colonies, persons without means of livelihood, sturdy beggars, female and male, and a quantity of public creatures were carried off. . . . Not the slightest care had been taken to provide for the subsistence of so many unfortunate people, either while in the place they were to embark from, or while on the road to reach it; by night they were shut up with nothing to eat, in barns, or in the dry ditches of the towns they stopped in, all means of egress being forbidden them. . . . They uttered cries which excited pity and indignation; but the alms collected for them not being sufficient, still less the little their conductors gave them, they everywhere died in frightful numbers.

This inhumanity, joined to the barbarity of the conductors, to violence of a kind unknown until this, and to the rascality of carrying off people who were not of the prescribed quality but whom others thus got rid of by whispering a word in the ear of the conductors and greasing their palms . . . Law, regarded as the author of these seizures, became much detested, and M. the Duke of Orleans repented having ever fallen in with the scheme.

No documents link Law directly to this storm trooper phase of French colonization, but it might have derived from his intelligence

if not from his instincts, for except for his one duel, he was not a
man of violence, and his sympathy for humanity in general appears
throughout his writings. But it is a cold sympathy. The fact that the
archers wore blue to identify them with the Mississippi project is
enough to suggest that Law made no attempt to dissociate them
from the company he had created and directed.

Cabaret lyricists lampooned the situation:

> It's not the thing to talk of the king
> Or the war in Spain. A new land of Cockaigne,
> Mississippi in the south is heard in every mouth.

One song had a pun on Mississippi—*Michepipi* (pronounced pee
pee). Some people were not sure what Mississippi was, and even
the better informed thought it was an island. Regarding the butcher
Quoniam they sang:

> Now all you husbands hear, if your wife should have a dear,
> When you find him in your bed, do not hit him in the head,
> For they'll ship you out to sea, straight to Mississippi.

Mounting protest brought the deportations to an end during the
summer of 1720. Rumors that Protestants secretly practicing their
rites might be sent to Louisiana reached the British ambassador,
who made it known that this would be interpreted as an act hostile
to England, and nothing came of it. Had Louis XIV allowed the
Huguenots to settle in Canada, France might have created in North
America a force powerful enough to have successfully rivaled the
English, but he had stubbornly rejected this opportunity.

If conditions en route to America were appalling, things were not
much better in the colony itself. Administration was chaotic and
food supply was a problem. There was war with Spain from April
1719 until June 1721. The Spanish raided the coast of Louisiana,
and Bienville, now a military leader, captured, lost, and recaptured
Pensacola and then had to withdraw as part of the larger peace
settlement. It was a waste of valuable time, money, and energy

that took a serious toll. At the height of Law's difficulties in Paris, in the summer of 1720, starvation was such a real threat to the colonists that they were forced to live on herbs and shellfish.

The reality was in a sense disaster. But so was Plymouth, where half the Pilgrims died the first year. Despite the misery suffered, Louisiana's population under Law rose from less than 1,000 to more than 7,000 by the end of 1720. A list of the classes of inhabitants has been preserved: 122 officers, 977 soldiers, 43 clerks, 302 company laborers, 119 concession overseers, 2,462 concession workers, 1,278 smugglers, thieves, and deportees, 1,215 women, and 502 children.

A foundation had been laid and in time Louisiana would prosper —but not as a French colony. Its eighteenth-century history is one of continuing economic difficulty, and with the French defeat in North America by the British, Louisiana was ceded in part to Spain and in part to Britain in 1762–63. Napoleon reacquired the Spanish sector by the secret treaty of San Ildefonso in 1800, but three years later sold it to the United States for $15 million when he feared it would be seized by the British. This tremendous area later became Jefferson's great Louisiana Purchase.

John Law's association with Louisiana is not admirable, but he should have credit for giving it an impetus hitherto lacking. He had the good sense to restore Bienville to the leadership of the colony; he encouraged the establishment of New Orleans and gave that great city its name.

But Louisiana was his own undoing. Had Crozat not relinquished his concession in 1717, Law might have been forced to confine his energies to developing his bank. He saw in America what he thought was his chance, and it led him step by step to abandon sound economic principles in order to build an empire on paper. By the end of 1719, when some shares of the Indies Company traded as high as 20,000 livres, forty times their price in the spring, it was necessary to pay a dividend and to give an accounting of what his System was accomplishing. But before that, John Law had to make his first communion.

15

A Portfolio Is Worth a Mass

Years before the Revocation of the Edict of Nantes (1685), Louis XIV had tired of tolerating the powerful Protestant minority, and his officials had already begun to harry them, to force them to forswear their Calvinism and convert to Catholicism. Priests were allowed to enter the homes of dying Huguenots and pressure them into denying their faith with their last breath. Official sanction was given to *dragonnades*, military raids on Protestant communities by royal troops known as *dragons*—dragoons in the British army—tough fire-breathing soldiers, who would abuse and torture the obdurate until they agreed to march to a Catholic church to receive communion. Protestants were forbidden to hold offices and could not even be grocers.

After the Revocation of the Edict of Nantes had purged the country of anywhere from 200,000 to 400,000 of the strongest Huguenots, the harmless remnant was given a respite. But shortly before he died, Louis again struck at the Protestants by denying them legal status and arbitrarily declaring them Catholic by virtue of their residence in France. This stirred a rebirth of Protestantism and churches of the "desert" were formed secretly. France, however, had become fixed as a Catholic nation.

In the circles frequented by John Law, Catholicism was not ardent. Louis XIV and Mme. de Maintenon's stiff adherence to the dogma and pageantry of the Church had turned off a multitude of courtiers. The publication of Cardinal de Retz's *Memoirs* in 1717, describing the intrigues of the Fronde, did nothing to inspire confidence in the princes of the Church. Orleans had read his Rabelais during Mass, had tried to converse with Satan, and was an agnostic whose conversation at the moment of his fatal heart attack was alleged to have turned on the question: Is there a God? He had toyed with instituting a policy of toleration for exiled Huguenots wishing to return to France. And he knew one thing: he could not give a minister's portfolio to John Law until Law had joined the Church. This was a political necessity.

John Law had no more strong religious convictions than Orleans. In a sense, he was the beneficiary of religious persecution in Scotland, for had his grandfather not been forced out of his parish of Neilston, John Law's father would not have been apprenticed as a goldsmith and might have become a clergyman. Religious controversy in England had the result of secularizing the Laws, and John Law's religion was a matter of convenience, not conviction. He was untroubled by the problem of trying to observe during the week the humble Christian ethic preached on the Sabbath. Unlike Orleans, he did not speculate at all about spiritual matters. His Protestantism was a habit, and the Calvinist emphasis on self-reliance had carried him buoyantly through life. If he was one of the elect, then God intended him to be a minister in the government of Louis XV.

Accordingly, he put himself in the hands of the Abbé Tencin—and vice versa. Tencin, one of the rising provincial churchmen, "a fellow of debauched habits and shameless life," according to Saint-Simon, destined to wear a cardinal's hat, was let into the inner sanctum of Law's System so that he could make a fortune. Law took Tencin's religion, and Tencin took Law's stock certificates, with which he speculated successfully in the rue Quincampoix. An anonymous observer sarcastically describes the nature of the transaction as follows:

The secret of this commerce [speculation] as of every other kind, was to know just when to buy and sell; this is to say, sell when stocks were at their highest and buy when they were at their lowest. But as this alternative was pretty much in the hands of the famous John Law, author of this system, he [Tencin] believed it was a good idea to get to know such a man, in order to see what was in the stacked deck of cards and thus be able to gamble on a sure thing.

Tencin, a highly cultivated man who had taken a doctorate at the Sorbonne, proceeded to insinuate himself into the Law household following an introduction by that other worldly abbé, Dubois. Tencin's sister happened to be Dubois's mistress. A little like Molière's Tartuffe, Tencin courted Lady Catherine Law, with the intention not of seducing her, but of winning her husband's confidence. Eight years younger than John Law, Tencin became the platonic *cavalier servente* of Mme. Law, holding her hand when she climbed into her carriage, pouring her tea, sealing her letters, handing her a powder puff when she made herself up. His gallant gestures pleased Mme. Law, and his polite stories made her laugh. Soon Law was obliging the priest with stock at a knockdown price, and when he was not courting Law's wife, Tencin was trading Law's shares in the rue Quincampoix.

It was only natural that Law should turn to Tencin, then, for advice on becoming a convert. Tencin thought it over and proposed a family trip of twenty-five miles to the town of Melun at the end of the summer, and there, on September 17, 1719, John Law abjured whatever Protestant faith he had. The eleventh-century romanesque Church of Notre Dame in Melun could be a moving experience, and who is to say that Law did not feel some of the awe expressed about it at a later date by the great sculptor, Auguste Rodin:

On entering this old church, it seems to me that I enter into my soul. My most personal reveries arise and come to me when I have pushed the door open. The impression moreover is that of a crypt or a tomb. What silence! How far away one seems to be! But shafts of light at the end allow, nay counsel hope.... Now children enter the church and then in a few minutes go out to play. They are like the exquisite Renaissance ornaments added to the entry. Who knows? perhaps they will have retained something from this catechism of stone. Happier, wiser than their parents who pass the church without going in, without even seeing it.

Abjuration was not followed, as was often the case, by immediate communion. Three months of instruction by Tencin for Law and his family followed. It is hard not to conclude that Tencin took his time so that he could be instructed by Law in the art of speculation.

So caught up was Tencin in the activities in the rue Quincampoix that he declined a call to be Bishop of Grenoble, where he had been raised in an upper-class family. With what he was making through John Law, he could buy himself a cardinal's hat. To be close to the future controller general of finance was infinitely more useful than to endure the tedium of an Alpine bishopric.

Indeed, the rue Quincampoix was becoming so heated in its transactions that prices in November were now rising to unbelievable highs—15,000, 16,000, 17,000, or 18,000 livres per share for stock originally issued at 500 or 1,000! The Christmas season failed to slow down the frenzy of speculation, because the prices fluctuated wildly and there were bargains to be had during a drop in the market. On Christmas, the street remained open to a crowd shopping for presents in the form of capital gains for themselves. If *Père Noël* (the French Santa) was anywhere that day, he was on the rue Quincampoix.

At the same time, on the other side of town at the Church of St. Roch, M. and Mme. Law were taking their first communion from the hand of Abbé Tencin. An eyewitness reported that Law "received the holy eucharist with the magnificence of a man who had all the Kingdom's money in his vaults." A gift of 500,000 livres in stock was Law's Christmas present to the church, for completion of the nave of one of the most striking Baroque interiors in Paris. That evening, Law gave a ball in celebration of his receiving the holy sacrament.

However cynical it all was, Law sincerely accepted his new faith, his first true confrontation with religion. When he died in Venice years later, his closest companions were two Jesuit priests whom he saw much of during his final illness. Tencin went on to be Bishop of Lyons. He was made a cardinal in 1739 by Pope Clement XII despite considerable opposition, particularly from Jansenists, who cited his disgraceful speculation and the quick conversion of John Law among examples of behavior unbefitting a prince of the Church. At one point, he had been convicted of simony by Parlement and had paid a fine. No matter. His career as a diplomat under Louis XV was creditable, but his sister is the one more remembered, because in 1717 she became the mother (out of wedlock) of D'Alembert, one of the great philosophers and mathematicians of the eighteenth century, a leading encyclopedist, and an outspoken voice for tolerance.

Once Law had made his first communion, his appointment as controller general of finance followed with embarrassing swiftness on January 5, 1720. Perhaps, in a day without a daily press to expose such a coincidence, it did not strike either Law or the Regent as a particularly brazen move. The cabaret lyricists made fun of the conversion, saying Law was on the road to eternal life because of his *bonnes actions*, a pun that cannot be translated because *actions* in French means shares of stock as well as actions.

There was a pressing reason to place in Law's hands the powers of a great minister. His desire for a portfolio had been stirred at first by vanity and by his scorn of the Marquis D'Argenson. But these trivial motives were now replaced by a recognition that his System was being threatened by speculation and inflation. John T. Flynn, whose account of Law in *Men of Wealth* is written from an arch-conservative anti-New Deal point of view, put his finger on something when he wrote: "Perhaps in October Law saw that for the first time gold and silver were leaving the Royal Bank. Therefore when he renounced his ancient faith at Christmas and became Controller General, it was not merely to crown his triumph with the trappings of high office, but to put into his hands the supreme power he required to begin the battle to save his System."

To those still paying wild prices for Mississippi stock, the System looked very sound indeed. But these were johnnies-come-lately to the rue Quincampoix. Shrewder traders, especially those from abroad, had begun to sense that the market was approaching its peak. They did as the modern adage bids all speculators to do: be a bull or a bear, but not a pig. But neither Law nor anyone else had any experience with such a volatile situation. Law sensed the danger, and he thought he could avert it by a combination of chastisement and powerful sanctions. Having put into circulation a billion livres in paper money by January 1720, nine times the amount in existence a year before, he well knew that all the gold and silver in the kingdom could not support the Royal Bank if a run should occur.

Until late in the fall, the bank had been the beneficiary of the general prosperity, and gold and especially silver poured in as the public sought the paper notes because of their stability after the summer devaluation. But now the old prejudice in favor of metal currency was beginning to reassert itself, and against this deep-rooted instinct Law was determined to do battle with a ruthlessness never before seen in the realm of economic affairs. For Law, paper was the foundation of his System—paper representing not gold, silver, jewels, or unfarmed land but thriving production and commerce. To be useful it had to circulate, and he compared it frequently to the bloodstream of the body. To immobilize this flow of paper by converting it into the dead weight of treasure, however valuable, amounted in his eyes to a capital economic sin, a treason against the King, to punish which any forceful measure was justified. The practice Law hated most was hoarding, because it tied a tourniquet on the arteries of commerce. His revulsion is widely shared today. Hoarding is a pejorative term, but it is generally seen less in terms of an unsocial act than as a symptom of economic uncertainty and lack of public confidence. It was Law's mistaken belief that this symptom could be eliminated by edict. Early in 1720, he wrote a memorandum, a statement that exposes the harsh frame of mind that came over him once he was controller general: "As defiance mounts, it is necessary to have recourse to authority to induce the public to contribute to their own happiness."

These are the words of an angry man, who felt that the public for which he had done so much was now, in its infinite stupidity, threatening to wreck his System by greed. It is the familiar mood of the revolutionary when the tide turns; it is Luther denouncing the Peasant Revolt: "Therefore let everyone who can, smite, slay, and stab, secretly or openly, remembering that nothing can be more poisonous, hurtful, or devilish than a rebel."

It might be said that as winter came on, Law had an attack of snow blindness—the blizzard of paper had blinded him to a fact apparent to the most ignorant: the yield on his stocks had been drastically reduced by the unreasonably high prices they commanded right into January 1720. He himself believed 10,000 livres was a reasonable price, and quite soon the market retreated to that level. But before it did, Law held a meeting of stockholders on December 30, 1719, where he announced a 40 per cent dividend. But this was based on the par price of 500. At a price of 10,000, the return was only 2 per cent. But he ignored this momentary meagerness and talked of giving "more dividends to shareholders one day than the annual interest on money loaned at 20 per cent. . . ." It was jam yesterday, jam tomorrow, but never jam today. And he blamed public ignorance for overpricing the shares: "One must open his eyes to this vulgar misconception and no longer regard stock certificates as a simple equivalent of specie, not believe in an imaginary wealth because the shares sell for more than all the gold and silver in the Kingdom. It is the immense profits from foreign and domestic trade that constitute the value of the certificates. . . ."

The sad thing is that like Law's own bank, his company, the vast Indies Company conglomerate, was in sound condition. Scholars have quarrelled over the figures, but Paul Harsin, after sorting it all out, arrived at a profit for fiscal 1719–20 of 88 million livres, which justified the dividend of 40 per cent on a par value of 500. This 200 livres a share was to be paid on the 424,000 shares held by the public. The 200,000 shares held privately by the company, Law, the King, and the Regent would get no dividend. And future prospects were good, too. The company owned thirty large ships and, with its smaller vessels, had a bigger fleet than the English East India Company. By June its assets included 105 new buildings purchased or constructed. In 1721 its capital was valued at 67 millions. The largest source of revenue was the government debt, on which the company received 3 per cent, an income of 48 million. For collecting taxes, it earned 20 million and the mint returned 6 million. The rest came from tobacco and import-export business. The company was heavily dependent on the state for its business.

The state was involved in another way. The Royal Bank was used to finance certain speculators at low interest rates to the tune of 450 million livres in loans. The bank, too, bought shares in Law's enterprises. This interlocking of bank and company is reminiscent of the relationship of the Bank of Amsterdam and the Dutch East Indies Company. But never did any government put so may of its fiscal eggs in one basket. Little wonder that eighteenth-century critics accused the Regent of deliberately allowing Law to do whatever he wanted in order to mask a scheme for enriching himself and his followers. Law himself told Saint-Simon that the Regent's extravagance was an embarrassment to his System. But this was the pot calling the kettle black, because Law's own extravagances were manifest, and the Regent's extravagances were made possible by Law's selling him huge blocks of stock at par when they were worth ten or twenty times as much. In exchange, the Regent gave Law a free hand; he could not understand all the hocus-pocus, but it appeared sound because all the wealth at the moment was so palpable. There was no evidence that the System was unsound until the winter of 1720, and even then the Regent supported Law's most extreme edicts. For Law to blame his troubles on the Regent was hardly fair. They were collaborators in an enterprise that carried them both away.

It must be remembered that all this was taking place at a time when amazing changes were being worked on men's outlooks. Science had passed from the age of alchemy to the highest place of honor thanks to Isaac Newton's genius. The world was being made to look like a new place. Old ideas were being challenged by men like Voltaire, Locke, and Defoe. Law's apparent transformation of a bankrupt country into a cornucopia that all Europe was dipping into impressed not only the greedy but the savants too. On

December 8, John Law was named to the French Royal Academy of Science, of which Newton himself was a member.

Those who like to moralize will find it easy to point to the hubris of John Law, which was at its highest at the end of 1719. At this time, when visitors to Paris were paying black market prices for coach tickets from the provinces, when speculators were arrested for being in the rue Quincampoix after hours, when the Indies Company dispatched eighteen ships to Africa and Asia, when Law paid a million livres to the Marquis de la Carte for a chateau in Brie, no Cassandra appeared to spoil the holiday mood with predictions of a troubled New Year.

THE CRASH

The ruin of Law's System was due to the absurd
prices to which speculation carried the shares of
the company, and to his endeavors to maintain
fictitious valuations by the purchase of shares at
vastly more than had been received for them.

James Brett Perkins

16

Winter of Discontent

The System that Law had developed rested on credit, on a belief in the future growth of the economy. Another word for this kind of credit might be *credibility*. So long as everyone believed in the new institutions, everyone supported them enthusiastically. But let doubt appear, let people wonder why stocks fluctuated and were on a downward trend, let bondholders grumble that they were being cheated by the System, then people would naturally look back to the one fact they had always known: that things of value are better to have than pieces of paper that authorities *claim* are valuable. In January, John Law had palpable evidence of disenchantment among his most enthusiastic followers. The evidence was this:

In a playful mood, the Duke of Bourbon had once sent Law two cartloads of ice as proof that he had won a wager of 1,000 louis d'or that the ponds of Chantilly would still be frozen in March. Law paid off this minor loss cheerfully. But nine months later, the Duke called for money of another sort: he asked Law to exchange many millions in paper money for specie. And the unscrupulous Prince of Conti, whose greed was unimaginable—piqued that Law, who had been encouraged in his theories as a young man by Conti's father, would provide him with no more shares at bargain basement prices—sent three wagons and asked that they be filled with gold in redemption of his paper fortune!

Law was aghast, but he was terrified that if he hesitated, either or both of these powerful noblemen would cause a run on the bank by spreading word that there was insufficient coin for the paper in circulation. He paid them both as stealthily as possible, and then hastened to Orleans, who called each on the carpet separately. He raged so against Conti that the prince was reduced to crying for mercy, according to Saint-Simon. This was a small price to pay for getting out of the System while the getting was good, and there was no way that Orleans could force these men to restore their treasure to the King's bank. Sensibly, Bourbon kept quiet about it, for all he wanted was sound money, and Bourbon remained a friend of Law and protected him when things became much more difficult for the Scotsman. Conti, though, was so peevish that he took out on Law his rage over being humiliated by the normally affable Regent; his petty revenge was to spread vile rumors about the controller general. But since everyone knew how much money he had made through Law, this cheap talk only had the effect of further lowering Conti's reputation. A verse satire of the day presented this imaginary dialogue:

> Prince! Speak of some deed.
> What have you done for your glory?
> —Quiet, you idiots! And go read
> The story of the rue Quincampoix.

Yet Law had been put on the defensive, and his reaction was far from cool.

The London *Gazette* of January 5–9, 1720, carried the following dispatch from Paris: "Mr. Law is made Comptroller General of the Finances and on the 7th instant was sworn into that employment." Not long after that, he was also made superintendent general of finance, a post that gave him the administrative as well as the ministerial power. He was now absolute in the economic realm—more powerful than Colbert under Louis XIV, the most powerful minister since Richelieu—for the Regent now gave him a free hand. He could do as he liked, and he began to move without sufficient reflection, for he was dismayed to realize that the fickle public could criticize as well as praise him.

In response to complaints that the bondholders who were supposed to cash their bonds were unable to replace them with stock because of the high prices, Law on January 10 issued an edict ordering the Indies Company to give up its own shares to them, and three days later put a time limit of April 1 for the exchange. This generous gesture had the effect of supporting the stock at a level of 10,000, considerably below the giddy prices of November—but still no cause for alarm. Yet even this price had no sound basis, and the fact that he was putting more stock on the market to stimulate trading is one measure of the confusion that assailed his usually orderly mind. He had become convinced that speculation had got out of hand, yet here he was encouraging further speculation, since the bondholders who got stock at par would naturally throw it on the market at once, par being 5,000 and the market double this.

In fact, Law was furious with these bondholders, who in his view were standing in the way of the entire nation. "There are more than 18 million people in France; is it fair that they should suffer so that a small number of their fellow citizens can live idle and useless to the nation through these obligations that are so burdensome and ruinous for the government?" wondered Law, unjustly lumping all bondholders in with a class of rich people living off their means. In less than a month, when the stock market sagged further, he expressed his feelings about these bondholders he was trying to help by threatening on February 6 to reduce the value of their holdings by 50 per cent if they did not come and get the stock they were entitled to.

Just when he had reached high office, John Law's luck was turning against him—and he was not used to losing. In the coming months, his strength would not be equal to the force of successive adversities. Even in little things, he ran into unexpected difficulties.

Saint-Simon records an instance where a "mere trifle had changed into spite and indignation" against the great man:

This is the trifle. The Marshal of Villeroy, incapable of inspiring the King with any solid ideas, adoring even to worship the deceased King, full of wind and lightness and frivolity, and of sweet recollections of his early years, his grace at fetes and ballets, his spendid gallantries, wished that the King, in imitation of the deceased monarch, should dance in a ballet. It was a little too early to think of this. This pleasure seemed a trifle too much of pain to so young a King [10]; his timidity should have been vanquished by degrees, in order to accustom him to society which he feared, before engaging him to show himself off in public, and dance upon a stage. . . .

Reflection was not the principal virtue of the Marshal of Villeroy. . . . It became necessary to search for young people who could dance: soon, whether they danced ill or well, they were gladly received; at last the only question was, "Whom can we get?" Consequently a sorry lot was obtained. Several who ought never to have been admitted, were, and so easily that from one to the other Law had the temerity to ask M. the Duke of Orleans to allow his son, who danced very well, to join the ballet company! The Regent, always easy, still enamoured of Law, and to speak truth purposely contributing as much as possible to confusion of rank, immediately accorded the demand and undertook to say so to the Marshal of Villeroy.

The Marshal, who hated and crossed Law with might and main, reddened with anger, and represented to the Regent what in fact deserved to be said: the Regent in reply named several young people, who although of superior rank were not so well fitted for the ballet as young Law . . . and the financier's son was named for the ballet. . . .

It is impossible to express the public revolt excited by this bagatelle, at which everyone was offended. . . . At last the public was satisfied. The small-pox seized Law's son and on account of its keeping him from the ballet caused universal joy. The ballet was danced several times, its success answering in no way to the expectations of the Marshal of Villeroy.

We must allow for Saint-Simon's hyperbole; he hated the idea of "confusion of rank," and perhaps the number of people appalled by what they took as Law's effrontery was limited to Saint-Simon's circle. Still it was a powerful circle to alienate, and Law would have done well to forgo this social chance for his son (though from his point of view he was asking no favor, since his son would have improved the mediocre dancing).

But he was shortly to arouse a justified hostility for his intention to make paper money the exclusive legal tender of the realm. In his youth, his claims for paper money's virtues were more modest than they had now become, and the original backing for the paper money he proposed in Scotland was land. At that time, he saw a need for correlating the value of notes with something tangible, and he chose land because it was constantly growing in value. Then, in his *Banque Générale*, he had been scrupulous in paying out specie on demand, giving the impression that paper was simply a more convenient form of coin. But when the bank was nationalized, Law began to deprecate gold and silver, first by promising never to devalue the King's banknotes and then by devaluing the coin in order to underline the superiority of paper. By the fall of 1719, merchants charged customers between 5 and 10 per cent extra if they paid in coin rather than in paper. In three years, Law's paper money had become preferable to coin in a land conditioned for two centuries to worship the gold and silver of Latin America.

So far in this evolutionary process, Law had used psychological devices for convincing the public of France (as well as foreign countries) of the worthiness of paper money. He relied in high councils on his persuasive memorandums and forceful logical discourses to gain the support of the Regent and others like Dubois and Saint-Simon. Although Law had not stated in so many words the concept of a free market, he acted and wrote as if that was what he believed would carry his System forward. He thought the public had sense enough to know that a stable paper money was preferable to coins, which might be clipped or devalued arbitrarily by the government. He wanted the public to have access to freely flowing goods that were not impeded in their progress across provincial borders by customs houses that choked the growth of the economy. Thus, freely circulating goods and freely circulating paper currency was what he wanted his System to provide for the nation. The Indies Company was one means to increase commerce, a pace-setter that would stimulate the business community to think of expansion. Despite his experience in the business world, there was a strong rationalist character to his theorizing. Like Descartes, he had worked out his System logically so that it ought to have run like a clock, and at one point he does compare himself to Descartes.

It began to enter the public mind even in the fall of 1719 that paper money was useful for buying things and especially for paying off debts. Paper money flowed from Paris to the provinces in profusion as mortgages were settled and millionaires traded their banknotes for chateaux and estates, even though real estate prices were doubling and trebling. One property was bought for 700,000 livres and sold in a few months for 2 million. It is significant that when the smoke cleared and the government attempted to settle more than half a million claims by people who had been injured by the System, three-fifths of these claims came from outside Paris. The city operators were putting it over on the country people by paying with paper money for valuable land and buildings. Paper was also being used to buy jewelry and silver and gold objects, as well as carriages, horses, furniture, and clothes.

In a sense, the public was only fulfilling its part of a bargain. "Bank notes should not be regarded as a simple promise to furnish gold and silver equivalent to the denomination," Law wrote at this time, "but as a reciprocal agreement between the King and his subjects to give and take mutually through the circulation of this paper money, not just specie but also things of real value."

But of course those who rid themselves of paper in preference for necklaces, for example, did not continue to seek more paper; they were hoarding their wealth instead of letting it circulate. "Those who want to amass and retain [wealth] are like parts or extremities of the human body which would want to stop the flow of blood that irrigates and nourishes them," Law wrote with singular naiveté, baffled to explain why, in January 1720, paper money was no longer bringing a 5 or 10 per cent premium. How dismaying to find that sellers might not accept paper at all, and that others raised prices for those who paid in paper. This had to be stopped. James B. Perkins puts the situation bluntly: "Law now began a series of violent measures, by which he sought to sustain the tottering credit of his institutions." As always, he acted with lightning swiftness, which momentarily won for him the first objective in his battle with an ungrateful public. Paul Harsin, who is generally detailed in describing Law's operations, confines his description of the few weeks in January and February to this sentence: "A series of specie devaluations spread over several weeks and executed in between two small augmentations, followed in turn by devaluations cleverly worked out, caused a crowd of people to bring their specie to the Bank." This was still a psychological thrust, and the public was responding as free agents. They brought in their coins because specie had been deliberately unstabilized while paper remained steady in value. Law's objective was to eliminate specie from commerce altogether. But to do this required more persuasive and less attractive means than he had been used to employ.

His next series of edicts was nothing short of draconian, and the grossest interference in the personal lives of millions. "Few men in history have wielded more power than Law possessed," Earl Hamilton has written. Law's bandoliers handled a few thousand unfortunate people at the bottom of the social barrel, but Law struck out now at the middle and upper classes still unwilling to go over entirely to the concept that wealth and paper are coterminous and indistinguishable. He decreed: (1) No one could wear diamonds or other precious stones without permission. (2) No goldsmith could make or sell gold-plated objects, and no one should import them. An exception was made for princes of the Church: episcopal rings could be purchased and worn. (3) Paper currency was the almost exclusive form of money, no payment in excess of 100 livres in coin being allowed. (4) No one could keep more than 500 livres of gold or silver.

These measures were promulgated on January 20, February 4, 18, and 27, and they were backed by harsh sanctions and police state techniques of search and seizure. Not only were fines substantial; rewards were offered to informers. The detested atmosphere of the hated 1716 *visa* against war profiteers recurred, but now a vast population trembled as the police did the bidding of the Indies Company and followed leads provided by servants and disgruntled relatives. "Servants lodged information against their masters, brothers against brothers, a son against his father. When a charge had been made, the officers suddenly took possession of the house. Floors were torn up, garrets ransacked, gardens ploughed and spaded in search of the treasure," as told by Perkins. Even churches were forced to disgorge coins from poor boxes. "You should have given them to the poor," the police would say to the pastor. According to Saint-Simon, "A certain Adine, employed at the bank, had 10,000 crowns confiscated, was fined 10,000 francs, and lost his job. Many people hid their money with so much secrecy, that dying without being able to say where they had put it, these little treasures remained buried and lost to the heirs."

At the same time, Bourbon defied them to find the gold he admitted having, and the police prudently withdrew without searching Chantilly, for fear that this powerful man could take his own revenge on them. His exemption became public knowledge and increased bitterness. Law's rivals, the Paris brothers, lost 7 million in gold to the treasury.

All this was carried out with efficiency and without apology. Indeed, Law was at pains to justify himself in a series of three letters in *Mercure de France*, patronizing in tone and insensitive to the feelings of his constituents. Regrettably, this was but the beginning of public suffering, and succeeding months would see that the other side of the coin of the preceding year's euphoria was chaos and ruin for thousands. Law reverted to his youthful swaggering arrogance, which had served him so badly in London.

Among the arguments he put forward in defense of his confiscations, the most extraordinary was the claim that the Royal Bank, once in possession of the public's silver and gold, would succeed in multiplying the national wealth by ten: "It is a maxim generally accepted by bankers and businessmen that well managed credit will exceed deposits ten times," Law stated. This, in truth, is not so far from the modern practice that allows the banking system of the United States to keep on deposit only 17 per cent against money created for public use. But Law went further in threatening the public with a reversion to the financial practices of Louis XIV if they failed to oblige in supporting the System by giving up their precious metal to the bank, reminding them of the usury, stagnation, and repudiation of debt that had characterized the days of the Sun King. "I say, despite the initial fear the man in the street might have, take your silver to the King, not as a loan, whose interest will cost him money, nor as taxes, which ought properly to be eliminated, but as a pure deposit with the bank, to be drawn against as needed."

In other words, the bad king, or rather the king without the System, took your money either as a loan or in the form of taxes; the good king, with the System, takes your money as a deposit and gives you paper as you need it, while using your silver or gold to create an enormous national wealth. The trouble was that every deposit of gold or silver required that more paper be issued, and other steps Law took during the winter of 1720 had the effect of doubling the quantity of paper money. Thus, by summer, there was two and a half billion circulating, while the bank held only 300 million in specie.

Law's letters to the editor make interesting reading for economic historians, but their effect on the public was nil. What faced the public now was a frightening inflation and the fear on the part of merchants of accepting paper money. Prices rose by 20 per cent in January; the cost of bread had risen five times in a year, and now it was going higher; wages lagged behind this jump in the cost of living. Yet a *sauve qui peut* attitude prevailed at the Palais Royal, where Orleans acceded to pleas of hardship among his friends, as Saint-Simon faithfully records:

In the midst of the embarrassments of the finances and in spite of them, M. the Duke of Orleans continued his prodigal gifts. He attached pensions of 6,000 livres and 4,000 livres to the grades of lieutenant-general and camp-marshal. He gave a pension of 20,000 livres to old Montauban . . . of 6,000 livres to the Duchesse de Brissac. I obtained one of 8,000 livres for Madame Marechal de Lorges. . . . M. of Soubise and Marquis Noailles had each upwards of 200,000 livres. Everybody in truth wanted an augmentation of income on account of the extreme high price to which the commonest, most necessary things had risen. . . .

Among others rewarded was the Count of la Marche, age three, who received 60,000 livres at the request of his brother, the infamous Prince of Conti!

No one has ever been able to make much sense of the seemingly endless and often contradictory edicts that poured forth from the controller general as he attempted to restore faith in his System. At a stockholder's meeting on February 22, he announced that the Royal Bank and the Indies Company were to be amalgamated; bondholders would be invited to subscribe to 500 million livres in new shares. The next day all of Law's offices dealing in securities were ordered closed. In the amalgamation, 100,000 shares of the Indies Company in the King's name were sold to the new firm at 9,000, to be paid over a ten-year period. This was supposed to keep the price of stock at 9,000—but it did not. Stubbornly, Law determined to support this price level by offering on March 5 to pay 9,000 livres for any and all shares. For this purpose he reopened all the offices he had closed on February 23. He reasoned that those who wanted to invest in a stable security returning 4 per cent in dividends would buy stock, and this would put an end to speculation.

Queues soon formed, and Law eagerly awaited large purchases of his shares. Instead, those who could get only 8,000 livres the day before turned in their holdings for 9,000 livres, and Law was suddenly confronted with a mass conversion of one kind of paper, stock certificates, for another, bank notes. Never had Law received more than 5,000 livres for any of his stock, and much of it had brought only 500 livres a share. Now he was obliged to pay 9,000 livres, using the new bank-trading company as purchaser. The golden eggs were turning to brass.

The scale of the redemptions was overwhelming in size and utterly ruinous to the new organization, amounting to 2 billion livres, which represented a loss of almost a billion and a half. So inconceivable was this setback that defenders of John Law maintained that the conversion edict of March 5 had been forced on him by enemies, but this theory was nullified by Law's own acceptance of full responsibility in his memoirs. He reasoned that he owed it to the stockholders to sustain the value of their shares, and in fact before he did so publicly, he had the Royal Bank buy them periodically at 9,000 even before the month of February. Earl Hamilton attributes Law's stubbornness (he overrode the strong objections of advisors such as Dutot) to the erroneous conviction, arrived at in 1702, that stock was a form of money and must not be allowed to depreciate. The result was that he monetized the stock of the Indies Company.

But look what this led to: in order to buy up the shares, Law had to have *a billion and a half* livres in bank notes printed in a few weeks' time, using nine presses in Paris for the purpose. Thus, the stockholders he was trying to help were given for their certificates other pieces of paper, which they found inadequate to meet the high prices now demanded everywhere. The public knew nothing of finance, but it could plainly see that the country was awash with paper.

Ambassador Stair, now unfriendly to Law and for that reason no longer welcome at the Palais Royal, on his way back to London commented sarcastically on his old friend's situation: "I can't doubt Law's a Catholic since he established the inquisition after proving transsubstantiation by changing specie into paper."

This circumstance was the more depressing because other edicts were eliminating specie from legal circulation. Six days after the stock conversion privilege was announced, it was declared that after May 1 gold could not be used in payment of debts, nor silver after August 1; and whereas in February the amount of gold or silver allowed to any individual was limited to 500 livres, after these dates the only people authorized to hold *any* precious metal were goldsmiths.

"France for a short time enjoyed the distinction of being the one civilized country where a man could not pay his debts with gold or silver, a state of affairs which had no parallel since mankind passed from the era of barter and chose the precious metals as the medium for exchange," says Perkins. In his colorful way, Saint-Simon wrote: "It was pretended that since the time of Abraham—Abraham, who paid ready money for the sepulchre of Sarah—all the civilized nations in the world had been in the greatest error and under the grossest delusion respecting money and the metals it is made of; that paper alone was useful and necessary; that we could not do greater harm to our neighbors—jealous of our greatness and of our advantages—than to send to them all our money and all our jewels."

And so the paper prophet reached that point in his financial odyssey that had appeared from a distance to hold the nongolden paper fleece he was seeking. Perhaps fleece is an unfortunate image at this time, for there was no doubt that thousands had been fleeced. And why was this? Today, we live comfortably with exactly the condition John Law envisaged. The difference lies in the limitations put on the quantities of money issued or on credit, which should correspond directly with the volume of general economic activity. This correlation is possible today because of the enormous statistical records available to banking authorities, while John Law had to "wing it." His *Banque Générale* never increased the money supply by more than 3 per cent; the Royal Bank was forced to ignore all limits because of its redemption policy after its fate was interwoven with that of the Indies Company.

Law, of course, knew that there was too much paper in circulation; he was like a science fiction chemist who has created life only to find it a monster that he must somehow tame by administering a yet-to-be-discovered nostrum. Yet he was loathe to blame himself. On whom or on what *could* he heap opprobrium? It was human greed and the love of speculation that he blamed. He saw himself as the savior of France, whose financial health he had restored; and now a few wicked people were infecting the fiscal body. As he wrote in the *Mercure* to one complaining bondholder: "I don't know whether in your present state of mind you will excuse the amusing example of the doctor who brings down his malediction on a city where everyone is healthy." Years later, he wrote of "the great infidelities in stock trading" that forced him to try to end speculation by pegging the price of stock on March 5, 1720. "If one considers it a fault of judgment, one should at least approve the motive," he pleaded.

But pegging the price could not put an end to speculation. To do that, Law would again have to resort to arbitrary sanctions.

17

Crime in the Streets

Law needed a plausible excuse to put an end to the stock speculation that he alone had generated through his Mississippi schemes.
He found it in the ugliest of modern developments—urban crime.
It was expected that there would be counterfeiting of paper money,
and stern measures controlled this obvious felony. But easy money
attracted marginal types to Paris, and these preyed upon the new
rich, who were held up on the streets and lost far greater sums in
paper money than they would have been able to carry in coin.
Burglars made off with the silverware bought after profit-taking on
the rue Quincampoix. Especially after the bloom was off the rose
and inflation made life horribly expensive, a crime wave swept
Paris in 1720.

Two criminals in particular drew the attention of Barbier, Buvat,
Marais, the memoir writers of the day. The most astounding was
a Mack-the-Knife character called Cartouche, whose legendary
crimes were such that when his name was called in an indictment,
some wag called out: "Present!" and half the spectators fled the
courtroom. He was a man of great mystery; some doubted his existence, and others colored his character to fit their romantic fantasies. He really was one of the first crime lords, a gang leader on
a scale that would be remarkable even today. More than 500 crim-

inals were discovered to have worked directly for him in crimes of the worst nature.

Born in 1693, he rose from the gutters of Paris, and after a time as a soldier he returned home to organize a criminal band of both sexes along military lines. He was a charismatic leader, who disciplined his worshipful horde and confounded the public and the police by wearing disguises, occasionally appearing as a gentleman in the best finery, no doubt someone else's. There were other refinements. No one robbed was to be murdered—except in self-defense; no one robbed was to be robbed again, and cards were handed to victims as a sort of passport to be shown if they fell afoul of a Cartouchian again! Stolen items that could not be sold were returned.

Not all his practices were so considerate. Like the Mafia, Cartouche and his cutthroats were for hire when someone had to be killed. It is recorded that Cartouche and three thugs, mounted on horses and wearing masks, stopped the Lyons diligence, hauled out a well-bred young lady, raped her, killed her, and rode away without molesting anyone else. Later, it was learned that they had been paid by a marquis who tired of her when she became pregnant and wanted her killed.

Cartouche may have inspired criminality in high places. A man robbed of his money, clothes, and wig went to a house, where a nobleman sympathetically clothed him and sat him down to dinner to recover his poise. After a few bites, he became ill and left the table. It was a pretext to get his host out of the room and advise him that the two holdup men were among those elegantly dining. They were two barons, part of the household, and their rooms were found to be full of stolen property.

On October 14, 1721, Cartouche was betrayed and forty men, like an FBI squad, moved in on the master criminal, who was sleeping with six loaded pistols beside him. Two bodyguards warming themselves at the fireplace were at once strangled, and the little man (he proved to be surprisingly small) was hauled off to jail. There he was interviewed at length by a writer named Le Grand, who quickly mounted a successful play at the *Comédie*

Française called *Cartouche, or The Thieves.* On opening night, the rascal escaped jail, but he was soon recaptured and tortured until he confessed his crimes and gave enough information for the courts to try 400 of his accomplices. Unlike our own practice, such cooperation did not bring any diminished sentence, and Cartouche was broken alive on the wheel at 2 P.M., November 28, 1721 in the Place de Grève. An enormous mob had begun to assemble there for the spectacle two days earlier, provisioning themselves with food to sustain them during their long, impatient wait.

After that, public hangings and torture were multiplied, in order to put the fear of the law into the hearts of the Paris underworld. Corpses were left hanging on the Pont Neuf. Torchlight executions were carried out to terrify people further. Cartouche's fifteen-year-old brother died by hideous torture, and another brother, too young to die, was allowed to age in prison until he was old enough to hang. As late as July 1722, there were eight or nine Cartouchians executed each day.

The other criminal, and one whose crime had an immediate impact on John Law, was the twenty-two-year-old Count of Horn, a rakish nobleman from abroad, whose mother was the daughter of the Grand Duke Arenberg of Spain. He was related to the Dutch hero, Admiral Horn, and also to the Duke of Orleans himself. Horn had a history of embezzlement and had left the army to gamble in the rue Quincampoix. In the winter of 1721, he was among many whose luck gave out, so he persuaded two fellow officers to join him in a cold-blooded plot to recover their losses. Horn struck up a conversation with a wealthy broker and offered to sell him some stock for cash at a favorable price. The broker agreed that such a transaction might be more pleasantly carried out over a bird and a bottle in a private dining room upstairs at the fashionable restaurant *L'Epée de Bois*, corner of the rue de Venise. The bourgeois broker, flattered to be doing business with such a distinguished youth, asked for no proof that the amount of stock offered was in fact in his possession. The date was set for March 22, Good Friday (there was little fasting in the financial district). M. Lacroix, the broker, arrived with 150,000 livres in paper money.

Shortly, the two accomplices went to work. The Marquis de Lestang stood watch on the stairs, and the Count de Mille remained in the room. Suddenly, Horn threw a napkin over the unsuspecting Lacroix's head to stifle his cries, while de Mille stabbed him with a dagger. But de Mille failed to dispatch the unfortunate broker, who struggled and cried out. Horn completed the stabbing himself.

The noise drew the attention of the innkeeper, who went up to the room. Lestang lost his nerve and rushed downstairs into the street. For some reason, the landlord had the presence of mind simply to lock the door on his guests while he sent for help. Perhaps he had opened the door and seen the bloody murder. In any case, Horn and de Mille were obliged to go out the window. De Mille limped off, jarred by the drop onto the cobbled street, and was soon caught. Horn, realizing the job had gone awry, tried to claim that he, too, was the victim of robbery. But de Mille was found to have secreted some of the money under his armpits and in his socks, money covered with blood, and the wallet belonging to Lacroix was found in the lavatory of the police station, to which he had been taken. He then implicated Horn and Lestang, who was subsequently caught, and all three were taken off to prison for further interrogation under torture until all the details were drawn from them.

This was no ordinary crime. It was the culmination of a wave of murders and robberies that had terrified Paris. Eleven murders in one week! Victims were left mangled and cut to pieces. The public was outraged and demoralized.

Horn and his accomplices were convicted and sentenced to death on the wheel. This sentence for Horn was a shock to the aristocracy, for such an ignominious death was reserved for the rest of mankind; noblemen were decapitated or hanged, but never *roué*. A number of noblemen appealed directly to the Regent to at least change the sentence to a respectable death. The Regent reflected on the arguments put to him. This degrading spectacle, execution on the wheel before a mob, would weaken the very fabric of nobility. To treat Horn like a common criminal, execute him with men of lesser birth, was to excite revolutionary passions. The nobility's sentiment for decapitation was almost universal. There was no question of saving the Count's life.

But then John Law had some comments to make. Forgetting his own escape from the death sentence, he strongly urged the Regent to uphold the court's sentence. The criminal statutes did not exclude the nobility from their consequences. This crime was punishable by the wheel no matter who committed it. To yield anything on behalf of Horn would be to condone an outrage on the rue Quincampoix. This could further undermine public confidence in the administration of finance. Horn must therefore be broken like his accomplices—and at once. Dubois likewise urged the hard line on the Regent.

The debate over Horn's sentence brings out in bold relief the basic anxiety of the privileged classes. It was not death, inevitable and common to all, that they feared; it was the symbolic character of death that concerned those who had come to feel that a title set them apart in a special way from the rest of the human race. It is easy to ridicule their attitude. But is it so different from the noble Roman expectation that the hero return from battle with his shield or on it—but never without it? Charles I's beheading was a disgrace to Cromwell, not to the King. *Vanquished in life his death/ By beauty made amends*, wrote Lionel Johnson of that beheading. There could be no beauty in the horror awaiting Horn.

The Regent held fast against even his mother, who had a special interest in Horn since he was related to the most distinguished German families, including her own. "All right," he said in his sardonic way, "*I'll* share the shame. That ought to console the other relatives." Then he quoted Corneille: "The shame lies in the crime and not the scaffold."

On March 26, four days after the murder, Horn and his accomplices were led to the Place de Grève for execution on the wheel. Horn himself had measured up in the end. He refused to take poison brought to his cell at Chatelet by the Prince of Robecq-Montmorency and the Marshal of Isenghien, and he asked that his accomplices be spared. "I deserve the wheel," he told the prison chaplain. "I hoped for my family's sake to have my sentence changed to decapitation. I am resigned to the worst, in order to obtain God's pardon for my crime." Then pitiably he asked, "Do you suffer much on the wheel?" It took half an hour to kill a man by crushing him to death, but the chaplain spared the Count this foreknowledge. In his innocent way, Horn had never witnessed such an execution.

After watching his companions in murder expire, he died as manfully as the means permitted. But this was not the end of the affair. Whatever he had owned was confiscated, and his brother, the Prince of Horn, arriving the next day in Paris, blasted the Regent in a letter: "I don't complain of my brother's death, but I do complain that your Royal Highness violated in his person the rights of the kingdom, the nobility and the nation." The disgrace tainted the Prince and other close relatives, and for three generations some of them were excluded from noble chapters and orders in Germany. The memory of Count Horn persisted well into the nineteenth century, but, as one commentator noted, only the nobility spoke of it, and always with bitterness.

And now John Law, satisfied by the execution, saw in it the perfect pretext for damping down the speculation he had come to believe was a curse, despite his own responsibility for creating and encouraging the mania. Now it was the cupidity of these conscience-less traders that was damaging his System. Two weeks earlier he had revealed his new-found contempt for speculation in a letter to *Mercure de France*, in which he rather petulantly explained that there had been a misunderstanding that threatened his System.

The rage to pile up money came from the extraordinary growth of securities. Most people, surprised at their own profits, believed that they ought to turn them into gold and silver pieces, which they called profit-taking. They have not realized that the appreciated shares represent less actual money than capital, worth many times more than their old contracts. But the truth of this should have been evident from the astonishing heights to which these shares had risen, for they actually surpassed in value all the gold and silver that will ever be in the kingdom.

This intemperate attack on human logic led him to the mistaken conclusion that the habit of speculation he had induced in people could be cut off on command. What he had made, he could unmake. And with his instinct for timing, he took the bold step on the very day of Horn's execution of closing the rue Quincampoix as a stock exchange by official edict. It was psychologically impressive, but from a practical point of view as ineffective as the Eighteenth Amendment; shares continued to change hands in the rue de Venise and the rest of the financial district.

A week later came another edict banning the trading of securities throughout Paris at a heavy penalty to violators. This only created a black market, and by summer there was an open market carried on ironically in the Place Louis-le-Grand, where Law lived and much of which he owned. Eventually, the racket and traffic obstruction led a sleazy nobleman, the Prince of Carignan, to obtain a monopoly from the King for the garden of his home, the Hotel de Soissons. For outrageous sums, one could rent a booth on the premises, and it was in this once-elegant, urbane, walled garden that brokers and customers noisily traded their shares in the closing days of Law's System.

Symbolically, Horn's crime and death killed the rue Quincampoix, and though Law himself closed that famous or infamous street and returned it to oblivion, he was also unintentionally signalling the coming collapse of his System.

18

Inflating the Bubble

Since his ascent to high office, Law had been under a tremendous strain. "In many respects the political powers Law had under an absolute monarch were not good for him," Earl Hamilton has said, a considerable understatement. It seemed that from the moment Law became exalted and absolute, both events and people turned against him. Some of his troubles he brought on himself, and his refusal to admit his mistakes until later in life damaged his mental balance at moments, at times in 1720 he showed signs of a disordered personality. In a way, he reflected the instability of the financial system he had created.

His alienation of the Earl of Stair is an example of the damage his extreme behavior could do his reputation for clear-headedness and urbanity. He had been boasting during the days of enchantment on the rue Quincampoix that his System would put the Dutch and British businessman to rout, an apparently harmless bit of competitive advertising. But Law was capable of mesmerizing himself as well as others. In a foolish attempt to disrupt the London stock market, he proceeded to sell short £180,000 sterling in British East India stock to Thomas Pitt, Earl of Londonderry. (Pitt was the uncle of the future prime minister, William Pitt, and the son of Diamond Pitt, whom Law had helped out in the sale of his famous gem to the Regent.) This short sale was taken as an affront to England, and Stair, still ambassador to France, became convinced that Law was a menace. Even though Law had guessed wrong and the East India stock rose in price in the summer of 1720, Stair continued to be openly critical of the new controller general, whom he had characterized as virtually prime minister of France.

Stair, a man about town, spread stories of Law becoming unhinged. One, attributed to servants, was that Law was behaving like a madman in his own home, talking to himself, cursing, shouting, singing, and stamping his feet. One night his wife was so frightened by his behavior that she called for help because she feared to open the door to his room. On entering, they found the minister in his nightshirt dancing around two chairs.

Stair also retailed a story of the Regent's fury during an interview with Law, conducted as was the quaint custom while Orleans was seated on the *chaise percé*. The Regent grew so infuriated that he rushed at Law with his pants down around his ankles, and denounced him as mad and unfit for anything but the Bastille.

If true, these incidents suggest symptoms of a breakdown. Certainly, the reversals of fortune and favor would have been extremely damaging to Law's image of himself, and he would not have been human had he not reeled and staggered. But he did not lose his equilibrium, and in fact in all the long years of harassment and vain hope, John Law maintained his personality intact, so much so that he overawed Montesquieu when that great writer finally caught up with him in Venice in 1728, six months before he died alone. This ability to live with himself and by himself, a true friend of but a handful of people besides his wife and brother William, made it possible to withstand the blows to which he was henceforth almost constantly subjected.

He was a tiger, and he struck at any and all who appeared to him an obstruction. He should have been flattered by Stair's concern; they had known each other from boyhood, and Stair, whose father was for a time the leader of the Scottish government, had always supported Law and had helped to build his reputation at Whitehall. But now in a way they had become rivals. Stair was almost as flamboyant as Law. He gave huge parties, and upon being advanced from minister plenipotentiary to the rank of ambassador, he arranged a magnificent parade through Paris in 1719. But he lacked any sense of money management and was always low on funds, while Law grew richer by the day. Although Stair claimed to disdain speculation, he may have played the market—and lost.

Certainly, Law's fame in London now exceeded his, although Stair was a war hero from Marlborough's time, and Law was supposedly responsible for the outbreak of "bubble" mania in the City of London. In 1719 the South Sea Company sought to improve its flagging fortunes by converting government securities into company stock on terms similar to those secured by Law's Indies Company when it offered to fund the national debt of France. This very much interested the chief minister, Stanhope, to whom Stair reported. The immediate result in London was a substantial profit to the South Sea Company, and accordingly the spectacle of the rue Quincampoix was recreated in the English Exchange Alley. For a moment, some people contemplated entering into the fatal combination of Law's System by conglomerating the South Sea Company, the Bank of England, and the British East India Company.

Prudently, this temptation was resisted. Instead of grandioseness, the South Sea Company confined itself to something Law never stooped to, enriching the managers of the enterprise through blatant stock manipulation and widespread bribery of Parliament. As the stock soared from 114 to 850 in less than a year, so many new questionable stock companies suddenly appeared out of nowhere that a Bubble Act was passed to suppress them.

The gullibility of the English exceeded that of the denizens of the Paris financial district: stock was sold in companies that purported to insure against death from rum, to insure female chasity, to furnish funerals throughout Britain, to make a wheel of perpetual motion, and so on. Hundreds of such ventures found investors— and critics. A pack of South Sea playing cards appeared satirizing the goings-on, but the jokes were scarcely distinguishable from the reality—Puckle's Machine Company for discharging round and square cannon balls to revolutionize warfare, for instance. Swift pictured subscribers "Each paddling in his leaky boat,/ And here they fish for gold and drown." Defoe used the image of air: "Divide the empty nothing into shares,/ And set the crowd together by the ears." And Pope pontificated, "At length corruption, like a general flood,/ Did deluge all." The story of the man who made £2,000 by issuing stock for a project to be announced later has been declared apocryphal by modern scholars, but it will stand as a "true legend" of man's capacity for self-deception.

All this, occurring in the spring of 1720, disgusted Law, and for years afterward he was at pains to denounce any comparison between his carefully conceived and well-constructed System and the felonious South Sea Bubble, which burst in August 1720 and brought disaster and ruin to people of all classes (Isaac Newton, for instance, lost 20,000 pounds) and death to two estimable men. The Earl of Stanhope, called by his colleague, Lord Townshend, "the only Englishman I know possessed of a universal spirit," dropped dead in the House of Commons defending himself and colleagues against verifiable charges of corruption; while Craggs, the secretary of state, committed suicide. They avoided the fate of the chancellor of the exchequer, Aislabie, who was sent to the Tower for having taken £70,000 to promote necessary legislation.

Law's later comment: "The South Sea directors have worked *against* England; I have worked *for* France."

As tension between Law and Stair mounted, Stanhope decided to recall Stair in April 1720, thinking that he could use Law as a channel to the Regent—just as the relationship between the Scotsman and Orleans was growing strained. In truth, Stair was a high-strung man and must take responsibility for losing the objectivity a good diplomat strives for. The breach between him and Law was symptomatic of a general irritabilty in France, growing from the uneasiness about money.

In breaking with Stair, Law may also have undermined his friendship with the anglophilic Dubois, who, when the going got rough, furtively jettisoned Law. But then, Dubois was without scruple and would probably have dropped Law anyway once the System foundered and threatened Orleans's regime.

It should not be thought, however, that Law's ministry was without its constructive side from the beginning. Along with edicts affecting the finances and suppressing the rights of citizens, there were edicts suppressing taxes and privileges. On January 22, government advances to contractors were abolished, and three days later the salt tax, the hated *gabelle*, was completely eliminated. All exemptions from the direct taxes, the *tailles* or income taxes, were revoked on February 9, and subsequently a series of measures relieved merchants of debts to various tax collectors—like wine inspectors and others, who had to be paid for supervising the filling of wine casks. The jobs of inspectors of fowl, commissars of rubbish collection, verifiers of tin content, and others were swept away with the stroke of a pen. Consuls who enriched themselves by pocketing port fees in the Levant and on the Barbary Coast lost these privileges.

There is no doubt that had John Law survived his troubles, he would have tried systematically to do by edict in 1720 what was only achieved in the heat of the most turbulent feelings following peasant insurrections in the summer of 1789, when the nobility voluntarily surrendered their ancient feudal rights. He probably would not have been able to make his reforms endure, for they were too threatening to the whole concept of privilege on which the hierarchically organized French society had gradually been constructed. Law had insufficient understanding of the organic nature of communities, and he failed to see that French social injustice was so wide and so deep that all but the poorest classes profited from it in some measure, and that for this reason the unscrupulous at the top received support from the petty beneficiaries all the way down the line. The problem today is summed up in the British phrase, "I'm all right, Jack," or in the hard-hat support of the businessman in America. It was not until many peasants had grown prosperous enough to gather strength to rebel against the increasing injustice of exempting all but themselves from paying the cost of governing France that this despicable arrangement could be overthrown. Law was no *philosophe*; he had none of the passionate hatred of iniquity characteristic of Voltaire, Montesquieu, or Rousseau. He was moved by a desire to clear the arteries of commerce of the sclerotic blocks occasioned by taxes and privileges that worked only on behalf of the "haves" of France. He wanted the "have nots" to have more certainly, but this was really to satisfy his conviction that the time had come for a massive expansion of economic activity. His was the point of view of a liberal businessman who saw that the wealth of France was largely agricultural and insufficiently developed. He urged reforms in order to create a boom.

For the nobility and the clergy, a more limited objective seemed satisfactory, and throughout the eighteenth century they pursued their selfish goals with blind stubbornness, creating that comfortable, genteel world characteristically portrayed in the paintings of Fragonard. Law had drawn up fourteen rules for a fair system of taxation, which would never have been acceptable to what are collectively known as the corporate estates of the aristocracy and the Church.

The fifth of Law's rules states: "that taxes be of a nature so as not to harm commerce"; the sixth: "that taxes be general and that exemptions and privileges are abuses contrary to the general welfare of the State and even to the special interests of the privileged"; the seventh: "that the share of taxes be proportional to the ability to pay." And so on, to condemnation of arbitrary taxes and frauds and to an insistence on the probity of the King himself in balancing the budget and using his people's money wisely and constructively. The relief of the peasants, he foresaw, would result in higher production and greater profits for landlords.

But landlords had no reason to be dissatisfied with the present situation, and it would require the envy and frustration of a new class of merchants and lawyers, encouraged by the writers of the Enlightenment, to displace the ancient privileged nobility—and then only by violence and not with complete success.

Law's tax reforms were not original. For a generation, the fiscal system that had been in existence since the sixteenth century was under attack by thoughtful and sensitive observers like Fénelon, by economic theorists like Boisguilbert, and by businessmen themselves. Louis XIV had instituted a tax reform known as the Dixieme in 1710, but it was not enforceable. Law, however, was the first man in France with the energy and the power to eliminate nuisance taxes, internal duties, and lucrative sinecures. Even as his System was sinking into chaos, he clung to his dream of a bountiful country with economic justice (if not liberty) for all. But his good works were lost to sight amid the growing dissatisfaction over high prices and the dying stock boom.

Even the enlightened Montesquieu could not accept the idea of a *sound* money system; being an aristocrat, he feared that the entire nation would develop into a pack of money grubbers. In *The Spirit of the Laws*, written in 1748, he observed that paper money in an absolute monarchy "supposes money on one side and power on the other, which is to say, the option of having everything without power, and on the other hand power without any option." Money is democratic when it is made plentiful by a credit system; it redistributes wealth, putting it in the hands of those who have no responsibility for governing and thereby deprives the King of the power to govern. Montesquieu might not hold these views today; only dictatorships refuse to adopt liberal credit policies, thus keeping the power *and* the options in the hands of oligarchies like the Communist parties of Eastern Europe or the Falange of Spain.

The nineteenth-century socialist, Louis Blanc, appreciated the thrust of Law's reforms: "In his secret heart [Law] conspired against the tyranny of money, against privilege and idleness. No one guessed this at first. . . . Later when they began to see it, he fell. . . . To make the state the depository of all wealth and capital, of all industry, etc. . . . this was Law's conception." Law has been seen more than once as a collectivist trying to abolish inequality through a munificent state that would distribute the wealth according to some unstated principle of equity. The trouble with this interpretation is that Law believed very much in a class system; he had not an egalitarian bone in his body. He once expressed the hope that his reforms would allow a wealthy man to acknowledge it proudly instead of hiding it to deceive the tax collector. This has never happened. Two hundred years later, H. L. Mencken remarked that the businessman "is the only man above the hangman and the scavenger who is forever apologizing for his occupation."

Madame, the Regent's now-aging mother, who had genuinely liked Law (an unverifiable and improbable story is that they were momentarily lovers), wrote in October 1719, "Mr. Law is a clever and honorable man. He is extraordinarily civil and courteous to everyone and is a man of the world." And in November, "Nothing else is thought of but Mr. Law's Bank . . . the god Mammon reigns an absolute monarch in Paris." But on March 30, 1720, her views had changed decidedly: "I should like to see Law go to the Devil with his System and wish that he had never set foot in France."

Law and his System would be gone soon enough, but in the spring it was too early to dispense with either. He was allowed to continue manipulating the value of specie, to make it appear unstable and less attractive than bank notes. The value of silver, he announced, would successively diminish monthly beginning in April until December, at which time it would have one-third the value it had in March.

"It is impossible to understand Law's tactic," Paul Harsin says. "Bank notes were supposed to take the place [of silver]. It was thought that under these conditions paper money would not be excessive, given the high prices . . . one might say that this edict virtually forced the circulation of bank notes exclusively."

Confidently, Law again wrote in April in the *Mercure* that "faith in the bank notes, once well established, is our assurance that it will no longer be necessary to devalue the coinage." He said nothing about his original fundamental horror of devaluation—"every devaluation of coin is unfair and not in the national interest" he wrote in 1706 in his *Memorandum on the Usage of Money*. Circumstances had altered his ideas; as he was forced to print more money on paper, he had to look on specie as noxious and vexatious, particularly because it did not always circulate but was held against a rainy day. He wrote some years later:

I am persuaded, that the right [to own] money must not be regarded as an absolute property right; it is only a right of transient possession which we cannot all share at once, but in which we take our turns participating. . . . It is no longer its possession which is advantageous, but its proper use. That is why avarice is condemned by God and despised by men, and the tendency to pile up money to safeguard it is the most ridiculous, the most fruitless of all passions and the most dangerous for the nation.

Hoarding money should therefore be punished just as hoarding grain is punished, he said.

There is little difficulty in grasping Law's point of view today in a world urged to fly now and pay later. Movie stars endorse travellers checks in ads that boast they never carry more than twenty-five dollars. In the twentieth century, money is not hoarded; it moves silently through checking accounts; savings in banks are turned over as loans for building houses, buying cars, and so on. We have only transient possession of our money. Avarice, however, has not disappeared.

The French public was not reluctant to circulate money when the supply was limited. It was the increase in bank notes, as much as the attempt to abolish specie, that was destroying the System. During 1719, bank notes had been printed to allow people to speculate and buy the massive issue of Law's shares that were to retire much of the national debt in a stroke. In 1720, they were issued to accommodate the policy of calling in gold and silver coins—and when the public learned it could get 9,000 at the bank for shares worth less in the marketplace, more paper had to be printed to give out as the shares came pouring in. Law did not want to overissue paper money, but his own policies, whose consequences he did not foresee, forced him to turn to the printing presses. He was like the father in the maternity ward expecting twins and watching the excitement as the delivery room door kept opening while his wife was giving birth to quintuplets.

No wonder, then, that in April a black market in securities and in coins sprang up, centering first in the Place des Victoires behind the Palais Royal. Furtive in the beginning, speculators and brokers huddled in knots that dispersed when a lookout cried, *"Les guets!"*

to warn of the police, some of whom were mounted and capable of dealing blows with the flats of their sabres. Tiring of these interruptions, the brokers shifted the scene to the more populous Place Vendôme, filled with shops and stalls, thronged with vehicles and pedestrians. There speculation again flourished, the police no doubt being paid off.

But the noise was too disruptive; businessmen and residents (Law among them) were unhappy. The chancellor, who had his office there, complained he could not hear anything but the shouts of speculators. Marshal Villars, perhaps the greatest French military hero living, sixty-seven and as crusty as he had been a decade ago at bloody Malplaquet, protested from his carriage against the goings-on and denounced the greed and speculation he said he had never engaged in. He was vilified and almost set upon. After that, the Regent told Law to find some place more suitable as a stock exchange.

This proved to be the gardens of the Hôtel de Soissons, on the rue des Deux Ecus, an establishment Law had once tried to buy from the Prince de Carignan, one of the Regency's less savory characters. He had run a gambling casino there at one time; now he was in debt. He did not hesitate to tear out flower beds and handsome shrubbery, jettison fountains, statuary, and espaliered fruit trees to make room for 138 stalls of the same size, brightly painted, looking like so many bath houses at Coney Island. These rented for 500 livres a month, and the prince was soon making more money than most of the traders tramping about his grounds.

He was, however, an aristocrat, and the Swiss Guards posted at the gate on the rue des Deux Ecus were instructed not to allow servants, lackeys, or even artisans to enter. The place became known as the Bourse, and later in the century it was the site of the commodities exchange, which is still there, housed in a round, late nineteenth century structure and called the *Bourse du Commerce*. (The word *bourse* means purse, but it became associated with exchanges in Bruges, where a great Renaissance marketplace bore the name of a prosperous family which, coincidentally, was de la Bourse.)

The failure to prevent speculation and a black market in coins ought to have warned Law that he could not long deal with the public in so arbitrary a manner. He knew that his popularity had vanished, to be replaced by distrust and a growing hatred that threatened to erupt in violence to his person, and he now ventured forth only with the protection of armed guards. The memorialist Charles Duclos commented:

Never was seen a more capricious government—never was a more frantic tyranny exercised by hands less firm. It is inconceivable to those who were witnesses of the horrors of those times, and who look back upon them now as on a dream, that a sudden revolution did not break out—that Law and the Regent did not perish by tragical death. They were both held in horror, but the people confined themselves to complaints; a somber and timid despair, a stupid consternation had seized upon all, and men's minds were too vile even to be capable of a courageous crime.

The insensitivity of the Regent and his crowd at this time was hardly a check to Law's conviction that he could maintain the System by some means or another, for its spoils were in the hands of those who loved display. The Opera, always a measure of prosperity, had never flourished as it did during this troubled year of 1720; receipts rose to 700,000 livres, more than ten times what they had been before. Inflation explains only some of this enormous increase. Law loved the Opera, so much so that as a gift he presented the management with a season's supply of the finest new candles.

The festivities of the annual carnival were particularly lavish, and Law attended along with the Regent, Bourbon, and their mistresses, all attired in the costliest costumes—though without jewelry. The controller general's presence among royalty was particularly resented by the people, who blamed him, and rightly so, for their growing distress. Royalty was none too happy about Law's elevated status, and this amused the Regent, who smiled first at Law's delight and then at the noblemen's frowns.

Law now posed for the court painter, Rigaud, paid him with

Indies Company shares, and did not discourage the distinguished portraitist in his heavy speculation. The Laws also resumed in the spring their friendship with the stylish Venetian, Rosalba Carriera, whom they had met years ago in Venice, who worked in pastels in the style of Watteau (but without his genius). Her renewed interest in Law appears from her diary to have been partly to benefit from his connections and obtain commissons; after his downfall she apparently disappeared from his life, and we hear of no meeting between them when he retired to Venice. But to her credit, she continued to call at the Place Vendôme long after everyone else had dropped him.

However good a face Law put upon the situation throughout the month of April, he could not avoid the increasing pressure of the Regency Council, which reflected the concern of Parlement over the rising tide of paper money. Between March 26 and May 17, about a billion and a half livres were printed, and the question put to Law was: how can the bills retain their value?

Law did not deny the difficulty. He agreed to face up to it and promised to work out a solution for retiring some of the paper money during the remainder of the year. By mid-May he had drafted the necessary edict. But again he was surprised by its effect. What he was unwittingly doing was providing almost all the nails needed for the System's coffin.

19

Fatal Edict

Paris is, and has been for centuries, a city for strollers. Its tree-lined streets and elegant public gardens, the Seine, the magnificent architecture under low scudding clouds, the special light, the open-air cafés tend to draw people out of doors in good weather, and never more than in the month of May.

But on May 21, 1720, people were in the streets for another reason—to commiserate with one another about John Law's newest edict. A bombardment could never produce the consternation that came over the entire city, for bombardments are selective and localized. Only Law could have struck so much dismay into an entire population. His edict touched not the hearts but (they thought) the purses of every citizen. Much fun has been made of the parsimonious character of the French, but on this occasion one did not have to be French to howl with pain. It was as if a poison gas had been laid down uniformly from St. Cloud to Notre Dame.

This is what he decreed in the name of the King: in order to check inflation and reduce the amount of paper money in circulation, the value of paper money was to be diminished by 50 per cent over a six-month period. That is, a 100 livre note would become by December a 50 livre note. The first of these diminutions would occur the next day, May 22, when 100 livres would drop by

20 per cent and become 80 livres. These moves, Law's edict explained, would benefit exports, since the prices of French goods were becoming prohibitive abroad. Devaluations are commonplace today and to an extent they are effective, but they are seldom so drastic as Law's.

The edict also stated that shares of the Indies Company would be forced down from 9,000 to 5,000 during the same period. This decline was less sharp than the currency devaluation, and Law expected the prosperous to turn in some of their paper money for shares; he would then retire some of the excess bank notes he had just finished printing.

Although the public would actually lose nothing in theory, since prices would presumably fall to accommodate the changing value of money, the man in the street felt as if he had suddenly been robbed of half his money. "The uproar was general and frightful. Every rich man thought he was ruined beyond redemption; every poor man believed himself reduced to beggary," said Saint-Simon.

While all Law's depressive edicts until then had been unevenly punitive, harder on the rich than on the poor, his latest announcement affected every adult in the nation who possessed bank notes. It was in vain for Law to plead that this measure was by no means arbitrary, that it had been under discussion with the Regent for two months, that D'Argenson, the former minister of finance and still Keeper of the Seals, stood behind it, all of the government convinced by the controller general's reasoning that it was time for a period of deflation to remove the excesses produced by speculation, after which credit would be restored. There was no television to reduce complex matters to understandable commonplaces. The immediate and lasting reaction was one of victimization.

There were mild demonstrations. Some people beat on the windows of the bank and demanded Law's head. But the chief reaction was pure indignation and frustration. What hurt the most was the loss of faith in the immutability of the bank notes, which Law and the Regent had solemnly on numerous occasions assured their holders would *never* lose their value, and which only a few months ago had been worth more than their face value. This betrayal was fatal—fatal to Law, fatal to the System, fatal to credit, and literally fatal to a number of people who died in mob scenes later trying to cash their paper for a few coins. Law himself subsequently admitted that this was the beginning of the end of the System.

Law's supporters claimed for a time that the edict of May 21 had been forced upon him by enemies out to wreck the System, but Law accepted full responsibility and wrote at length, as usual, in defense of his decision to try to stop inflation by a precipitous deflation. He knew it would unsettle the public: ". . . this decree could not help but throw the public into great consternation and to alienate every mind," he later wrote, ". . . but there were some enlightened people who thought otherwise, that this decree was the unique way to put affairs in order."

Perhaps so. But the enlightened ones were overshadowed by the host of powerful enemies of Law and of the Regent, who listened to the uproar of the alienated and concluded that Law had reached the nadir of his fortunes and could at last be brought to bay.

The public scrambled to rid itself of as much paper money as it could, but merchants were refusing to accept it. Crowds stormed the bank seeking coins and had to be driven off by troops. Civil disorder seemed imminent. Parlement, the only center of whatever organized opposition the government faced, studied the edict they must register and found much that was objectionable. Egged on by the treacherous D'Argenson, who claimed that he had only gone along with Orleans for reasons of expediency, the Parlement refused to register the devaluation and issued a remonstrance that the startled Orleans could scarcely ignore. Dubois added his weighty opinion to those of everyone surrounding the Regent, including his mother, who said that no matter how many times it had been explained to her, the System had always remained incomprehensible. The private bankers, silent for so long, sought audiences with Orleans—Crozat, Bernard, the Paris brothers, these were the men he would have to rely on if Law's System should really fail.

But the convincing voices were those of the crowds in the street. Lampoons were hastily printed, and the Regent came in for as much abuse as Law himself. The old stories about him of murder and incest were revived. The satires on Law were by now a familiar feature of the walls of Paris: "Law, son of satan/ Has turned us all to beggars." (Ironically, Law had tried by edict to rid Paris of beggars and vagabonds—by locking them up or shipping them to the colonies!) "Since Law became a catholic/ The entire kingdom is capuchin." The Capuchins were an order of mendicant friars. Law was seen as a doctor who had come to cure France and ended by putting everyone in a sickbed: "Observe this Scot cerebral/ Calculator without equal/ who uses the rules of algebra/ To put France in the hospital." The Regent did not like being linked to Law in such couplets as: "As soon as Law was seen to arrive/ The Regent proclaimed that the nation would thrive."

Some of the posters around town were menacing: "Sir and Madame, this is to give you notice that a St. Bartholomew's Day will be enacted again on Saturday and Sunday if affairs do not alter. You are desired not to stir out, nor your servants. God preserve you from the flames! Give notice to your neighbors." This appeared dated Saturday, May 25. The St. Bartholomew Massacres, in which thousands of Huguenots were slain in cold blood, occurred in 1572, but the memory of them had passed into the folklore of vengeance.

A popular uprising in the city was not to be feared at this time, however. There was no leadership among the mob, and none of the rich and powerful wanted an alliance with common people at this stage in French history. What was feared was something like the Fronde, the rebellion that so frightened Louis XIV. A rebellion against Orleans? By whom? That apparently lazy leader had established in the name of the King another kind of absolutism, looser and less obvious than that of Louis XIV, and it was for this reason that John Law under his protection could do as he pleased. Orleans, good natured, pliable, and a sometime believer in Law's reforms, was no sentimentalist, and his deplorable lack of rigidity, his wavering on so many matters, now seemed a necessary virtue. M. the Duke, as Bourbon was known, still holding much paper, upbraided the Regent, who silenced him with a gift of 4 million livres. Du Mesme, the president of Parlement, stopped by to say he would rather have 100 livres in silver than 1,000 in paper.

Still, Orleans temporized, while Law explained his strategy in a letter the *Mercure* refused to print. The editor was doing the minister a favor; the letter was too technical for readers of that official paper—it based the devaluation on the need to follow the course of the debased coinage, ignoring all prior debasements when the paper bills held fast—and its tone was enough to get Law lynched: "As for those who have a large amount of bank notes, their lot is not in truth as favorable as that of the stockholders: but that is their fault; why did they cling to their bank notes instead of converting them into shares?"

Law now had the bad habit of forcing people to do things they did not want to do, and he was audacious enough to believe he could continue his high-handedness indefinitely. To make paper money attractive and then chastise those who accumulated it was not only arrogant but blundering.

Brazenly, Orleans took Law to the Opera with him. In the corridors, the Regent learned, people were studying the *Memoirs* of de Retz. Was a coup possible? The doddering Duke of Maine could surely never lead it. But what about Bourbon—or Dubois? Someone told him troops were grumbling over losses of their own in the rue Quincampoix!

Orleans began to realize that the foundation on which the System rested was credit, and that this had been shaken by a repudiation of the King's solemn promise that his bank notes would never be tampered with. Without too much reflection, he called a meeting of the Regency Council, where, as he expected, all members favored an abrogation of the edict they had just passed. A restoration of the paper currency's status quo before May 21 was essential, they said. Law was present and was allowed to oppose this move, asking for patience to prove that his deflationary policy would work after the public realized that in fact they were no worse off than before, and that as credit reestablished itself, and the insanity of speculation died down, the country would be stronger financially than it had ever been. No hostility to Law was shown, and this should have alerted him to what would follow. Reluctantly, he accepted the reversal of his edict, convinced that it would badly damage the chances of restoring credit.

The council's decision preceded a meeting of Parlement, from which a delegation was named to go to the Palais Royal on May 27. But before this deputation could set off, the Regent sent one of his counsellors, La Vrilliere, to Parlement announcing withdrawal of the edict of the 21st. The coincidence led some people to believe that Parlement had forced the Regent's hand, and later in the summer this led to an overconfidence which the Regent had to deflate by banishing the entire assembly to Pontoise in the suburbs. But for the moment, Parlement rejoiced and attended a dinner at the Palais Royal, from which Law was conspicuously missing.

Perhaps for the first time since his happy entry into Paris, Law was not welcome anywhere in the capital. Next day he found it impossible to gain entry to the Regent's chambers, where he had been as much at home as at the bank. The rebuff shook him, and he hurried to his office, taking care to be inconspicuous among an uneasy and hostile public. Merchants held back to see what would happen. Law was still very much the villain. "The System has enriched a thousand beggars, and beggared a hundred thousand honest men," an observer noted.

A day passed. No word from anyone. Law noted that restoring the value of the livre did not seem to be restoring confidence; there was just too much paper money in circulation.

On the 29th Le Blanc, secretary of state for war, was announced at Law's house. Formerly, he had been just another minister over whom Law towered physically and in prestige. Now, from this minion of the Regent, Law had to hear that Orleans was relieving him of his portfolio as controller general of finance, with the usual ritualistic gratitude for services rendered the King. Outside, Law could hear horses and the rattle of sabers. A precaution, Le Blanc explained, for Law wondered if he might be under arrest. A Major Benzualde of the Swiss guards was introduced, and he promised that his sixteen men would insure M. Law against the treacherous swine in the streets who might attack him or his family.

"You are not popular," Le Blanc said. But Law remained uneasy; Benzualde's men might be considered by the public a precaution to insure Law's presence in the kingdom, and he deeply resented the implication that he might run away.

The dismissal Law could understand as an act of politics, but not the way it was done. He immediately requested an audience with Orleans, and from the Palais Royal came an escort, the Duke de la Force. This was a further insult, for la Force was the most notorious hoarder in Paris. He had cornered so much spice that Parlement conducted an inquiry to see whether he should forfeit his peerage, since noblemen were not supposed to take up the commoner's calling of merchant. A caricature pictured him as a street porter loaded down with bales of spice that only a giant could have carried; the caption read: *Admirez la Force* (admire the strength).

La Force took Law to the Regent's outer office, where they sat and sat and sat, until finally a valet announced that the Regent could not see M. Law.

This humiliation rattled around the court. Law had not only been cashiered, he was *de trop*, and it was expected that he would soon be departing the kingdom or be put in the Bastille. No one asked what would become of the finances. D'Argenson had also been sacrificed, relieved as Keeper of the Seals to be replaced by D'Agasseau, Law's old opponent; a functionary named Desforts was named commissar of finance. No controller general was appointed. D'Argenson, who had had enormous power as lieutenant of the police and great honor as Keeper of the Seals, retired to live in a convent, of all places. Saint-Simon passes off the scene of Law cooling his heels in an antechamber as a comedy.

Law bided his time without further attempting to see Orleans, who must sooner or later call him to interpret the figures of the bank and the company for Parlement's review of finances. Next day, he was called to the Palais Royal, escorted down a narrow hall to some back stairs and up into a room he had never seen before. There Orleans waited to embrace him. There were no hard feelings, he said, and Law was most necessary to the kingdom. As of now he was to be a state councillor and intendant general of commerce; of course, he would retain his place at the head of the bank and the company. *And* he was invited to attend the Opera with the Regent that evening.

Law had only one request: in view of the continued protection of His Royal Highness, it should not be necessary to waste the valuable Swiss Guards on his account, and Orleans agreed to withdraw Benzualde and his men. As a precaution, he advised Law, perhaps his family might retire to the country for a time. Law said he would think it over.

What Law did not know was that the Paris brothers, the private bankers, had been pressuring the Regent to arrest Law and liquidate the Indies Company. This he indignantly declined to do. He now asked Law what should be done for the finances. Law replied that a new program would be necessary to restore confidence, and he again deplored the refusal to uphold his devaluation edict. All was not lost, however, and he hurried off to draft proposals. Orleans may have fired a minister, but he still had the finest financial mind in Europe at his disposal.

Law made his memorandum short, beginning innocently: "If the discredit had not been carried so far, the arrangements for withdrawing [excess] bank notes would have reestablished confidence and specie [would have come into France from abroad]. But in the present situation it is necessary to have recourse to extraordinary measures." As if until now no extraordinary measures had been tried. You give a patient medicine, he refuses to swallow it; so you tell him to spit it out; then fatal pains begin to grip his bowels. Most doctors would walk out under the circumstances. Law's advice was to take the patient firmly in hand and administer another concoction, just as bitter tasting, but certain to be effective.

His concern was for the vast majority of Frenchmen. He distinguished between two classes, those with funds who were able to buy bonds and annuities, and "the little people who have nothing to invest . . . and it is these people who must be saved." The System was based on the conception that *all* should share in the productive wealth of the nation.

And it was in this that he was practically alone. No one in power cared at all about the little people. Not even Voltaire or Montesquieu had such sentiments, which only appeared in literature in *Manon Lescaut* (1731), Rousseau's *Discourse on Science and Art* (1750), and later in England in Laurence Sterne's *Sentimental Journey* (1768). Society was hierarchical, and those at the bottom could always be sacrificed in the name of stability, the nation, or some other idea that allowed those in power to remain comfortable. Law might have been well advised to smuggle funds abroad and depart, but the idea never entered his mind.

Persistently and courageously, he refused to yield the high ground of his convictions. If no one else cared for the little people, Law really did not care about those at the top. In this he was hypocritical, for to achieve his purposes he had fawned before the powerful. But having been an exile most of his adult life, leading a gypsy-like existence all over Europe, he belonged to no settled society and had no personal stake in a fixed order. This is why from the beginning he could so cavalierly propose reforms that would, if carried out, unseat thousands of the privileged.

This side of Law amused Orleans, who liked to tease the stiff aristocrats led by Saint-Simon. But in the final analysis he perceived Law as Daisy Buchanan perceived Gatsby. Law simply had to go—but not just yet. Law, with unshaken confidence in his own genius, failed to see that henceforth he might propose, but others would dispose.

His proposals came as no surprise. The paper currency must be saved at all costs, and he set down the means in almost shorthand form:

1. Reestablish authority. 2. Declare that there will never be investigations or penalties. 3. Declare that Your Royal Highness will support the

System. 4. Substantiate what has been done to strengthen the Company. 5. Carry out the decrees ordering bank notes to be received in all transactions. 6. Abolish the use of gold in purchasing silver at the mint. 7. Renew the prohibition of keeping more than 500 livres of specie without permission. 8. Open transfer [i.e. checking] accounts for businesses. 9. Set a limit on holding bonds on the city [of Paris]. 10. Begin new arrangements for retiring 600 million livres in bank notes. 11. The public requires that authority and the System be supported, it hopes that the bank notes and shares will recover their value, which will not fail to happen when the public is reassured against penalties and that some money sent abroad will come back. A favorable exchange once reestablished, silver being strong then will leave [the country]; but to reestablish a favorable exchange and the circulation of silver specie, it seems to me necessary to abolish gold money.

The reasoning about gold, silver, and foreign exchange is technical, but any layman can see that Law would be happy to have silver leave the country, gold be used for nothing but jewelry, plate, and industrial application, and paper money become the exclusive money of the realm. He also saw, too late, that for this to occur, the supply must be carefully limited in relation to the level of economic activity.

Law would have been willing to allow anyone to keep 1,000 or even 3,000 livres in specie if the Regent thought that would ease the situation, but in his memorandum he suggested the death penalty for hiding more than this "*sous les scelles*," under the floorboards! He concluded with a few words about doubling or tripling the government's revenues by simplifying the tax system, cutting down the expensive and larcenous bureaucracy, and eliminating arbitrary duties that impeded industry. He also noted that a high price of grain should become a government objective, since "landlord and peasant want a high price; when there is abundance, there is nothing to fear from high prices" unless you happen to be a *rentier*, an idle man living off a fixed interest income.

Law simply could not refrain from reiterated condemnation of anyone who derived income from bonds, annuities, mortgages, or other loans, although he himself had invested most of his original fortune in annuities and had an income of 100,000 livres from this source at the time he wrote. It was a blind spot, due perhaps to the competition of such securities with those of the company. Not all *rentiers* were rich and idle. But their capital was not available to *him*!

Law's memorandum was of course academic. The Regent was not going to make any public statement about the System; in removing Law from the ministry he definitely meant to clip his wings—in effect to alter if not abandon the System. Law was ignored, and new edicts were now issued permitting the use of specie again in transactions; the limit of 500 livres personal possession of coin was removed. "Alas, the permission comes when nobody has any left," said the chronicler Barbier. But as Perkins remarked, "The experiment of banishing gold and silver from the marts of the world was abandoned before it had been fairly made."

There is evidence that despite the French collapse, the idea of paper currency was not odious in places that had not experienced its inflationary consequences. Lady Mary Wortley Montagu, the great letter writer whose admiration of Law led her to successful securities investments in London, wrote to her husband from Rome on November 23, 1740: ". . . there is litterally no Money in the whole Town, where they follow Mr. Law's System and live wholly upon Paper. Belloni, who is the greatest banker not only of Rome but all Italy furnish'd me with 50 sequins which he solemnly swore was all the money he had in the House."

And so from June until December, John Law remained in Paris, forced to watch others undo in six months what he had created over a period of four years. The ancient forms of government finance, so profitable to the few and so fatal eventually to the *ancien regime*, were to be restored. The Regent, apparently absolute in his power, was only Regent and therefore a lame duck. The King was now ten. His time to rule was within sight. Powerful noblemen were preparing to resume the role that Louis XIV had denied them, and they would need the privileges which

Law's System had aimed to destroy. A young King, compliant and sensitive to their aims, would not stand in their way.

And with all these forces working against John Law—public hatred, private conniving, an indecisive Regent, a sinking currency, the violent emotions of fear and panic all around—nature itself struck what Law believed to have been the absolute blow: a terrible plague swept through Marseilles in June. For a year, Mediterranean trade, vital to the Indies Company, was largely closed to France, there was great fear of an epidemic in Paris, and the public became desperate for hard money.

20

La Peste

The twentieth century, an era of massive suffering, has been spared at least one horror: modern technology has apparently eliminated outbreaks of bubonic plague through the development of effective urban sanitation. The rapid growth of European cities, with their crowded tenements and systems of open sewage, made them particularly susceptible to this fatal fever, carried by fleas from hot eastern climates. John Law was born five years after the so-called "Great Plague," which killed a seventh of the people of London, and during his boyhood Vienna lost 76,000, and Prague 86,000, from this frightening scourge. Early in the eighteenth century, 283,000 people in Eastern Europe were struck down by it.

It was a disease of progress and commerce. It originated in the Orient and the Levant and travelled on rats by ship to European ports, where the rod-shaped bacteria thrived (the germ was isolated in Hong Kong by a French biologist named Alexandre Yersin in 1894). Knowledge of its consequences was widespread, and among the ignorant it was attributed to the devil; fear of the plague could lead to panic, riots, and torture of persons suspected of being agents of Satan.

Milan had just such a popular fright in 1630, and this may

bear on how the plague came to Marseilles 90 years later. For the ship that carried the disease, the *Grand-Saint-Antoine* out of Beirut, had as its destination an Italian port, Cagliari, the chief city of Sardinia, whose government was in the hands of a disappointed man named Saint-Remys. He had just been reduced from ruler of the island to a mere viceroy after the Duke of Savoy, John Law's old patron in Turin, had himself declared the first King of Sardinia. Saint-Remys was deeply troubled by the loss of his prestige and power, and early in May he had a nightmare, easily interpreted today as a reflection of his anguish and anxieties of the moment. He dreamed that the plague had overwhelmed Sardinia. His visions were horribly vivid and memorable. He saw the ranks of society melt away in disorder as the city became demoralized and maddened with fear. Matter was transformed by some mysterious process into ashes. He himself was a victim, and the very marrow of his bones was pulverized. In his nightmare, he all but vanished.

When Saint-Remys awoke, he remembered the continuing rumors of the plague and its awful visitation in 1656 upon Naples, when 300,000 died, and on Genoa, which lost 60,000. He may have heard through sea captains that recently Stockholm had seen 40,000 carried off by this pestilence, and that as a result of 215,000 deaths in Brandenburg, British ports were quarantining Baltic ships. Outbreaks had occurred in Constantinople in 1711 and in Hungary and Poland in 1719. There were no psychiatrists to reassure him that he was simply projecting in fantastic form the sense of loss he felt in his present depressed condition of deprived chieftaincy. It was his belief that he had experienced a genuine premonition that his realm was in grave danger, and he proceeded at once to act on it.

As viceroy, he was still the supreme commander of the port, and when he heard that the *Grand-Saint-Antoine* from the Levant was requesting permission to dock, he went into such a frenzy of denial that his subordinates thought he had lost his mind. Chataud, the ship's captain, had the sympathy of those on shore, particularly merchants awaiting cargo, but nothing could move

Saint-Remys, who gave orders to level the cannons of the port on the vessel, which he insisted was pestilential despite no visible evidence of illness aboard.

The *Grand-Saint-Antoine* hoisted sail and found its haven a few weeks later at the end of May in Marseilles, a city that already had pockets of plague, which were controlled by quarantine. The mystery is that the ship got through the supposedly elaborate port check developed in France to avoid England's experience of the previous century. The authorities were so efficient in registering crew and passengers that they were later able to report that everyone on board but the captain eventually suffered the plague! The captain, however, had concealed from health officers the fact that two passengers and four sailors had suddenly died during the trip from Sardinia. It seems probable that he and everyone else aboard knew then that Saint-Remys had been justified in his fear. In the tiny rue d'Escale, in the workers' quarter of Marseilles, the outbreak of the plague of 1720 began in June.

Weeks after the authorities believed that an epidemic had been avoided by putting cases into lazarettos and quarantining hospitals, fourteen people living on the rue d'Escale suddenly died in one day. A shudder of fear went through France and eventually all of Europe. A year before, the rue Quincampoix had been the symbol of an unforeseen benevolence that would enrich anyone with energy and wit to plunge into speculation. Now the rue d'Escale became the symbol of the *fléau*, the scourge of God. Too late it was learned that those aboard the *Grand-Saint-Antoine* were sick and some dying. Marseilles for the next year was *une ville morte*.

The infections of the body never reached Paris, but an infection of the spirit was carried beyond the borders of Provence. "I have said that if France had been exempted from this malady, the System of Mr. Law would have been upheld," Law wrote—he ocasionally used the third person in writing about himself.

It is ironic that Victor Amadeus of Savoy, the man who advised Law to take his banking ideas from Turin to Paris, may have inadvertently caused the governor of Sardinia to have the nightmare that sent the death ship on to Marseilles, a ship Law claimed was in effect the death of the System (he knew nothing of the Saint-Remys episode).

The terrible psychological and economic impact of this catastrophe is self-evident. To describe the pitiable scenes that occurred is to indulge in a kind of retrospective morbid voyeurism, but a few observations may be permissible in order to appreciate the state of mind the plague engendered hundreds of miles away.

The disease, which is glandular, took two forms, visible and invisible. The visible symptoms were ugly sores that turned from red to black and erupted like a volcano. The lungs and brain were assailed with feelings of suffocation and madness, which drove victims to public fountains screaming with thirst. When death came after a few days, the body turned hard as stone. But some died suddenly with no symptoms at all, as if from a heart attack, yet autopsies could reveal no vital organs damaged, save for a blackness in the blood and in the head. Men congratulating themselves on their immunity might drop dead while shaving.

In September, a thousand people a day were dying in Marseilles, and the effect on the society of the city was one of almost total disintegration. As a group, the clergy stood fast, led by a fanatical bishop named Belzunce, who, in addition to genuine administration of relief, led dramatic religious processions seeking divine intercession and incidentally taking advantage of the occasion to denounce the liberal Jansenists in the community.

Since most of the population of any city is made up of humble people who do the heavy work, the labor force quickly vanished until there were not enough hands able or willing to remove corpses, which piled up in hospitals and then in the streets in a grotesque tangle of rock-like limbs. Shoving them into the harbor could only mean that they would be washed up against the shoreline. The living slept next to the dead in many instances, and in a few cases the healthy were driven by some demonic desire to seek sexual satisfaction among the dying and dead.

Thousands fled, deserting families, seeking pure air. Those with boats went to sea. The rich could find sanctuary in the countryside without much trouble, but they also might die there, and eventually the plague spread throughout the towns of Provence. The poor might sleep in the open or climb the cliffs around the city and hide in caves to avoid the infection.

All values broke down in the disorder arising from the fragility of day-to-day living; money, rank, privilege meant little, since nothing could guarantee immunity. Famine and speculation in commodities increased the chaos. Only caring for the sick seemed to have meaning. Hundreds of priests, nuns, and city officials upheld the dignity of civilization, and many of them also became infected. Not all who got sick died. Doctors worked heroically, but they were baffled, and they were criticized for their conflicting observations, particularly about contagion. In general, the infection comes from a flea bite, but there are instances when it can come in other ways. The rats of Marseilles were not dying, so in this instance contagion was a justifiable conclusion.

The stench led doctors to adopt the bizarre custom of wearing the kind of bird-beak masks seen during carnival season, in which were conveniently stuffed deodorants and disinfectants. Long cloaks, wooden platform clogs on the feet, and gauntlets completed the garb of these crows, as they were called, and they were the heroes who stayed on to comfort the afflicted, and often to die themselves.

It was well that photography and television did not exist to provide instant horror shows of the scene for the rest of the world. Communications were rapid enough, and they were terse and sensible. The officials of Paris and London effectively sealed their cities against any visitors or merchandise from southern France or the Near East until satisfied that the plague was not being transmitted. A *cordon sanitaire* sealed off the whole of Provence and Languedoc.

The public elsewhere was uneasy, especially in London, where the scars of 1665 were visible. The author of *Robinson Crusoe* was so moved by what he heard of Marseilles that he composed *A Journal of the Plague Year*, a narrative of events that supposedly occurred in London when Defoe was five. Plans were made to evacuate the city should infection reach it.

The Regent ordered all galley slaves to Marseilles, and these criminals and political prisoners worked to help keep the city together, some giving up their lives in the process. John Law provided 275,000 livres in silver to the city at a time when the bank desperately needed it, and through agents of the company there he tried to prevent commodity speculation.

John Law envisaged what might happen to English credit if the plague had spread there:

Suppose it broke out in one English county; every family would seek silver coins to buy food in the countryside, fearing that the disease would spread across the kingdom. There are 100,000 families in London and all the specie in England would not suffice for half the people of this one city. The demand on the Bank [of England] would not have been as mild as it was when fear of the Pretender (1715) put the credit of that establishment in danger—but only for three or four days.

Law's knowledge of the Bank of England included, as he shows in this memorandum written after he left France, the fact that the Bank of England prevented a run by counting out money slowly and in small coins, or by inserting friends in the line who would return the money they withdrew, so that the funds were not exhausted and confidence was restored. Such expedients would not have worked during a plague lasting six months, and Law paints a picture of England in the condition of depression that occurred in France in 1720.

Mr. Law had surmounted the difficulties that occurred after the edict of May 27, 1720 [the third-person memorandum goes on]. The Regent, well aware of the situation, could no longer stand what his [Law's] enemies were proposing in an attempt to restore credit. This Prince had always appreciated Mr. Law, and sensed the necessity for putting him back in charge, which he did; and it has been presumed that credit would have been reestablished if the plague had not occurred.

This, of course, is a self-serving judgment, but it is not without support. A French scholar, Charles Carriere, after studying the business situation in Marseilles before and after the plague, concluded in 1956 that "Law was in a way the victim of the plague in Marseilles." During the four years Law was active in France, trade with Africa increased sevenfold. The closing down of Marseilles and other ports of entry in southern France in 1720–21 was not what Law was referring to directly; it was the loss of confidence that followed the news that Marseilles was being ravaged by disease. The fear that it would spread northward turned the growing distrust of paper money into a genuine panic in Paris and other cities, where a pitiful craze developed for coins and produced the saddest scenes of the days of System. At the same time, the knowledge that plague was interfering with Indies Company shipping helped to depress further the rapidly dwindling value of its shares.

In October, as the weather cooled, the severity of the plague was sharply reduced, and it disappeared entirely in April 1721. But not before 60,000 dead were counted in Marseilles and 40,000 in Aix, Nîmes, Arles, Toulouse, Avignon, and the countryside. Recovery from *la peste* took years.

It is probably going too far to say that if there had been no plague, things would have turned out very differently for John Law. But this affliction aggravated the economic difficulties that had become so infuriating to everyone by the summer of 1720 and certainly added to the almost insane desire among ordinary people to exchange their paper money for coins. The Regent grew more unpopular.

> That the plague is in Provence
> Is not the worst of all.
> It would be better for France
> If it struck the Palais Royal.

So went a summer song.

By the time the fear of an epidemic in the north had subsided, Law's efforts to restore credit and save his System had attracted so little confidence anywhere, in the government or outside of it, that as things turned out, he was lucky indeed to save his life.

THE END

Who sees with equal eye, as God of all,
A hero perish or a sparrow fall,
Atoms or systems into ruin hurl'd,
And now a bubble burst, and now a world.

Alexander Pope, Essay on Man

21

A Splintered Carriage

Where would it all end? That was the bewildering question everyone was asking in the summer of 1720. What a difference a year makes! Looking back twelve months to the giddy days of the rue Quincampoix, people could not believe that a boom had ever existed. That was all a dream, and the present was surely but a nightmare. An evaporation of reality seemed to have occurred. There was no longer any talk of gold or silver mines in Mississippi. There was no substance to that fancy. But worse, instead of new wealth flowing into France from Louisiana, it appeared that what wealth there had been before had simply vanished into thin air. There were no coins to be had anywhere. Fear of confiscation had turned everyone into hoarders.

And all there was, was this confounded paper! How on earth could it ever have passed for the real thing? It was not money; anyone could see that it was just paper with numbers on it. The government could print as much of it as they wanted to, give it to the public for gold and silver, and pass that around to the Bourbons and Contis and the *roués*. It was all a maddening swindle. And as punishment for our stupid greed, some simple minds concluded, God has cursed France with a plague! We will not only not be rich, we won't even be poor. We'll be dead!

This sentiment was not shared by the middle class, which was neither superstitious nor reverent, and prudently looked for a way out of financial difficulty. Some shrewd people who kept their heads even made some money from the general distress. The Abbé Tencin wrote his brother on June 4, 1720: "I have sent you one hundred and fifty thousand livres. . . . See to it that all of it is invested in some way even if it should be without income for some years, which is not important. Lose no time. . . ."

It was to the investing public that Law looked for support— not of him personally; he was not a public figure so much as a functionary by now. He needed belief in the possibility of a stable situation so that credit could be reestablished; then credit would reestablish *him*!

But the System and Law were inseparable; if Law no longer had any credibility, the System was finished. The subtle and fragile confidence in his credit mechanism, so carefully developed over a long period, was irretrievably gone. Yet those who suspected him of malfeasance were confounded by a Parlementary report in June on the condition of the Royal Bank and the Indies Company, both of which were sound and, if not exactly flourishing at the moment, had promising prospects if the crisis could be ridden out. There was wide amazement and admiration at the impeccable accounts Law had insisted on, and the double entry bookkeeping, though well known outside France, seemed to the jurists, who were unskilled in finance, an absolute marvel.

Moreover, Law's administration of his System turned out to have been a model of efficiency and orderliness. With one or two exceptions, he had chosen highly capable and honest executives to manage all that he undertook, and some of these later had the courage and intelligence to publish defenses of the System in the greatest detail. Had there been the slightest chance of accusing Law of anything illegal, it would have been seized upon in the summer of 1720 by Law's enemies. But no public accusations were ever raised charging him with a single act of fiscal impropriety. In fact, so awesome were the voluminous ledgers examined by Parlement and so sweeping was Law's grasp of money matters in every corner of the kingdom, that wise men drew back lest this giant of finance have concealed somewhere figures and information that might compromise *them*. How many people were let in on the ground floor of the System will never be known.

The idea that Law had concealed something became a cruel weapon that was used to torment and impoverish him later. Law, they said, had put a fortune aside in some other country. The fact was that he had brought his fortune of over a million and a half livres into France and was going to leave the country with nothing; and he was never able to reclaim his loss because of the insistence on blackening his reputation with stories about gold and jewels he had hidden in Belgium or England. Even Law's brother, William, believed he must have set something aside in another country.

But this came later. For a moment, after the discovery that the bank and the company were not just so much legerdemain, Law's enemies were forced to regroup. Keeper of the Seals D'Argenson was finally forced into retirement. Daguesseau, another old opponent of Law, took his place. But though Law was still allowed to carry out certain measures he hoped would reduce the amount of paper in circulation, he was no longer the complete master of his System, a fact he could plainly see in the long sad queues every day outside the various offices of the Bank. Since paper could be converted to coin now, thousands stood by the hour waiting a turn at the teller's cage to cash in their bank notes for a few coins.

On June 11, Law conceived the brilliant idea of publicly burning the bank notes as they came in, to convince the public that because of their growing scarcity they should be worth more. He had long recognized that too much money was harmful and had written prophetically in 1715: "Not only the scarcity, but also too great a quantity of silver money in public hands is harmful to the state." Eliminate the word silver, and you have a truism that the simplest mind can grasp. A huge cage was set up outside the bank, and here ceremonially from time to time for the next several months officials burned up retired bank notes and stock certificates. A poet might see in this bizarre rite a purging of the ailing financial body, to use the familiar image, akin to the practice of bleeding the sick for almost any ailment. Law hoped that a phoenix would rise from the ashes in the form of a common sense acceptance of a credit system that was sound so long as speculation was kept within limits, so long as the government was keeping the money supply in better proportion to business activity. (This still eludes the money managers of the twentieth century on occasion.)

A different interpretation was put on the smoldering paper by the miserable sector of the public: paper, they concluded, was the last thing a sensible person would want to keep in his possession, and the lines outside the bureaus of the Bank lengthened. The provincial branches were likewise besieged. During the warm summer nights, people got up before dawn to reach the rue St. Avoie or the rue Vivienne ahead of the crowd and waited long hours to clutch a single silver coin in return for the little paper money they owned.

Charles d'Ivernois, a young Paris banker, wrote to his brother on June 21, 1720, "If the bank no longer pays out silver, people will soon cut their throats for a few coins . . . and I'm unable to pay my laundress, who only wants silver."

The amount of paper turned in to the bank was not always small. Those with large sums could afford to send employees to stand out in the hot sun all day. By the end of August, over 700 million livres had been burned. In a technical sense, Law's strategy was working. But the psychology was so wrong that Law's enemies adopted it after he left France; it was a convenient way to prove that the System was being consigned to the ash heap.

Less dramatic means were adopted for absorbing another billion and a half in paper money by offering to open checking accounts for businessmen and to provide annuities of various kinds. There were credit balances in state accounts and in accounts of the company that were also liquidated by burning these deposits of paper. As a result, in October the amount of paper in circulation had been reduced by more than 50 per cent; the mistake made in March of having the bank buy up shares at 9,000 had been rectified. All the printing press money issued during the spring was retired during the summer of 1720.

The number of shares issued by John Law were also drastically reduced—by more than two-thirds. The company's own holdings of half the shares issued were burned, as were the King's 100,000. By this gesture, Law sought to convince investors that the profits of the company could now be distributed more generously among the reduced number of shareholders. The trouble was, though, that the shares had been monetized in March, so that the public was unable or unwilling to distinguish them from paper money. If paper lost value, the shares must also lose, no matter how many were outstanding. Ivernois quotes the price of the company stock as 4,800 on July 5—in spite of the devaluation.

Paper money continued to lose value all during the summer. Taking June as 100, a 100 livre note was worth only 53 livres in the beginning of September. The supply had been considerably diminished, but there was no demand; everyone wanted *coins.* Had someone in the government, not necessarily Orleans, given some public reassurances, confidence might have been restored, because the situation was not as bad as it appeared; the mess was being cleaned up. But of course, the finances of the government were now returning to the hands of those who never wanted Law's System in the first place, and by their silence they condemned his sensible measures to oblivion.

Law had learned his lesson too late. Humbled by Orleans, he brought his activities down to the sensible level they were at when he had organized the *Banque Générale.* He was prepared to forgo popularity and honors, and work in obscurity. He seemed to have won back the Regent's confidence, and that wavering leader might have been able to keep Law in the kingdom if a terrible thing had not occurred at the bank on the night of July 17.

Queues had reappeared on June 1, after the bank had been closed for ten days following the unfortunate announcement of devaluation on May 21. In the beginning, 100 livre notes were redeemed for silver, but as the silver supply ran low, Law did as he had seen the Bank of England do under similar circumstances; he slowed down redemptions by refusing to accept anything but 10 livre notes. This naturally increased the lines and shattered the nerves of thousands. Bullies took advantage of their strength and fought their way to the tellers' windows, some swinging through trees like apes, on occasion inflicting serious injury. Observers reported deaths of men and women from trampling, and a soldier killed a man during a melee.

The mood of the people grew sullen and ugly, and there were little outbreaks of violence directed at Law. Once Law's daughter was spotted in a carriage and surrounded by a mob, which began to stone the carriage. According to an eyewitness, there were shouts about Law's failing to redeem 10 livre bank notes, proof that not everyone who stood in line got to a window before it closed (hours eight to noon, three to seven). The thirteen-year-old Catherine got away with minor injuries. Elsewhere, a woman mistaken for Madame Law was thrown into a duck pond and nearly drowned by peasants. "It was a marvel all Paris did not revolt at once," Saint-Simon remarked.

Parlement, sensing anew what they thought was a weakness in the Regent's armor, supported the people by challenging him on an edict that attempted to strengthen the company and support paper currency. By the edict, all its trading rights were extended in perpetuity and the monopolies on tobacco, the mint, and tax collecting were reconfirmed. With a new issue of 70,000 shares of stock, the company was to retire more than half a billion livres in paper money if fully subscribed. This looked as if Law was starting up all over again, when the purpose was but another feeble attempt to create confidence.

Members of the Parlement, encouraged by businessmen and bankers, resolved to defy Orleans, who had pushed the measure through the Regency Council on July 16. Paris was full of rumors that the government was in danger. People spoke of the possibility of the plague reaching the north.

During the night of July 17, an enormous crowd began to gather in the narrow rue Vivienne, everyone determined not to be turned away from the bank, which would open at eight o'clock the next morning. By dawn, 15,000 people were jammed in so tightly that suffocation was occurring. There was an arrangement

just outside the door to provide orderly lines. Solid wooden bar-
riers had been erected for the purpose, and within these chutes
the worst losses of life came. Ivernois claimed that 300,000 people were around the bank—half the population of Paris! Allow
for the exaggerated estimate, and say that it *seemed* as if the entire city had got up early that day.

Gradually, bodies were passed out until sixteen dead had been
counted. Subdued and guilty for their own selfishness, the hushed
mob withdrew when the bank posted a notice that it would not
open that day.

But once separated into viable crowds in more open streets,
and no longer threatened with suffocation, the people breathed
deep and let out terrible screams of anger, frustration, and re-
morse, and a series of riots broke out. Mounted troops rushed to
protect Law's house from being stormed. But the sympathies of
the soldiers were such that they did not block a spontaneous parade that headed for the Palais Royal bearing three corpses on
a stretcher. From the square, the people shouted their demands
to be let in and heard. This was the first time during the Regency
that the seat of government had been menaced, and troops from
the Tuileries were posted around the edges of the crowd, while
spokesmen for the government talked soothingly to the leaders.
Meanwhile, another body was exposed under the King's window
at the Tuileries itself. Ugly knots of people throughout the city
threatened those who appeared well-to-do. The Palais Royal
was secretly reinforced by dressing fifty soldiers as civilians and
letting them in a back door.

Now the gates of the Palais were thrown open, and a mob of
thousands swarmed into the outer court, filling it in a few moments. The secretary of state for war, LeBlanc, appeared, surrounded by the plainclothes guard, and began talking to the
leaders. The Duke of Tresme, governor of the city, arrived in a
carriage, which was allowed to pass through the crowd. He tried
humoring the people by tossing them coins. They ripped the lace
cuffs from his sleeves, and he withdrew to safety. A widow of
one of the dead broke through and grabbed LeBlanc by the col-

lar. He graciously instructed the soldiers who had seized her to let her go.

Then someone, seeing the corpses in the sunlight surrounded by this seething mass of people, suggested that this was no way to treat the dead and invited strong hands to help carry them to the nearest church. As expected, the widows and relatives followed, and with them went the sobs of anguish that had so moved the people. Gradually, the crowd withdrew. Amazingly, there had been little violence, and the troops had not been forced to take any action. It was not yet noon and the city was calm. Most of those who had been up all night went home to sleep. Sometime during the morning, John Law managed to slip into the Palais Royal without incident.

The Regent was more concerned about Parlement than about the *soupe au lait* that had boiled over in the courtyard, but he did appreciate Law's vulnerability, and for the second time a Parlementary rebellion obliged Orleans to offer the financier quarters at the Palais. Mme. Law and her two children were out in the country with the Bourbons. Orders were given to send Law's carriage away, but it was spotted by a roving band of belligerents, who blocked its way. The coachman told them Law was not inside, but they harangued him and he called them *"canaille!"* (riffraff). With that, the crowd moved in and vented its fury on the beautiful carriage, while the coachman was roughed up and let go, limping. Shortly the vehicle was pillaged for souvenirs, the wheels removed, doors ripped off, and the plush upholstery stripped, until within an hour all that was left was a pile of splintered wood. It was more fun than hanging Law in effigy.

By the time rumor carried the stories around, they had it that Law was dead. The Parlement was in session when a wag broke in with a jingle: *Messieurs, messieurs, grand nouvelle!/ Le carrosse de Law est reduit en cannelle.* "Great news, gentlemen! Law's carriage has been reduced to kindling." The news for Parlement, though, was that the Regent was disturbed again, and the members waited nervously.

Saint-Simon, calling on Orleans, found him "very tranquil and

showed that you would not please him unless you were likewise."
In this calm mood, he issued the kinds of orders that absolute
rulers delight in: no public assemblies and the bank to be closed
down until further notice. A show of troops was made at high
points of Paris. Parlement's official refusal to register the company's edict met with the determination to chastise such unwar-
ranted disobedience. At first, the council suggested that the
members of Parlement be sent off to Blois without their families,
away from the pleasures of Paris. But there was no real fear of
the jurists, and the Regent decided to slap their wrists by sending
them to Pontoise. In the eyes of Saint-Simon, this was so close to
Paris as to be a vacation rather than a punishment:

The chastisement became ridiculous, showed the vacillating weakness
of the Regent, and encouraged Parlement to laugh at him. One thing
however was well done. The resolution taken to banish the Parlement
was kept so secret that the assembly had not the slightest knowledge
of it.

On Sunday the 21st of July squadrons of guards with officers at their
head took possession at four o'clock in the morning of all the doors of
the Palais de Justice. The musketeers seized at the same time upon
the doors of the Grand Chamber, whilst others invaded the house of
the Chief President, who was in much fear during the first hour. Other
musketeers went in parties of four to all the officers of the Parlement,
and served them with the King's orders, commanding them to repair
to Pontoise within 48 hours.

Saint-Simon enjoyed any humiliation suffered by *noblesse de
la robe*, but he saw nothing funny in the Regent's provision of
100,000 livres in coin for Parlement's expenses, and five times
as much for the president of Parlement, who spent it entertaining
his fellow members in a magnificent house belonging to the Duke
of Bouillon. "Banishment to Pontoise was a fine punishment!"
Saint-Simon concludes sarcastically.

At the Hôtel de Soissons, 100 livres was quoted as being worth
only 40. In London, bets were being made that by September
John Law would be hanged.

22

Liquidating the System

Napoleon once said to a dilatory marshal, "Ask me for anything but time." It had taken Law three years to establish international confidence in his System of finance and credit, and this confidence had been destroyed in a few months. If there had been a chance for Law to recover his stride, it would have required another long period of sober, unspectacular management. Supported again by Orleans, he might eventually have reestablished himself with the general public, which, he remarked, "in France growls a lot but does not bite like the British."

Perhaps.

Before the end of July, he quitted the Palais Royal, but urchins hung around his house as lookouts for toughs, ready to spring on him if he was unprotected. This was the same house that the mighty had thronged to a few months ago. Now people avoided Law, and his very name could arouse a fury. As late as October, a coachman who was slapped by a passenger during an argument over the fare had the wit to denounce the man to the gathering crowd as John Law; the poor fellow only saved himself from the onlookers by hiding in a church. Law himself was careful to move only with bodyguards.

In his financial capacities, Law was now largely an unwilling spectator of undramatic events that saw the System dwindle and die out gradually in August and September. These were dog days in more than one sense. To insure against malnutrition or possibly starvation, the Regent sent 100,000 livres in coin to the bakers of the outlying town of Gonesse. Prices of everything suddenly shot up again, on the average by 60 per cent in August, but higher in some cases, reflecting the depreciation of paper money, which fell to 40 per cent by September 1. One group of workmen asked for treble their wages and took four days off until they got it, meanwhile "eating their money," as they said.

Despite price fixing by the Regency Council, merchants found ways to get what they wanted, one of them being to create false shortages. A candle merchant was caught claiming he had no stock left when his cellar was quite full, and his shop was closed for a month as punishment. Demoralization increased on August 15 as the government, not Law, decreed an end to the convertibility of the 1,000 and 10,000 livre notes, which could be used thereafter only to pay taxes or buy government bonds at 2.5 per cent, a ridiculous return on a dubious investment. It was only a matter of time before paper money would disappear altogether.

Law, on occasion, sulked. Madame thought his behavior cowardly. He was frightened and dismayed, powerless. "Law is like a corpse," she wrote. A disloyal few at the bank, which still existed but was closed to the public, left the sinking ship. A cashier vanished with some money, the only instance of its kind, but it came at a bad moment. A member of Law's secretarial staff departed for Italy on a pretext. The rumor was that Law would end in the Bastille and that those close to him might be dragged down by his fall.

The satirists were never more prolific or more clever.

> My shares which on Monday I bought
> Were worth millions on Tuesday, I thought.
> So on Wednesday I chose my abode;
> In my carriage on Thursday I rode;

> To the ball-room on Friday I went;
> To the workhouse next day I was sent.*

Announcements of burlesque books included "Dissertation on the Philosopher's Stone," by M. Law, dedicated to the Regent; "The Art of Converting Those Who Have No Religion," by the Abbé Tencin, dedicated to Law; "A Treatise on Christianity," by the Abbé Dubois, dedicated to the Regent.

The most remarkable work was done in Holland under the appropriate title, *The Mirror of Folly*. This long lampoon of seventy pages was illustrated with artistry and cleverness and accompanied by reams of doggerel. To it we owe the only detailed drawings of the rue Quincampoix. It shows too the bitterness felt in Holland, where Law's collapse was having an adverse impact on that model of financial stability.

For example, it was commonly said in the streets that Law's money was now good only for toilet paper. *The Mirror of Folly* illustrates its use as such. There are pictures of the mountains of Mississippi. Law is seen elsewhere as Don Quixote. And always there are mobs of people waving shares and paper money. A golden calf burps coins, while John Law inserts a bellows in the animal's rear. Frequent use is made of the idea of a bubble, for that word had been transplanted from Exchange Alley, and the wind is a frequent image in scenes depicting sudden wealth and sudden poverty at the whim of Fortune. "Wind business" was what the trading in Law's shares was called. And in the middle of most scenes, Law stands serenely in his wig and grand clothes, dispensing securities, unruffled.

Although Law wanted to outdistance the Dutch with his System, he admired them for their frugality and far-sighted business acumen. To be repaid for all his compliments to their financial and commercial genius with such caricatures was especially galling.

Beelzebub begot Law; Law begot Mississippi; Mississippi begot the System; the System begot paper; paper begot the bank; the bank begot

* The translation appears in H. Montgomery Hyde's biography: *John Law, The History of an Honest Adventurer,* London, 1948, 1969.

the bank note; the bank note begot the stock certificate; the stock certificate begot speculation; speculation begot the ledger; the ledger begot accounting; accounting begot the balance sheet; the balance sheet begot zero, and so all power of begetting was eliminated.

Such was the nature of the joking that went on as the System vanished. Some did not think the matter funny. E. J. F. Barbier, the librarian-diarist, wrote at the end of the year:

Last January I had 60,000 livres in paper. Its value was imaginary, to be sure, but I had only to cash in and turn it into money. I did not have the wisdom or the good luck to do so. Now it is worthless, and though I have neither speculated nor lost, today I have not enough money to give New Year's gifts to my servants.

Among those wiped out in this way were the widow of Racine, the great poet and dramatist, and Rigaud, who had painted Law's picture before the crash. Most of the Knights of Malta had sent money from their island in the Mediterranean to the rue Quincampoix for investment, and this was lost.

On August 15, the same day the convertibility of large bills was suspended, Orleans had a *tête à tête* with a rising young private banker, Isaac Thellusson, who had become imbued with a deep hatred for Law while still making money on the System. Law had tried to convince him of the soundness of his ideas, but Thellusson, only thirty, had coldly turned away when Law put his arm around him, and later Law heard the joke Thellusson started on its rounds in the financial community.

"I'm sure to make a fortune soon," he said. "I've rented every window that looks on the Place des Grèves, and when they hang Law, I can name my price for places at the spectacle." It was at the Place des Grèves that public executions like Horn's took place.

Law had reason to fear Thellusson's influence. He had strong connections with émigré Huguenot bankers in Holland, and in his meeting with Orleans, as Thellusson told it afterward, he discussed terms for helping the government over its financial difficulties with funds from abroad. He did not talk of executing Law, probably because the Regent had some good things to say about the Scottish wizard, but he did make it a condition of funding the government that Law be exiled. So at this date Orleans was already considering a restoration of the old methods of financing the King through usurious loans from private bankers. At this moment, the death throes of the System had their beginning.

Ivernois observed on September 19 that many people had sold their carriages and there was less traffic in the streets. He himself feared that silver plate would be called in to be minted in exchange for a mixture of bank notes and poor coins, so, with great difficulty, he sent his silverware to Switzerland. Shortly afterward it was forbidden to send such household objects abroad.

Law knew nothing of what was going on at the Palais Royal, and feared from day to day that he would be assassinated or executed summarily. Probably the Regent and Bourbon reassured him on this point, or else he might have taken flight as he had from London in 1694. He put as good a face on his situation as he could. He was virtually friendless. Dubois, though never openly hostile, kept his distance. Saint-Simon was no longer interested in receiving him at home. Madame had finally convinced her son that henceforth Law would only waste the Regent's time. So Law divided his hours between his house and the bank through the month of October.

Rosalba visited his home regularly, comforted Lady Catherine, who had returned from the country, and in September she started a pastel portrait of Law that was later acquired by Horace Walpole for his collection at Strawberry Hill (subsequently it disappeared).

By the end of the month, the bank's paper currency had reached about the same status that the old *billets d'état* had when Law arrived in France in 1714; the paper livre was at a discount of between 50 and 25 per cent and was hardly circulating at all. "Never has such consternation been seen," wrote Ivernois. "A large number of people fear they will die of hunger."

On October 10 an edict decreed that after the first of November all paper money would be withdrawn from circulation and could be used only for conversion into state bonds. The shares of the company were quoted at 2,000, which meant 400 livres in hard money—money that had been devalued several times since the shares were first issued. So by the end of the fall, both paper currency and stock certificates were worth so little that only speculators who specialized in holding paper over long periods of time were interested in having either of Law's creations (in years to come such people made a tidy profit, because the shares were manipulated back up to 3,000 in 1724). Voltaire remarked, "Paper money has now been restored to its intrinsic value."

Among the unverifiable stories that circulated at this time was that of the workman who killed his family and committed suicide by cutting his throat at a table piled with worthless money.

By the end of October, Law was virtually unemployed, though he went regularly to the bank. The Hôtel de Soissons gardens had been closed on the 25th. He no longer wrote memorandums. Instead, he pondered his future. The Palais Royal echoed with the jubilant voices of the Paris brothers, who had returned from their exile in country chateaux, and the talk now was of a new *visa*, another fiscal investigation that would attempt to satisfy hundreds of thousands claiming to have been badly damaged by the System and to penalize arbitrarily some who had made millions. Having witnessed disagreeable scenes during the *visa* of 1716, Law had no desire to be caught up personally in another. So he conferred with Orleans, who sought his advice about people to be appointed to run things in his absence.

The controller general's portfolio had not been handed to anyone since May. Law proposed his able but not too loyal assistant, Pelletier de la Houssaye; the Regent made the appointment early in December, after disregarding Houssaye's advice to throw Law into the Bastille! The bank, which Law said could still restore credit in France even in his absence, was to be dissolved as a matter of state policy. The victory of the private bankers was more complete than Law could have imagined, and he now wished to leave the country as soon as arrangements could be made. He trusted Orleans's word that the government would not molest him, but he realized that between Paris and the border of the Netherlands an ambuscade was always possible. He did not trust the provincial officials he would have to deal with, particularly the *intendants*, or royal governors of the provinces—the real rulers of France, Law called them, absolute masters of the territories they held for the King.

Another cause of his sleepless nights was the pending return of the Parlement from Pontoise. These fine arbiters of the law, who had once thrown together an ex post facto statute that aimed to hang him, might still have their way. His mind was made up, and he conferred again with the Regent, who was impatient to get him out of Paris and thus betrayed his own uneasiness about his ability to protect the man from whom he had obtained much, but who now constituted a threat to the stability of his regime.

It was agreed that Law would retire immediately to one of his chateaux, Guermantes, eighteen miles east of Paris, and there he would decide on his next step. A condition of his departure was that he must leave Lady Catherine and his daughter behind and travel only with his son, now sixteen and quite a worldly young man. His brother William would remain at the bank and look after Law's personal interests. As a final gesture, the Regent invited the entire Law family to share his box at the Opera the night of December 12, 1720. To the end, Orleans carried on his defiance of public opinion and kept off balance those who sought to use Law's disgrace for their own purposes. He thus kept alert the restored bankers, who were never quite sure of his intentions and were left to wonder whether some day John Law might be returned to favor.

Orleans would miss Law. There was no one else like him, and the prospect of a restoration of the fiscal anarchy of Louis XIV was unpleasant to contemplate. He was tired. Only forty-six, he was no longer strong. The plague was spreading through Provence, though colder weather always abated the fury, and Paris was protected by a rigid ʟordon *sanitaire* in the south. Nothing seemed to go well these days.

He listened gravely to Law's final words, reportedly as follows: "Sire, I agree that I have made grave errors. I am only human, and all men err. But I have acted always without malice or dishonesty." The Regent bid him rise from his bended knee. He needed no obeisance from his gifted financial adviser. It is said that he was deeply moved by Law's parting statement, and this is not to be doubted. However mixed his feeling, Orleans's actions until the collapse of the System showed that he grasped Law's purposes, which in general were in the interest of the King and the French people. It was dismaying, to say the least, that it all had to end so pathetically, that the forces of greed and selfishness they had both thought they could use for better purposes were to emerge more triumphant than if the System had never existed.

Next day, December 14, Law, his son, and a valet took their leave of Lady Catherine and Mary Catherine, and drove out of the Place Vendôme, five-and-a-half years after the family had arrived with such high hopes for a long and prosperous life in their favorite city. They were headed for a property Law had bought as an investment and which he had never even visited. Young John knew the chateau of Guermantes, though. A chip off the old block, he had made several visits there with girls he had picked up. But the old block was approaching fifty, and he had seen too much of life to be anything but depressed by his immediate prospects. His son's love life was the last thing he wanted to hear about as the coach, attracting little attention, swung onto the muddy road toward the Marne.

23

In Exile Once More

It was characteristic of Law not to have bothered to visit his property near the town of Lagny. He was strictly an urban man. In Scotland, none of his family had resided at Lauriston Castle, a short distance from Edinburgh. The possibility of staying in a retreat in France, perhaps farther away at another of his estates, Effiat in Auvergne, had been suggested by Orleans, but Law had requested that passports be sent for him and his son. He would die of boredom in the provinces—and he might be assassinated by some enraged victim of the crash. Law was uncertain, though, just how long he would have to stay in this district of Brie, famed for its cheese.

The chateau of Guermantes was known in the neighborhood as "*la belle inutile*"; the original builder had spent so much decorating it in bad taste that he had no money left to entertain in it. All but empty of furniture, it was looked after by a couple who were unhappy because through some oversight their wages had not been paid for months. It was a place to wait for passports. The sudden contrast between this vacant emptiness and the gay and comfortable life of Paris darkened Law's mood, and he longed for a reprieve from his banishment.

"Monseigneur," he wrote Orleans impulsively, two days after

arriving, "it is difficult for me to decide between my desire to with-draw from all public affairs so as to remove all cause of jealousy in those Your Royal Highness has put in charge of finances, and the longing that I have always had to contribute to your glory by the enlightenment I can give you on the way to reestablish public credit and strengthen a system that YRH adopted. . . ."

It was a naive and useless letter, which attempted to play on Orleans' well-known good nature and tendency to change his mind. What it probably did was determine the Regent on getting rid of the temptation either to consult Law or consent to hold him hostage to satisfy Parlement. There were those who wanted Law to suffer Fouquet's fate under Louis XIV—life imprisonment for peculation. Orleans showed the letter to the Duke of Bourbon and told him to get his friend across the border and see that he was taken care of abroad. Next day, M. the Duke sent the Marquis de la Faye to dis-cuss with Law arrangements for immediate departure. Something the Marquis said caused Law to write the Regent a second letter from Guermantes. Law protested his innocence in attempting to help in 1715 to put the Stuart Pretender to the British throne in contact with Spain, the mutual enemy of France and England. The accusation was probably by Dubois, blackening Law's name at the Palais Royal. All Law had done was to send the poor Pretender in Rome some money he had requested. Dubois's spies probably read the correspondence, and used it to suggest treason. "I have helped some unhappy people who lacked bread," Law explained in this letter dated December 17. In happier days, he would have had the judgment to ignore such gossip, but he was ill at ease in his state of suspension. Petulantly, he rejected a proffered sack of gold from La Faye and asked again for passports.

Finally, the passports arrived with an escort named Sarrobert, who delivered an impersonal letter signed by the Regent, which made no allusion to Law's correspondence. Father and son would travel to Brussels in a carriage belonging to Bourbon's mistress, the Marquise de Prié. They set out with Sarrobert early on December 20, avoiding Paris and arriving without incident at the northern border town of Valenciennes, fifty miles from their destination in Flanders. Here Law had a fright.

As bad luck would have it, the *intendant* of the province of Hainaut was the son of Law's old bête noire, D'Argenson. When the young man saw who was trying to pass out of the kingdom, he stopped him, despite the signature of the Regent on the two passports. With bureaucratic exactitude and considerable coldness, he announced that he would have to verify Law's papers, and it took two days for a messenger to ride to and from Paris, returning with an authorization signed by Orleans to let the Laws go on their way.

D'Argenson had no choice, but he could still do something nasty. Law was carrying 800 louis d'or, a sum equal to perhaps $16,000 today. It was all he had with him except a diamond—it explains his cavalier gesture of refusing money from Bourbon. D'Argenson confiscated the gold on the grounds that an edict of October 29 had forbidden all such removals abroad. He was technically within his rights, but it was a spiteful act he might have forgone. Law said nothing when D'Argenson attributed the edict to him; long before October 29, his power to issue edicts had evaporated. He was happy to be allowed to leave in one piece. Saying goodbye to Sarrobert, father and son went on to Brussels by night, where three days before Christmas they registered in the Hotel Grand Miroir, giving their names as du Jardin. It was the beginning of a new life for John Law.

Just a year before, the Abbé Tencin had led Law to St. Roch Church to receive communion, in a symbolic gesture that foretold ample rewards for his services to France. To be a minister of the King of France had been for Law the equivalent of a bishopric for Tencin or a cardinal's hat for Dubois. But tenure has never been a characteristic of government portfolios. Still, what amounted to banishment was a shameful disgrace in those civilized days, and it was all the more bitter because Law had that affection for France typical of successful immigrants who are grateful to their adopted country for the opportunity they fail to find in their native land. Now he was fleeing, with no thought beyond saving his skin.

He had entered France with a fortune and with a trunkful of

plans for its financial salvation; he was leaving empty handed, and his great plans were mocked by the collapse of the paper currency on which he had promised to build a French empire. Yet abroad there were important people who wondered if they might wrest from him the secret of instant riches. But it was no longer possible for Law to claim that if only he were allowed to establish a bank, he would do wonders for the credit of any nation. His future, as the saying goes, lay behind him, and he refused offers of new chances to show his wizardry.

In similar circumstances, good men have yielded to the death wish and committed suicide. Ivar Kreuger, the Swedish match king of the 1920s, comes to mind; but Kreuger was an out-and-out swindler, who forged Italian government bonds in attempting to cover enormous losses. Law had been guilty only of serious lapses of judgment, and the thought of doing away with himself never occurred to him. His object now was to redeem his honor and return to France. Meanwhile, he could count his blessings, because the Parlement had returned from Pontoise, and Houssaye before Christmas ordered the arrest of Bourgeois, treasurer, Revest, comptroller, and Fromaget, general manager of the company. They were sent to the Bastille, and Bourgeois and Revest remained there for some time, while Fromaget was restored to his job.

The tension over Law's departure was such that in the Regency Council at the Tuileries, with the King present, hot words were exchanged between the Regent and Bourbon over who was responsible for letting him leave the country. The Regent finally admitted that it was his wish that Law be gone, because he thought that would be helpful in restoring credit. Orleans also accused Law of issuing 600 million unauthorized livres in bank notes. In a series of cynical *beaux gestes*, most of the notables present agreed to give the government token sums because of the crisis; but these consisted of a few thousand shares of stock, worth almost nothing.

A report on this meeting, held Christmas Eve, reached Law through important people in Brussels, who insisted on feting him when they learned who the mysterious M. du Jardin really was. They included the Marquis de Prié, cuckold of the woman whose carriage had brought Law to town, bankers, and generals, all anxious to meet the great man, some hoping for a tip on money making. Law's great fear was of being seized by a French agent acting for creditors, since he now realized that he had been effectively stripped of his assets. His great need was to replenish at least a fraction of his lost gold, and this he accomplished through Belgian bankers who felt his credit was still good. He attended the theater and drew as much applause as the actors, and he responded graciously when toasted at a large banquet on Christmas.

A day later, he and young John disappeared from town. Brussels was too close to Paris for comfort: ". . . although the roads are very bad, I propose to continue my trip to Italy," he wrote Orleans. "The Regent desires that I withdraw to Rome; that makes me determined to do so. The enemies of the system would take umbrage to see me at the gates of France and would try to make trouble for me, even outside the Kingdom."

Alpine travel in January is still difficult today. John Law and son, obliged to go around France through Germany, took coaches up through the Rhineland and to Munich. En route, Law wrote Lady Catherine that she could write him care of the post office in Augsburg. They went over the Brenner Pass by coach and down into Italy, reaching Venice on January 19, 1721. They might have made a faster journey, but in Cologne they were held up by its ruler, the archbishop and elector, who unfortunately held 400,000 livres of Law's worthless bank notes. It required a few days to issue drafts on people who owed Law money abroad. The demanding cleric then released the travelers, and that ended the first of many harassments Law would suffer for several years to come. He was never again able to draw drafts, his credit having come to an end; all who owed him anything were considered debtors to the government of France. But in Venice he felt in a way at home, and there he was safe from his enemies.

An entire book has been devoted to Law's life between the day of his departure from Paris and his death in Venice in 1729. Jean Daridan in 1938 wrote *John Law, Father of Inflation*, telling the story, in a slightly fictionalized form, of Law's declining years. It is a sensitive and sympathetic study, based on much original research. More is known about Law's activities during this time than about his wanderings as a younger man before coming to Paris. But the fact is the story is somewhat anticlimactic and is essentially an account of false hopes and pathetic appeals for money, sympathy, and understanding of the System. The important thing that Law accomplished in his last years was to write voluminously and to leave behind a fairly orderly account of what he had done in France. There is not a great deal to say about a man who spends his life either at a desk or at a café table; much, however, has been published about Law's writings by students of money, banking, and economic history.

It remains, then, to account in somewhat summary fashion for John Law's movements during this time, and particularly for his new obsession, which was really but another form of his old obsession to establish a bank, issue paper money, and use credit to enrich a kingdom. This new obsession was to defend his ideas, his principles, his System, and his honor. While it was not successful during his lifetime, it must be deemed an ultimate success in view of the extensive literature that was subsequently written and continues to appear in praise and support of John Law.

It was Law's plan to settle in Rome, which welcomed refugees and protected them from foreign creditors with a grant of citizenship. Since creditors could always assign their demands to some citizen, however, Law decided against this move, which anyway the local British resident (ambassador) had advised against because of the continuing presence there of the Stuart Pretender. The British feared some kind of intrigue might develop. This left Law with much time and no money, and the story is he supported himself at the gambling tables of Venice. If so, he won hardly enough for all his needs.

Nothing discredits the legend that Law was a professional gambler so much as the way he gambled in Venice. It is a subject never mentioned in all his long correspondence. In more than sixty letters Law wrote between December and August, his need of money is one of the chief topics. He frequented the Ridotto casino, but his success was certainly limited. Montgomery Hyde says Law won

20,000 livres at one sitting, but even such a sum was a pittance compared to the demands of his creditors, and nothing is said of his losses. Law liked a sure thing, and a casino's odds favor the house. He enjoyed the social life to be found there, but it is ridiculous to suppose that Law was the kind of man who could break the bank at Monte Carlo.

"Last year I was the richest individual who ever lived," he wrote to the Marquis de Lassay, one of Bourbon's associates. "Today I have nothing, not even enough to keep alive." This was on June 14, 1721, a time when he was being dunned for £60,000 sterling by Cardinal Bentivoglio in the neighboring city of Ravenna. Pellegrini, who decorated the Mississippi room of the bank, was back in Venice, complaining that he had never been paid 100,000 livres and that Law should pay him personally. (Later the ceiling collapsed!)

Still, when offered a job in Denmark as director of state finances, Law wrote to Count Guldenstein, minister of King Frederick IV: "I want to live quietly. This republic pleases me. I esteem the princes who govern it. I am here comfortable, and I believe the longer I live here, the more I will like it." He concluded with a firm refusal to come to Denmark. He likewise refused an invitation from Fich, the Russian finance minister, to work for Peter the Great, saying that the Regent "had decided my situation."

Had he been younger and healthier—he complained now of rheumatism—he might have ventured forth again, but he must have realized how limited his energies now were, and his old aggressiveness was being crushed by the continuing pressure put upon him from France. Although few letters he wrote were answered, a day hardly passed without some new missive arriving demanding money. The cruel tactic of the French government was to maintain the fiction that Law had ample assets hidden outside of France and was just posing as a pauper for the time being. In Venice, this story was kept alive by the French ambassador, Fremont.

Why had Law not taken the precaution of hedging against the future with some deposits abroad? Law later explained it in terms of his naiveté and generosity, but there may have been more to it than that. "I had four diamonds worth £4,000. I gave them to my brother because of the law against export. He sent me one. That's all I took from France. I gave my brother my Scottish estates and with that income he supports my sisters, nephews, nieces who still need money."

This was his explanation in a letter to Bourbon in 1724 when he was being hard pressed by creditors. The letter continued:

If I had any plan I would have kept my brother in England where he wanted to stay. I gave daily to Frenchmen I scarcely knew more than is needed to put my relatives at ease. But I was French and consider relatives as strangers, being no longer established in France.

I have been offered the Principality of Massa in Italy and the Isle of Tabarque on the coast of Africa. M. Boissart proposed to reimburse me with sums the Dutch loaned the Emperor on mined silver ore. If I had been a dishonest man I wouldn't have missed the chance to make myself very rich and respected abroad. But, Monseigneur, my conduct has been the opposite, it has been that of a true and zealous servant of the Duke of Orleans and of France. My children, my brother, my parents, my friends can blame me for having so disinterested a conduct; I don't repent it, I have done my duty.

It is possible to accept this plea at its face value and at the same time wonder why a man who had always travelled light should *ever* worry about his material circumstances. Law had always landed on his feet and never had any serious worry about money since he was born. If he had been prudent, he would not have brought all his fortune to France. He had an irrational streak that caused him to behave in ways that proved self-destructive. The investment of all his capital in French annuities was hardly the act of a plunger, and it was putting all his eggs in one basket. Since most men are motivated by greed, it was not unreasonable for them to suppose that Law was consistently the same and had squirreled something somewhere against hard times. A man who considered himself the richest man who has ever lived may easily lose sight of the realities of fortune. Law was not the first millionaire to end his life penniless, for one reason or another.

In France, government accountants were busy adding up Law's debts, all of which were honorable and showed no sign of extravagance in view of the assets he had at the time he incurred them.

Because of the depreciation of paper currency and stock certificates, much of his wealth had indeed vanished—hundreds of millions!— but the indebtedness ought to have been similarly reduced. In any case, Law was solvent when he left France, but a few days later plans were made to confiscate everything he owned, and he was faced with debts only a bank or a government could ever hope to pay off. Eventually, the bill came to the ridiculous sum of more than 20 million livres. This was a new form of persecution, mental torture, in which Law's enemies took the satisfaction of suiting the punishment to the supposed crime.

Law was not the only victim. There were Lady Catherine and his brother William. It is at this time that the deep affection John Law had for his "wife" manifests itself in a series of rather formal letters. Whether his warm feelings were reciprocated at this time is a question. He complains of not having heard from her, but perhaps she was afraid to write to him often. She did manage to send him some money, which he thanked her for and explained how poor he was. But she could hardly feel sorry for him. French law now did its worst to make her circumstances difficult. The absence of any evidence of marriage made it possible for the courts to nullify the power of attorney Law had given her, so she was left at the mercy of handouts, forced to move to cheap lodgings with her daughter and sell off everything she owned just to pay bills—one from the butcher for 11,000 livres. Paris snickered about the Laws having lived in sin all these years. Actually, her husband was now dead and she could have formally married John Law had they been allowed to come together.

Plans were made for mother and daughter to come to Venice in the spring. In a long letter written on April 19, 1721, Law gives her elaborate instructions about traveling incognito via Innsbruck, not Munich, obeying health regulations in view of the threatened renewal of the plague as the weather warmed: "I want your company, and to live as we used to before I engaged in publick business. . . . I am better satisfied than when in the greatest plenty." He assured her that they could live wherever she liked.

Catherine found it impossible to obtain passports. Law wanted to believe that the problem was one of quarantine against the plague, and he hoped to meet her in Holland or England. "I am not satisfied you stay in Paris," he wrote on May 5. But he was up against a heartless bureaucracy, which was motivated by nothing but cruelty.

In May, for no reason, William Law was thrown in the Bastille. William was loyal to and proud of his great brother. He had come to France without enthusiasm when Law organized his bank, and had worked hard to assist him, rewarded generously with money, but never honored by an important title. He was no frequenter of salons or friend of the great, and he was not a threat to anyone. His only crime was one of kinship, and he paid for it with two years in prison. Naturally, he resented his treatment, and Law was not too sympathetic. "Brother," he wrote, like some Puritan minister, "I have received your letter, which tho full of complaints, yet I shall not take amiss." William learned something in prison, and that was that he could survive in France without John. It is a quirk of fate that John Law, who truly loved France, was exiled, his son never married, and so his family line died out; while William stayed on, raised two sons who served France with honor, and his line survives to this very day.

The combined impact of harassment by creditors, the absence of his wife and daughter, and the imprisonment of his brother changed John Law's mind about the Republic of Venice, especially as summer grew hot and moist. He had passed his fiftieth birthday in good health, and he was recovering his spirits and his *amour propre* sufficiently to want to move on. His restlessness was a sign that he was coming out of a depression that had led him to continue to address the most inappropriate letters to the Regent, Tencin, and Dubois. Pleading that he be allowed to recover the original 1.6 million he had brought to France, he offers to settle for 500,000 livres and ends with, "In case Your Royal Highness should find this too much, I shall be content with whatever you consider fit to determine." That was written to Orleans March 1. By June he is writing Lord Londonderry, to whom he is deeply in debt, "I can change the face of the affairs of Europe . . . I should never have engaged in the service of France if my pardon [in England] had not been refused me."

During July and August, Law's desire to return to England became a determination, and the way this came about is typical of the old John Law. He had been forgiven by the Wilson family for his crime of 1694, probably by arranging to pay them something, since impecuniousness was one of their characteristics. They had formally withdrawn the complaint that bound the courts to hold Law guilty of the murder of Beau Wilson in a duel. The legal document was in Catherine's hands in Paris, and Law wondered if it would be necessary to have it to obtain a pardon from the King. This technicality might be forgone with the help of his old Scottish friends, Lords Islay and Argyll, who were arranging for his return. Burges, the English resident in Venice, whom Law had been cultivating, got in touch with Whitehall, and enough assurances were given for Law and his son to leave Italy before September.

The ultimate means of getting to England are so curious, that no one has ever found out how Law arranged it. By this time he had learned the danger of documents, and he depended on Lords Londonderry and Carteret to clear the way in official circles. What he did was to travel secretly via Germany to Denmark, probably knowing that he could stay there grandly if anything went wrong because the offer to work for King Frederick was still open. He was received at court, but his interest was not in the Danes in Copenhagen but in his own countrymen there. Somehow, he cultivated the right people and managed, in mid-October, to be given a place aboard a British man-of-war, the flagship of Admiral Sir John Norris, which took him from Elsinore to the naval base called The Nore at the mouth of the Thames.

There was nothing secretive about the crossing, and two peers, Argyll and Londonderry, were waiting near by at the town of Rochester to escort the Laws to London. It was later to be asked pointedly in the House of Commons just how it happened that a felon seeking the King's pardon after a twenty-seven-year absence returned so grandly aboard one of His Majesty's naval vessels.

24

The Beau's Return

John Law's spirits on arriving in England were naturally higher than they had been on leaving France almost a year before. During that time he had not failed to keep abreast of what was going on in Paris, and once in London he came into possession of the horrible details about the *visa*, the investigation of finances, and the random punitive excursions against some of the "profiteers," the parvenu millionaires who became a convenient target for those trying to explain why economic conditions had soured. A veritable restoration of the old ways was in process, and this gave rise to a new hope in the breast of the former controller general that France would degenerate into such financial chaos that the Regent would be obliged to recall him. Like Napoleon on Elba, he longed to recover his lost power and glory.

In Venice, Law had had no serious objectives. He had lived from day to day, fending off creditors, receiving visitors such as the exiled Spanish minister, Alberoni, trying his luck occasionally in the Ridotto, writing letters about his impoverishment to everyone he could think of, trying to get his wife and daughter out of the clutches of the French. He was weary of this defensive posture. Now he would try going on the offensive again, aiming specifically to win over Orleans. The evidence seems to be that he was not discouraged in his aim by the Prime Minister of England, the formidable Robert Walpole, who eventually wrote to his ambassador in Paris: "If the Duke of Orleans is disposed to recall him, as Mr. Law's friends here are very sanguine of hoping, it is not easy to judge what is most to be wished for in this case, unless we know the competition and upon whom the favour and confidence of the Duke of Orleans might probably fall."

To get the British government into so positive a frame of mind that its leaders could see a benefit from having a British subject in charge of the finances of a great rival took John Law a year and a half, and he would be the first to say that it was French policy as much as anything that brought Orleans to reconsider the virtues of the System.

The *visa* that dominated the French domestic scene for several years was motivated by vengeance and greed, and its injustices were so manifold that it succeeded in its object: to turn back the clock and restore as much wealth, power, and prestige as possible to the *ancien regime*, which, lacking the mediation of a Louis XIV, spent the next fifty years happily digging its own grave. The policy of financial investigation had the support of a deceived populace. Saint-Simon, in an almost biblical style, observed:

Then the people saw at last where all the golden schemes that had flooded upon popular credulity had borne us; —not to the smiling and fertile shores of Prosperity and Confidence, as may be imagined, but to the bleak rocks and dangerous sands of Ruin and Mistrust, where dull clouds obscure the sky, and where there is no protection against the storm.

As history shows, in a dictatorship events can be manipulated to serve the regime. Although the System was fully supported by Orleans, he now fell back on the old excuse that he had been betrayed by Law. The books of the company and the bank had revealed no chicanery, but it was now accepted in the council on the Regent's word that Law had illegally overissued the King's bank notes. There was no substance to the charge, and anyone who thought about it would have realized that Law spent his last days trying to withdraw bank notes he had been obliged to print because of his policy of redeeming the shares at 9,000.

Saint-Simon would have us believe that Orleans had ordered Law to issue so many bank notes "to satisfy his own prodigality," but Saint-Simon had no understanding of what Law was doing, despite his weekly inspection of balance sheets. To overissue bank notes would have been to deliberately depreciate their value. The money was made by Orleans's friends on stock manipulations, and not on bank notes issued during the inflation.

Those in charge of the *visa* understood this well enough. The Paris brothers, whose anti-System Law had defeated and who had more or less been persona non grata in Paris for a while, were put in charge of the operation. They proceeded to turn it into a great bureau made up of no less than 800 clerks working in the halls of what had been the *Banque Royale*. Anyone holding either shares or bank notes was obliged to deposit them and explain what he had been doing during the more successful days of the System. Particular attention was paid to "those who had received shares or notes as favours due to their authority, and who could show no other title to them," noted Saint-Simon. His own monetary favors from the Regent, which he had used to substantially improve his property at La Ferté, were bestowed in such a way that no investigation could reveal them, but on this Saint-Simon was silent.

"Those who have lost are already ruined," said Barbier in his journal, "and now they wish to ruin those who gained."

Before this fiscal inquisition was over, 511,000 individuals had brought in 2.2 billion livres in paper money and contracts and 125,000 shares of the Company of the Indies. Whatever anyone failed to register was simply invalidated. It is a question whether some people would have done better by not reporting to the authorities. It was the obvious intention of the government to restore the status quo ante wherever possible, so that the comfortable classes who might have lost money were treated kindly and some were granted pensions (Racine's widow, for instance), while the millionaires risked being fined for their speculative audacity. The famous widow Chaumont, who had entertained so grossly with her win-

nings, paid a fine of 8 million livres for being presumptuous enough
to get rich quick. Some 187 million livres in fines were levied
against *parvenus*. Perkins observes:

> The crime consisted in the fact that a great deal of money had been
> made by people of small account. The government declared that those
> must be punished who two years before had been poor, and now pos-
> sessed riches above their condition . . . the name of no person of rank
> appears among those who were fined for their good fortune. The ex-
> emption of nobles from taxation was extended to their gains from
> Law's System.

An interesting example of restitution has been turned up by
Claire-Eliane Engel, who reports that the Knights of Malta recovered their losses incurred on the rue Quincampoix. Apparently
Law promised the grand master of the order, Zondadari, that he
would indemnify the Knights in the amount of 200,000 livres.
On January 5, 1721, Zondadari wrote reminding Law of the
obligation at a time when Law was en route to Venice and, of
course, unable to keep his word. However, one of Saint-Simon's
nephews, Claude Saint-Simon, had been trying desperately without
success to become a Knight of Malta, having failed as an Augustine
monk. An appeal to the pope had failed. It was a rule that no one
who had belonged to any other order was eligible for Malta.

Zondadari sensed the chance to revalorize the worthless shares,
and he had his Paris representative, brother of the president of
Parlement, find out just how interested the powerful Duke of Saint-
Simon was in his scamp of a nephew. When it was reported that
Orleans himself was concerned for the youth, the Grand Master
found means to waive all rules, and on October 5 wrote a note to
Orleans expressing appreciation for an expected annuity "which is
necessary to permit our religion to be able to sustain its obligations."
Claude became a Knight of Malta, and the Knights got their money
back!

The 2.2 billion livres in paper of one sort or another was declared valid to the extent of 1.7 billion livres and converted into
bonds at 2.5 per cent or annuities at 4 per cent. The shares were

cut down from 125,000 to 56,000, which were considered bona fide. The Regent intervened on occasion to protect friends, mistresses, or *roués* from an overzealous bureaucracy.

Then, finally, when the clerks had swept up all the paper, the authorities imitated John Law's procedure and began to burn everything publicly, just the way he had in the summer of 1720. If the smoke and flames had a sacrificial character, it was public probity that was being consumed, for into the fires went all pertinent records that could ever accuse the government of giving favors—or its favorites of receiving them. Those fires continue to inflame historians who search in vain for a detailed accounting of the distribution of Mississippi stock; no stockholders of record are listed anywhere. Economists are forced to rely largely on Law's own records in their discussions for and against the merits of the System, and in this sense the flames allowed John Law to have the last word.

John Law felt it vital that he be treated with respect by important people, especially when his own condition was so reduced, and he was angry to find that no plans had been made for his reception by the King of England. However, through Mrs. Henrietta Howard, mistress of the Prince of Wales, Law was presented to the non-English speaking George I of Hanover, who carried on with Law in French and granted him the pardon he sought. This reception at court, he discovered, advanced him little, since the King's incomprehension of English caused him to withdraw from public affairs and permit ministers to run the country.

Nor was the applause Law received at the theater or the stream of visitors who called at his lodgings in Conduit Street more than a passing solace. His continuing penury reduced him to begging for relief. To Mrs. Howard he wrote: ". . . is there nobody that could have good nature enough to lend me one thousand pounds?"

If people flattered him to his face, behind his back they blamed him for the South Sea Bubble. To de Lassay in Paris, he wrote shortly after landing: "I compared the credit of France with England's. You can see by this comparison that the directors of the

South Sea Company worked against England and that I worked for France." But in truth, Law's System had a worse effect on France than the South Sea Bubble had on England, where thousands may have been ruined but the Bank of England and the nation's credit were unscathed. He was never able to convince many people that there was a distinction between his bubble and England's. It all looked the same to anyone who had lost money in Paris and then in London; Law's high-minded intentions carried no weight.

Perhaps public incomprehension decided him on his project of justifying the System. He writes de Lassay that he is working on "a very curious task. It's the history of my administration." And so over the next several years he wrote and wrote, revising his theories as well as recording in great detail what he had sought to accomplish in France. When his *Money and Trade Considered* was brought out in Holland, he repudiated it, saying his ideas had changed since its appearance in 1705, at which time he had proposed that the Bank of Scotland issue paper money backed by land. He was not writing for posterity so much as for the purpose of reinstatement by Orleans. On November 17, 1721, he wrote Guldenstein in Copenhagen, "I now know the Regent will render me justice."

His desire to get back to France was apparently motivated as much by the need to settle his own affairs as by the desire to gratify his vanity. The money he had lost impulsively by selling British East India shares short had been assigned for collection to a man named Mendes, who pressed Law hard for £15,000 and threatened to have him thrown into debtors prison. "My affairs are come to a *crise*," Law wrote Catherine in January 1722. The text of his unusually candid letter to her on January 8 shows his confused feelings:

I had a line from you this morning of the 2 January which makes me a little easy, being you are better satisfied with the usage you meet with. I owne to you I have been much out of humor, when I reflect on the treatment I have received from France, and that is the reason why I don't write much. I would divert myself from thinking of it, lest I should say what perhaps might be taken amiss. Your retention, my brother in prison, my reputation attackt in the basest manner, my estate kept from me, and several engagements I had taken for the publick service, occasioning demands on me while I have not the necessary for my personal subsistence; I owne to you these reflexions animate me sometimes to that degree, that I'm not master of my passion. At the same time I'm solicited very earnestly to reingage myself in publick business, and have great offers made me. If I should accept one of them, I'll send my son to you. And since they won't let me have the satisfaction of living quietly with my little family, I'll show them that I'm not to be retained by ill usage. Those who advise the Regent to such measures venture a great deal, for my person is not indifferent. I'll finish my letter, for I grow angry.

By March, Law constantly fears arrest for indebtedness, and he offers to send his son to France as another hostage. "There is nothing I would stop at, rather than be reduced to that extremity [debtors prison]," he writes Catherine on April 11. This might sound like a suicide threat, but his despair was never that profound. Like a sensible Scot, he exercised to restore his spirits, frequently going horseback riding with his son.

Law's capacity for analyzing political and financial situations remained unchanged, but his views reflected not only a loss of boldness but also a growth in human perception. Although he knew it was in the Regent's interest to recall him, he wondered in a letter to de Lassay: "But where do you find men who know their true interests? Men are good and the difference is not in degree, it is that we make wrong judgments of men—the least and the most clever."

And to de Rosenberg, Serbia's finance minister, who had inquired about starting up a bank: "Your intentions are good, but you will, as I have already said, run into difficulties. Princes for the most part are badly advised, and follow false objectives. They seek to extend their influence, when they ought to be working to make their people happy. The honest man who wants to act in the public interest, finds so much opposition that if he succeeds, it is some kind of miracle. If men were reasonable it would be easy to help them find their interest in righteousness. But there are so many who prefer to profit from the present disorder, that it is too difficult to establish order."

Reflecting on English government to de Lassay, he remarked: ". . . here Lords are born legislators and think in terms of the government's interests." He added his analysis of France's foreign relations, saying that the Regent above all wants peace and is stronger by virtue of not engaging in wars. "In expanding industry France will be stronger than by conquests." So long as the Regent ruled, Law said, Europe would have peace. Of all Law's views, his most consistent was disapproval of war of any kind.

From the spring of 1722 until the following spring, Law lived obscurely and managed somehow to stay out of debtors prison and to write. He renewed his correspondence with Dubois, now a cardinal and the Regent's prime minister, and kept up his campaign for being recalled. A pension was granted him around April 1723 by the Regent, retroactive to his departure from France, and his hope of returning to Paris now appeared to have a solid basis. "If I were to start again, I would act otherwise," he wrote de Lassay in May 1723. "I would go more slowly but more surely and I would not expose the state or my person to the dangers which necessarily accompany the disruption of a general system." This message Law expected de Lassay to take to the cardinal and to the Regent. Another friendly omen was his brother William's release from the Bastille at this time.

With the pension came word that some claims against Law were recognized by the company as a sort of government debt, and he was relieved for the moment of the pressure of creditors. During the summer, Dubois began to fail, and his impending death led to speculation at home and abroad about the prospective nature of Orleans's government. Law advised the Regent in a letter to act as his own prime minister, and when Dubois died at sixty-seven on August 10, 1723, Orleans did just that.

Dubois had made many enemies. He had been ambitious, greedy, worldly, and treacherous to John Law, but he was an able man who understood Orleans and he had guided France's foreign affairs with consummate skill, maintaining peace and reestablishing French prestige abroad. This fact was acknowledged by those who disliked him, and the stock market sagged when his death was announced, a recognition that no one his equal would replace him. Law by this time must have realized that the cardinal had not been advocating his return. There would not have been room in Paris for both Dubois and Law, who were rivals for Orleans's attention.

Law probably shed no tears as his hopes soared. Jean Daridan's account of what happened during the next four months has the tone of a novel. In Paris, the story goes, Orleans was being importuned by the *roués* and others whom Dubois had banished from the Palais Royal to bring Law back and restore the golden days of the rue Quincampoix. In England, Law's friends celebrated his expected return to power in France with parties and arranged for claques at the theater and in the street to applaud the man they expected would soon enrich them. Supposedly, Law pressed Orleans hard by mail for an invitation, and was told by Orleans in reply to be patient and take a trip elsewhere until the time was ripe. The Regency Council considered the Regent's idea of recalling his old wizard of finance, and was blistered by the Duke of Bourbon, who said that public opinion would never tolerate such a thing. The Regent temporized, and then on November 28 said that he would make his decision in a week. He threatened *lettres de cachet* against the private bankers, who had put the finances of the King in a state worse than they had been in in 1715.

At this point Bully, a member of the council, wrote Law, according to Daridan, to return at once without waiting for a formal invitation, because he was certain that the Regent would reinstate him, if not as a minister, certainly in some financial capacity.

On December 2, Orleans was at Versailles, symbolic of the recovery of the *ancien regime's* influence. In the morning he drank some cocoa but ate nothing, and in the afternoon he continued to work at his desk on papers he planned to take to the King, now thirteen, in the evening. At six he spent a few moments with his son, a twenty-one-year-old royal playboy, and then the Regent received the Duchess of Fallari, his favorite mistress of the moment. She reported later to the British diplomat, David Crawford, that she knew at once the Regent was not well, and she asked him if he needed something. He replied that he had been upset by an argument between Saint-Simon and someone else over a minor appointment.

The Duchess, a pretty young thing, sought a minor favor for a friend, which Orleans agreed to with a heavy sigh; he then appeared to doze off and began snoring. Having had three attacks of apoplexy, his energies were limited and there was nothing new in this relaxation. He awoke, apologized, dozed off again. Then she heard a rattle in his throat and went out in fright to call servants. When they got back, Orleans had slid to the floor, and fifteen minutes later he was dead.

The traditional story was that Orleans died in the midst of a conversation in which he had asked her if she believed there was a God, and a heaven and hell, to which she replied affirmatively. Then, said the Regent, you are unwise to lead the life you do. The Duchess is said to have answered that she hoped God would forgive her. This is a legend, according to Claire-Eliane Engel, the most recent biographer of Orleans, who finds the report of Crawford, based on what the Duchess herself told him, not only more credible but more dignified.

Orleans was not deeply mourned by his contemporaries, and historians have dismissed him for his vacillating administration and self-indulgence. He deserves better. His willingness to allow John Law to reshape government finances and the national economy marks him as a man of vision who dared to explore means for a sounder and more just economic system. For all his personal extravagance, Orleans sensed the injustices that eventually had to be corrected by the fires of revolution. He was a man of peace, and he and George I gave Europe a much-needed surcease from war. He was circumscribed by his position as less than king, a role he would gladly have filled if Louis XV had died as a boy.

He was like Law in failing to associate with his equals in intellect.

The *roués* amused him but did nothing to lift his spirit. Law did that for him; he provided the break with convention that Orleans needed and which men like Dubois and Bourbon, with their ambition and greed, could never give him. His vacillation in matters of policy reflected his inner conflict between visions of what is noble in life and the glittering but largely empty character of the life of nobility in France.

The Regent was only forty-nine; not all men lived on like Louis XIV. With Orleans's death came the end of the Regency and the end to all hope that John Law might return to France. No new regent was named and the Duke of Bourbon became Regent de facto until Louis XV's majority in 1725 at the age of fifteen. Bourbon, who had profited from Law's System, wanted no part of John Law, and permitted the continued and needless persecution of the financier by the crowd of bankers who remained firmly in charge of the French finances for the next half century.

25

Death in Venice

Although all hope of returning to France in any capacity ended for John Law with the death of Orleans, he was only fifty-two and not yet prepared to settle for the life of a pensioner. Again, a veil is drawn over his activities. During the year 1724 he lived in London on Hyde Park with his son, who seems to have been overshadowed by his father, as so often happens to sons of the great. Young John followed the pattern of Law's own youth to the extent of debauching himself as much as his means allowed, but he apparently had neither industry nor talent, and he became totally dependent on his father, who no doubt was glad to have someone devoted to him at his side.

In the twentieth century, a man in Law's straits would be taken care of by a foundation or a university, and he would be encouraged to expound on his System by students and scholars and to write his reminiscences for learned journals and the mass media. He might even pick up pin money on TV talk shows. But, in 1725, all he could do was apply to the prime minister for work, not a pension, but a job of some sort. Law was once again penniless, the remittances from Paris having ceased after the Regency ended. But conversion to Catholicism, the very act that had assured him of high office in France, now blocked his entree into public service of any sort in England, where religious tolerance extended only to freedom of worship. Everything he had done in the past seemed to mock him, and he was an exile in his own country.

Why did he not try to publish his memoirs? Probably from fear of complicating his life. The public had deceived him once, and whatever he said could be misinterpreted. There was no money to be made, except by journalists or the famous who were supported by patrons. Law was not a literary man, despite his clear style of writing; he was a monetary theorist and polemicist, whose work was written for individuals he wanted to influence directly. By this time, he was through with money, and that was the only subject he could write about.

Walpole recognized Law's capacities, however, and he did manage to help him with a mission to Bavaria, which was to be carried out informally and without diplomatic sanction. Law's instructions were to pose as a man touring Europe for his health and to use his renown to insinuate himself into the court of the Elector of Bavaria. The objective was somehow to win this member of the Austrian Empire over to the English, with whom Austria had recently fallen out. It is worth noting that the cause of the disaffection lay in the presumption of Savoy, an Austrian client, in seizing Sardinia. Once again, Law's old friend Victor Amadeus was a hidden factor in his life.

So Law for a time became a secret agent in His Majesty's service, and he played the part with some gusto. First, accompanied by his son and a nephew named Hamilton, he went to Aix-la-Chapelle on the German frontier in August 1725 to take the waters. Law in fact was aging rapidly; he had asthma, and there were signs of a nervous disorder in the form of a facial tic and a sagging mouth. Sometimes, his hands shook uncontrollably. But he was as alert as ever, and his conversation was engaging and forceful. He entered into the lively social life that gathered around the baths of the imperial city, wrote letters to Whitehall in French so the King of England could read them, and signed them "Hamilton." He demanded instructions on the one hand, and offered grandiose diplomatic gestures on the other—such as going to Vienna to reconcile the Emperor Charles VI and King George I. Finally, a worried foreign minister, Townshend, ordered him to Munich in November, and in no uncertain terms discouraged any broadening of Law's mission.

Law was amply paid and in no evident hurry, for he spent a month in Augsburg, a day's journey from Munich, which he did not reach until January 2, 1726. There he made an immediate impression on the ailing Duke Maximilian Emmanuel, sixty-three, who wanted Law's financial advice and particularly needed a substantial loan at less than the 10 or 12 per cent interest demanded by usurious Augsburg bankers. Law saw an opening for England, and he suggested that arrangements might be made to obtain cheap money in London. The elector was delighted, and Law wrote at once to Walpole. Unfortunately, the Bavarian ruler died on February 26, 1726, and Law made no headway in getting to know his successor, Charles Albert. He did, however, win the heart of Maximilian's widow, Cunegunde, a Polish princess his own age, and that was one of his most gratifying accomplishments. He filed unwanted reports on the size of the Bavarian army and scouted the situation in neighboring Hesse-Cassel, but he sensed that he was not cut out for the role of secret agent, especially since the new elector turned out to be already very hostile to Austria. At the end of the year, Law asked to be relieved of his mission, and no doubt there were sighs of relief in Whitehall.

Law could have engaged in "consulting" in one or another German principality, such as Hesse-Cassel, but he was tired of being asked the "secret" of his System, which implied that some kind of necromancy rather than intelligence lay behind his theories and their application. By this time, his passion for finance had been diminished by a conviction that no place on earth was ready for his System because of the human limitations of those in power. He was alone, ill, tired, and afraid that he might again be the victim of arbitrary punishment if any difficulties arose in a country where he was employed to improve the financial situation.

In the winter of 1727, Law retired to Venice, assured by the Bavarian dowager electress, Cunegunde, that she would join him discreetly after a visit to Bonn, which she did. But Venice was not for her, and after a short visit, she and her retinue of six couples and thirty servants moved on, in fourteen carriages, leaving John Law with his son to enjoy his last days in the city he loved best after Paris.

Law was still plagued with millions of livres in debts claimed by the Indies Company, but no attempt was made to collect from a man who obviously had put nothing aside in other countries. The debts were quite specific, and Law objected to them on two grounds; namely, that he did not owe some of them, and those that were legitimate charges against him could be amply covered by the assets held in his name by the French government.

The sums were enormous: 450,000 livres for money sent to German families "in my own name. I did this to encourage the growth of Louisiana," Law explained to Bourbon. To Lady Tirconel was owed 100,000 livres; for lead for ships, 32,639 livres; sent to Marseilles during the plague in the name of M. Chavigny, 275,184 livres; and 7,435,342 livres for bank notes (which had been declared worthless in November 1720).

Law's explanation of this last sum reveals the corruption that existed at court. Law said he had transferred the notes to his account to be paid out to friends of the Regent for shares at 10,000, 12,000, and 13,500 shortly before he left France, when they sold for a few hundred. Why should anyone want worthless currency? Evidently, the Regent assured his friends that some arrangement would be worked out to exchange the paper for other securities. Law mentions a Mme. de Lauzun, who got two million livres of this seven million.

Law was said to owe a man 4.5 million livres for bonds, although he had a receipt showing that the man had received his money, and there was another charge of 3.5 million livres against Law for money he had paid out as subsidies to foreign powers on the King's account. Law worked up a very precise set of figures on what was owed *him*. He owed the company nothing by his reckoning, and the company in fact owed him 5.3 million livres. The current value of the original fortune he had brought to France was 2.3

million livres, but Law said he did not want to profit from devaluation and would settle for 3 million livres altogether.

He got nothing, and Crozat, the richest man in France, billed Law for 684 livres for a wall that had been built between their properties in the Place Vendôme! Law's properties bought during the boom were sold off at bargain prices to friends of those in power—79,000 livres for Charlevel, which cost Law 400,000; 8,600 livres for a house on the Faubourg St. Honore for which he had paid 73,000; only 26,800 livres for another called the Grand St. Martin, which Law had brought for 210,000.

It is supposed that Law now supported himself exclusively by gambling at the Ridotto, but the evidence is inconclusive and based on hearsay passed along by the French ambassador, Count Languet de Gergy, with whom Law had become friendly. It is impossible to know whether he had put aside some of his salary as Walpole's agent or whether the dowager electress provided him with an income. How else could he have afforded to resign as Walpole's agent? He now lived simply but in comfort like a gentleman, and the story that he died an absolute pauper is exaggerated; genteel poverty is more like his condition. It was his wife who really suffered from sheer penury. Driven from one lodging to another, she watched her belongings being auctioned off to pay creditors, and still she was not allowed to leave France. Presumably friends kept her alive with gifts for food and rent, a terrible humiliation for a proud woman.

Daridan has painted a word picture of Law in Venice in the style of a Canaletto painting—in a black cape and tricorn, brooding in the great Piazza San Marco, being greeted as a great man by the curious, ocasionally buying pictures, chiefly pastels. (Earl Hamilton believes he may have made a living as an art dealer.) That he was well known in the small, gossipy republic there is no doubt. Hyde believes he was received by the Stuart Pretender during his visit to Venice not long after Law settled there. His renown was sufficient for young Montesquieu to look him up, and there is a six-page report by the author of *The Spirit of the Laws* on the long conversation they had on August 29, 1728. This was the only event of importance that occurred during Law's final months on earth.

Charles Louis de Secondat, Baron de la Brède et de Montesquieu, then 39, was already renowned for his satirical *Persian Letters*, published in 1721, in which Law and his System were thoroughly derided. Law had not read the book, and this astonished the aristocratic philosopher, who assumed that everyone had. Law would no doubt have declined to talk to him if he had read Montesquieu's mythological fable about a child, son of Aeolus, god of the winds, who by age four had learned to count on his fingers uninstructed. Grown to manhood, this unnamed hero travelled the world with the blind god of chance until he reached a land called Bétique (*bète* in French means stupid), where he delivered himself of this speech:

"People of Bétique, you believe you are rich because you have gold and silver. I pity your mistake. Believe me, leave the land of vile metals; come to the Empire of the Imagination; and I promise you riches that will astonish you all." He then opened one of his bladders full of wind and distributed his "merchandise." (Montesquieu believed that money is the equivalent of existing merchandise in a country.) When the people of Bétique grew recalcitrant, he cried:

"I *advised* you to imagine and you are not doing so. All right now, I *order* you to." Finally, he diminished their wealth by 50 per cent, collected all their silver and gold, and made off with three-fourths of it.

Montesquieu's attack was savage and popular, but it laid everything at John Law's doorstep and neglected the eager collaboration of the Regency in the System. In dismissing the French as stupid, he was able to portray Law as the great corrupter of the people, whom Montesquieu as an aristocrat patronized. His distaste for paper money was rooted not in an objective examination of the nature of money itself, but in his fear of the revolutionary effect it had on society, which was opened up to opportunists, on occasion at the expense of the nobility.

Montesquieu was one of the greatest spirits of the Enlightenment, and the *Persian Letters* was the opening gun in a campaign against social injustice. It is to be regretted, therefore, that his conversation with Law turned out to be in a sense a dialogue of the deaf. Law obviously recognized in the young *philosophe* a superior intelligence, because he gave him as a present the only copy known to exist of a memorandum on "The Reestablishment of Commerce," written in 1715 but never presented to the members of the Regency Council, for whom it was composed in less than two months. Montesquieu did not think enough of this remarkable and sharply critical history of French commerce, which was found among his papers, to comment on it, and his own views on paper money remained fixedly negative. They can be found in Book XXII in *The Spirit of the Laws*, published in 1748. Harsin refers briefly in passing to Montesquieu in his *Monetary Doctrines* as contributing nothing to monetary theory.

What Montesquieu should have learned from Law was his tax theory and his application of it. Instinctively, they were both opposed to the status quo, but there was more than a generation gap between them. What Law might have learned from Montesquieu was how to talk persuasively with someone with whom he did not agree.

"He is hypercritical and argumentative," Montesquieu commented to the French ambassador, "and looks for a fault in your reply that can be turned against you." He added that Law remained brilliant, full of ideas and figures, and that he was motivated not by material gain but by a passion for his theories and concepts.

Probably neither of them knew that at the height of the System, when the Regent was profligately dispersing gifts of money Law had helped him make, a pension was accepted by the Montesquieu family. It has been noted that the nobility was amply protected by the *visa* from the adversity occasioned by the System. Moreover, with profits made on the rue Quincampoix many a nobleman paid off his debts in cheap money, and some sold their country properties at fabulous prices. But this to Montesquieu only confirmed the System as the great corrupter. His ideal aristocracy perished under Louis XIV, who destroyed the greatest noble virtue, the sense of honor.

Only a few more months remained to Law. Venice's damp climate was not good for him. In March 1729, a cold he had had for two weeks turned into pneumonia, and his death appeared imminent. The importance of this impending event may be judged from the attention given to the dying man by Gergy, the French ambassador, and Burges, the British resident. Both were friends of Law, but they also recognized his international significance. Since Law's important work had been undertaken in France, Gergy was more attentive, to the point of being overbearing—perhaps because the System had cost him almost 100,000 livres. But he genuinely liked the Scotsman; he had been his companion at many of the colorful Venetian festivals, parades on the Grand Canal, and fireworks celebrating the birth of the princesses of France.

Now Gergy, a devout Catholic, asked Law if he might bring a priest to administer extreme unction. Law consented and received the pope's ambassador to Venice. Daridan claims that because it was feared that Burges would attempt to wrest Law's soul from Rome, two or three Jesuits were stationed in his apartment until he expired. Burges confirmed their presence in a sarcastic dispatch to London, but since Law had never belonged to the Church of England, Burges had no interest in his soul.

To the end, Law was very much the materialist, and he scrupulously drew a will, which Hyde says was technically a *donatio mortis causa*, effective only if he died from the illness he suffered when it was drawn on March 19, 1729. Everything was to go to "Milady Cattarina Knowel" (the text was in Italian and Latin). Law was evidently concerned that if he referred to her as his wife, French courts would invalidate the bequest.

But what had he to leave her? He had reason to believe that Cardinal Fleury, now the chief of the government (he was not called prime minister), would have a new acounting made that would restore Law's French assets sufficiently to take care of the family. Concern for their future was thus one of Law's last emotions. His son John was present when he finally died on March 21, 1729, eight years and three months since he had seen Lady Catherine and their daughter.

Thus quietly passed away the financial meteor who considered himself to have been for a while the richest man in all history, and who certainly was one of the most renowned of public figures in his time. At a solemn high requiem mass in San Gemignano on the Piazza San Marco, sung by the papal nuncio, many leading Venetians and foreigners were present, and his remains were interred there, covered by a stone inscribed in Latin.

JOANNES LAW   WILLELMI FILIUS   EDIMBURGI SCOTORUM
IN SUMMO LOCO NATUS   REGII AERARII IN GALLIA
PRAEFECTUS   OBIIT VENETIIS ANNO SALUTIS
MDCCXXIX.   AETATIS VERO LVIII

His body was removed in 1808 to the Church of San Moise, and a more elaborate inscription now marks his final resting place:

Honori et memoriae Johannis Law Edinburgensis, regii Galliarum aesarii prefecti clarissimi, a MDCCXXIX aet. LVIII defuncti gentilis. Sui cineres ex aede D. Geminiani diruta huc transferri curavit Alexander Law Lauriston, Napoleoni maximo adjutor in castris, praefectus legionis, gubernator Venetiarum a MDCCCVIII.

It seems somehow apt that the memory of the ambitious financier should be linked to the overreaching Napoleon, who controlled Venice from 1805 to 1815, and that one of the governors of Venice, Law's favorite city, should be his grandnephew, Jacques-Alexandre, Marquis de Lauriston.

Epilogue

John Law was a financial genius who failed in the application of his monetary principles because he in fact deserted them. Distracted from his original and reasonable purpose of establishing prosperity in a depressed France, he allowed himself to be carried away by visions of personal grandeur. He careened to disaster after losing his sense of proportion. His own analysis that he should have proceeded more slowly is hard to disagree with. He had been afflicted with the modern disease of megalomania.

Perhaps on paper Law was for a moment the richest man in Europe. Who knows? What marks him out as exceptional, and not just one more acquisitive financier, was the keenness with which his mind penetrated the workings of international money exchanges, and the intensity of his vision of what really underlies the complex network of economic relationships and interdependence of groups of people. He saw that all commerce is a kind of gamble based on faith in the future. Credit can be obtained only when men believe in the stability of the society they work in.

For this reason, Law was a man of peace, for war is a destabilizer. In the Regent, he found a man friendly to the hated English and opposed to war for his own reasons. They came together quickly once Orleans had a clear idea of what Law was proposing.

But having helped with his bank to inspire a certain confidence among French businessmen, Law proceeded to expand their expectations as his own reasonableness gave way to fantasy. There is a term in psychopathology taken from the French, *folie à un, folie à deux*, meaning that the madness of one person can inspire madness in another—or, in other words, insanity can be contagious. The crowd caught Law's foolish optimism, and the fever of speculation was like the ravings of a lunatic.

Law's vicious response to adversity was that of one who for too long had had his own way and could not stand opposition to his wishes and hopes. But there was probably no way he could have saved the System once public confidence in it had faltered. The fatal flaw in his thinking and in his whole behavior was the belief that *any kind* of system is needed to establish a reasonably stable economy. All history before and since testifies to the stubborn resistance of men to a centralized "system" designed to determine their economic well-being. Even planned societies like the Soviet Union have, within the so-called system, many systems for evading its authority. We may talk of a capitalist system, but this is to give another meaning to a word associated originally with regularity of function—our bodies have digestive systems; the motions of the stars are systematic. The Newtonian spirit of that day inspired the model for Law's economic system.

He sought to bring the multiplicity of human wants and the infinitude of exchanges of goods and services under the governance of a single benevolent hand, his own. So long as he enriched the participants, he was rewarded with their adulation and gratitude. The collapse of his bubble was to some like the end of a dream and to others the beginning of a nightmare. In either case, rage and not reason dominated, so that for years it was impossible to perceive that Law's original conception was sound. Today, we implicitly accept what Law preached. Our money has value to the extent of our faith in a viable tomorrow and not to the extent of the gold and silver we believe we can obtain for it.

Was Law a charlatan, a scoundrel? Let us say he was not in the class of swindlers like Kreuger, the Swedish match king who printed phony Italian bonds for collateral. Law did not steal or embezzle. On the other hand, he did nothing to discourage the public's gullibility in believing that Louisiana was a new Eldorado. To say the least, his stimulation of the stock market in the rue Quincampoix was irresponsible. Much that he did would be impossible under the federal regulations governing Wall Street. He must answer for a great deal of human misery that followed the crash of the System.

Of course, the company John Law kept was worldly, and the Regent and all his crowd were the more reprehensible for making the luckless Scot their scapegoat. None could match Law's intellect, but most of them were shrewder than he—and greedier. That no one attempted to find a way to ease Law's old age with a decent sum of money, money that had been made by the System, says a great deal about the selfishness that was the chief energizer of the whole episode. Yet Law was incapable of making true friends who would stand by him. We can only guess that his early experience in London with the wrong kinds of people put him on his guard against intimacy and fixed in him a fatal self-reliance that was useless when his powers waned.

Little is ever said of the traumatic effect banishment had on Law. He was compelled to live abroad most of his adult life to save his skin. He made the most of the situation, but he was restless, as if searching for something he had lost. His obsession with banks and paper money, while characteristic of the period, was carried to a further extent by an enormous passion to prove himself. Perhaps he would never have amounted to much had he been able to settle down in London or Edinburgh.

His last years are rather pathetic, but not without dignity. His energies had been spent—in those days, to be in your fifties was to be in old age—and he was stunned by the sudden end of the System. To him it was quite clear that he had worked for the general good. And who can say that in jarring the status quo he did not set the French people to questioning the privileges of the *ancien regime* that restricted the rising middle classes?

It is not easy to see any lasting effects of the System, but it just may be that the fear of another bubble made it impossible to re-form French finance. The French Revolution, after all, was pre-cipitated by the King's summons of the Estates Générale, which he did for one reason: he needed *money*.

Appendix:
John Law's Legacies

Law's last hope that Cardinal Fleury would do posthumous justice to him through restoration of sufficient assets to support his family was not without basis. On June 18, 1729, three months after Law's death, an edict issued by the Council of State wiped out the claims of the Indies Company against him and his brother William. But the statutes were quite clear that any assets remaining after other debts were settled could not be distributed either to Lady Catherine or to her children, since she was not Law's legal wife, and the children were bastards and therefore had no legal existence. As for brother William's chances of inheriting, they were nullified by the fact that he had failed to take out French citizenship.

At this point, William bestirred himself on behalf of *his* large family of two sons and three daughters. He consulted a very clever nobleman jurist, Monseigneur Arman, whose clerk, Denis François de Montferrey, upon examining the records of John Law's estate, decided that no less than *4 million livres* might be left for distribution after everyone had been paid off at home and abroad. This money, less lawyer's fees, belonged by right to William's children, who were citizens and could inherit under the law. With this prospect in view, de Montferrey agreed to take charge of the education of William Law's children while he pursued matters through the courts.

John Law had not been in the least litigious, nor had his brother, but once de Montferrey was delegated to try to obtain the enormous fortune, John Law's brother and then his nephews and nieces were in the courts for decades. First, it took five years to obtain a declaration that John Law's nephews and nieces could in fact succeed to whatever assets there were. But the assets, managed by the court-appointed receiver, Péchevin, consisted largely of debts owed to John Law for various transactions and loans. If these were collected, there were the old creditors to pay off. Only Dickens could do justice to this case of the Laws "in chancery." Such was the system of inherited offices that, as the case dragged on, Péchevin was succeeded first by his son and then by a grandson, as receiver of assets that proved as illusory as the value of shares in the rue Quincampoix after 1719.

Perhaps it was as well that Lady Catherine was permitted to leave Paris in 1731 for Brussels to be near her son, John, now in the army in the Lowlands. John, who never married, died of small-pox in 1734. His mother finished her days in a convent in Liege, dying in 1747 at the age of about eighty-one. It was thirty years since her salon had been the center of Paris.

William Law died in Paris in 1752 and was buried in the same Scots College where his father had lain since 1683. To complete the story of the inheritance sought by de Montferrey (who by this time has disappeared from view), in 1779 a settlement was finally made on William's two sons and two daughters, one daughter having died. Daridan concludes his account of this legal comic opera:

Forced to give up and renounce their claim, the inheritors could finally add up precisely the inheritance of the richest of all uncles, reduced to the point it was carried to over fifty years by the most paternal of justices: they were obliged to divide in four the piddling sum of 37,545 francs and four sous.

John Law's daughter, Catherine, found herself rich in the end. Her husband, an Englishman named Viscount Wallingford, left her childless and a widow in 1750, but he also left her enough to live in a large house in London for forty years, where she was a well-known hostess. This brought to an end John Law's line. His brother William's descendants were more fruitful, and one of them was illustrious. Whatever prejudice remained against John Law did not carry over to his nephews, two of whom made successful careers in the Indies Company. Jean Law was both a general and governor of Pondicherry.

William Law's daughter, Jeanne, was the mother of the most prominent Law relative, Jacques-Alexandre, who was born in Pondicherry in 1768. When he was fourteen years old, his family succeeded in getting him ennobled by a decree of the *Conseil d'État*, and he became the Marquis de Lauriston. In justifying this sudden discovery of blue blood, an expert named Maître Alexandre Nisbet produced evidence from something called the *Traité Heraldique* to show that the Laws were descended from a long line of barons reaching back to the thirteenth century—*Law de Lawbridge, de Bogness, de Bogis, de Netherour, de Law-Burnton, de Newton, de Burntwood, de Canare, de Rumcois-Orientali.*

It may well be that John Law had it in mind to acquire a title, for he is pictured in some of the satirical cartoons with a rooster, which is part of the coat of arms the marquis took over, presumably from a Baron Law of Bogness. It is possible that John Law used a coat of arms, for his carriage was easily identifiable.

Lauriston became one of Napoleon's marshals, and it was he who arranged for his great uncle's reburial in Venice when the Church of San Gemignano was demolished in 1808. The count's name will be found today inscribed with those of other Napoleonic warriors in the Arc de Triomphe simply as Lauriston. Napoleon once wrote to General Lauriston in 1804, perhaps to spur him on: "Death is nothing, but to live defeated and inglorious is to die daily."

Lauriston had the distinction of being the only Napoleonic marshal to become a peer of France during the Bourbon restoration. He ended as a marquis, and his name is preserved for posterity in Paris in the rue Lauriston in the chic 16th arrondissement. His descendant, Count Louis Law de Lauriston, lives in Normandy. Family records now indicate that John Law himself was titled in France by virtue of estates he bought, and ingeniously it was discovered that the Laws in Scotland had claims to noble birth. Perhaps John Law might have sought a noble title had he been successful in France, but there is no evidence that he used the titles attached to chateaux which he had bought as investments.

The papers in Law's quarters in Venice, more than a hundred pounds in weight, were made into thirteen bundles and delivered by his son to Ambassador Gergy, who (with what right?) dispatched them to the Quai d'Orsay. The foreign minister, Chauvelin, kept them as his personal property, for the most part, and they simply disappeared. One set turned up in the Mejane Library in Aix-en-Provence. A few pieces of correspondence were given by Gergy to the British government and are in the archives. The fate of the remainder is unknown, and there is little likelihood that more will be found. What remained of his writings constituted his most valuable legacy, however, and has kept discussion of the System alive for more than 250 years.

During the eighteenth century, important defenses and condemnations of Law's work appeared in France, written by those who knew the finances at first hand. Then, in 1790, his *Money and Trade Considered* was republished in the French version, *Considerations sur le Numéraire* of 1715. Until 1775, memory of the System was the chief factor impeding the establishment of another bank in France. The confusion of the royal finances and the scandals of the Marquise de Pompadour discredited sensible but belated reforms under Louise XVI, and the leaders of the French Revolution, just like the Duke of Orleans, finding money hard to come by, eventually subjected France anew to a disastrous experience in paper money.

Law's memory was being restored by the publication for the first time of some of his memoirs (edited by General E. de Senovert), but his warning that he would have gone more slowly was ignored by the young revolutionaries, and the catastrophe of issuing too much paper money was almost a complete reenactment of the events of 1720, except that the agony went on longer and the amounts issued totaled more than a dozen times what Law had printed.

The *assignats*, as the money was called, began as 5 per cent government bonds secured by Church lands, which were declared to belong to the nation, but by August 1790, these so-called bonds had turned into paper money. Emigré propaganda discredited the new money by assurances that it would be repudiated under a restoration, and after war broke out in April of 1792, the bills were worth only 30 per cent of their face value. The bills were stabilized by price controls, but these controls were dropped at the end of 1794, and the ensuing inflation obliged the printing of more and more money, already at a total of 8 billion francs. John Law's old tactic of suppressing specie to force the use of paper was repeated, and with the same consequences. After two riots in Paris in the spring of 1795, the *assignats* were down to 3 per cent of their face value. When finally abandoned in the winter of 1796, the *assignat* issue came to a total of 36 billion francs.

Probably, the anonymity of the heads of the state treasury prevented an earlier demise; there was no John Law to blame this time, and another kind of *parvenu* made millions at the expense of the established middle classes, many of whom were wiped out by cheap money. The only element missing was stock market speculation in the order of magnitude seen on the rue Quincampoix.

As industrialization took hold in France after the Congress of Vienna in 1815, interest in Law's ideas was revived by both capitalists and socialists. Those looking for ways to fund the enormous projects of French railroad building saw in his notion of credit something of creative value, while socialists like Louis Blanc saw in Law's government-directed economy, as well as in his tax reforms, the spirit of state capitalism in which the control of money would rest with the government acting in the interests of all the people. During the nineteenth century, interest in John Law was widespread in France, and to a limited extent in England and the United States. Historians such as Michelet and Thiers wrote sympathetic accounts of the System, and Dumas fils dashed off a racy biography.

More of Law's papers appeared in 1843, edited by Eugene Daire, but the *Complete Works of John Law* (in French) in three volumes were not issued until Paul Harsin, after prodigious research, put them out in 1934. Some day, perhaps, these will find an English translator and will be edited for wider readership. Certainly, the hostility to his conception of credit has been diluted not only by time but by financial evolution. The world has long since accepted fiat money unbacked by land or gold (except in settling international balances), and is passing beyond the limited idea that money must be represented by a piece of fancy paper: a figure in a computer or on a bank statement is quite acceptable to almost everyone as evidence of the reality of any value from one dollar to billions. "To conclude that Law did visualize a paper money system similar to that employed today does not seem unjustified if one gives his writings the interpretation which he obviously intended." So wrote Frank Herman Beach.*

It is true that Law's writings are limited by their obviousness, and that his passionate arguments and defenses have a certain quaintness today. It is rather the man himself, his career, the boldness of his administration, his overreaching, and the injustice of his subsequent treatment by ungrateful and envious men of power that remains fascinating and indeed relevant to the frequent monetary crises that now shake the world.

Jean Starobinski, the French critic, has recently written: "The eighteenth century is remote enough to be another world, yet near enough for us to recognize here in their infancy our modern values, our political doctrines, and our intellectual disciplines. Exploring the eighteenth century is an indirect but useful way of examining ourselves." † To his list can be added monetary theories and practices, and we might say that Wall Street is but the rue Quincampoix institutionalized and better regulated.

---

* Frank Herman Beach, *Monetary Theories of John Law* [abstract of thesis] (Urbana, Ill.: University of Illinois Press, 1933, 10 pages, paper).
† In the *New York Review of Books,* March 22, 1973.

Another legacy that Law himself never spoke of after his disgrace was Mississippi itself, or more properly Louisiana. In France, Mississippi was a bubble, but in America it was a reality, and that was thanks to John Law. When he took it over from Crozat in 1717, the general area was scarcely inhabited—700 people lived there precariously. When he left France, there were 6,000, of whom 600 were slaves.

Historian Pierre Heinrich is hard on Law, particularly because of the forced emigration of colonists of dubious usefulness to the venture. Still, he credits the dreamer of overseas empires with giving the colony "a new life." *

Law's attention to his overseas responsibilities lapsed once he became controller general, so he really devoted only a small portion of his time to the management of the company's foothold on the Gulf of Mexico. The collapse of the System was ruinous for Louisiana, and the population soon declined from death and emigration. Its chief problem was the lack of food, which had to be largely shipped from France.

Its subsequent history, prior to the Louisiana Purchase of 1803, was not illustrious. The Indies Company never prospered, and in 1732 it had, like Crozat, to abandon its concessions and become a crown colony and a financial drain. It was therefore not entirely with regret that France, after defeat in the French and Indian War gave up New Orleans and the territory west of the Mississippi River to Spain in 1762, and that east of the river to England. During the American Revolution, Spanish Louisiana supported the colonies.

The Mississippi River had by this time become an important commercial artery and New Orleans a prosperous port. Cotton was not yet king, and Napoleon was first consul in 1800 when the secret Treaty of Ildefonso returned the Spanish sector to France. Napoleon's objective was to cultivate grain in the western plains and supply the island of San Domingo (Haiti) once he had subdued the rebellious black liberator, Toussaint L'Ouverture. French reacquisition of Louisiana by stealth alarmed the young American

* Pierre Heinrich, *La Louisiane sous La Compagnie des Indes, 1717–31* (Paris, 1907).

republic, and this led to the famous $15 million Louisiana Purchase. Napoleon's failure to crush the black republic of Haiti had taken the heart out of his American plans, and he accepted Jefferson's cash in order to strengthen his army for a British invasion that never came off.

Hodding Carter has written a history of Louisiana, entitled *John Law Was Not All Wrong*. Law's development of Louisiana was of course ad hoc, an accident of fortune. He needed a project overseas in order to satisfy his conviction that, with sound credit, France could compete with England and Holland in foreign trade. Crozat's abandonment of his concession in the bayous was that of a shrewd businessman cutting his losses. The trouble was that Law had not informed himself about the territory and then worked out a development plan that involved some sense of time. Had he done so, he probably would have lost interest in proceeding. He was a man in a hurry, and the gestation period for Louisiana appears to have been about one century.

It should not be overlooked that Law was not alone in his project. Little effort was necessary to inflame the public imagination in what became, in Mackay's phrase, an extraordinary popular delusion. The colonial examples of England and Holland provided ample warrant for a belief that a bigger, richer, and more powerful France should have its share of the new wealth, and it was justified, too, by a certain success in Canada, particularly in the profitable fur trade, which Law quickly assimilated in the System.

Law was correct in asserting the need to place large numbers of people in Louisiana, but he was at a loss to implement it. When the California gold rush ocurred in the following century, no less than 30,000 Frenchmen made the long journey to California to seek their fortune, drawn by exactly the same kind of propaganda that had failed to impel emigration in Law's day. By then, passenger sea transportation had become a profitable business, and like the airlines now, shipping companies lured customers with pamphlets entitled "The Gold Harvest," "The New World," and "Eldorado" (a term frequently used for Mississippi during the System). San Francisco's first trolley car line was built by a Frenchman, François Pioche, a financier who unlike Law settled abroad, but like Law lost his fortune (and committed suicide).

Law, for all his faith in colonialism, had no desire to visit the New World. It might have provided a new chance for him in the 1720s, but by then he was too obsessed with the past to look to an adventurous future in America. His concession, in which he invested heavily, was among the assets of his estate that were never realized in the final accounting of the probate court in Paris.

Louisiana led Law into the slave trade, and brief though his administration was, he stimulated its expansion, particularly in the port city of Nantes, famed headquarters of the Catholic League, where toleration of the Huguenots was promulgated. In a subsequent period of seventy years, 263,000 slaves were traded by the businessmen of Nantes, who built a magnificent classical square above the port from which they shipped their "ebony," as they called the Africans. Nantes became second to Marseilles in commercial activity. This was a discredit to civilized France, but even Voltaire, while denouncing slavery, invested in it.

Finally, Lorient in Brittany developed because of Louisiana from a fishing village into a substantial port during Law's time; it was for all purposes a company town.

A few years ago, when the American government was campaigning to increase the number of European tourists to the United States, among the full-page ads appearing in the French press was one dominated by a picture of a Mississippi River paddle steamer. Madison Avenue had been advised by Paris that the romance "du Far West," as Mississippi is thought of, is not dead in the French imagination.

Selected Bibliography

Much of the material related to John Law is in French and available only in libraries with extensive French language collections. Only a few of the most important of these sources are listed.

WORKS OF JOHN LAW

Money and Trade Considered with a Proposal for Supplying the Nation with Money. Edinburgh, 1705; New York, 1966.

Oeuvres de Jean Law. E. de Senovert, editor. Paris, 1790.

Economists Financières du XVIIIe Siècle. Eugene Daire, editor. Paris, 1843.

John Law, Oeuvres Complètes. 3 vols. Paul Harsin, editor. Paris, 1934.

Law's unpublished letters are in the Bibliothèque Mejanes, Aix-en-Provence. Other unpublished materials are in public libraries and archives in Paris, Nantes, Brussels and London.

BIOGRAPHIES OF JOHN LAW (in chronological order)

Wood, John Philip. *The Life of John Law of Lauriston.* Edinburgh, 1824.

Cochut, Andre. *Law, Son Système et Son Epoque.* Paris, 1853.

Thiers, Louis Adolphe. *Histoire de Law.* Paris, 1858.

Oudard, Georges. *The Amazing Life of John Law.* Translated by G.E.C. Massé. New York: Harcourt, Brace & Company, 1928.

Daridan, Jean. *John Law, Père de l'Inflation.* Paris, 1938.

Hyde, H. Montgomery. *John Law, The History of an Honest Adventurer.* London, 1948, 1969.

ARTICLES

Carriere, Charles. "Le Commerce de Marseille et le Système de Law." *Actes*, 1956.

Davis, Andrew M. "Law's System, an Historical Study." *Quarterly Journal of Economics*, VI, 1886.

Hamilton, Earl J. "Prices and Wages at Paris Under John Law's System." *Quarterly Journal of Economics*, November, 1936.

Mann, Fritz K. "Les Projets de Retour en France de John Law." *Revue d'Histoire des Doctrines Economiques et Sociales*, 1910.

Pereire, Emile and Isaac. "Le Systeme de Law." *Enquete sur la Banque de France*, 1865.

Sicard, Roger. "Les Consequences du Systeme de Law à Toulouse." *Actes*, 1956.

Wasserman, M. J. and F. H. Beach, "Some Neglected Monetary Theories of John Law." *American Economic Review*, December, 1934.

Wilson, E. B. "John Law and John Keynes." *Quarterly Journal of Economics*, May, 1948.

MEMOIRS

d'Argenson, Marquis. *Journal et Memoires*. Paris, n.d.

Barbier, E. J. F. *Journal*. Paris, 1847.

Buvat, Jean. *Journal de La Régence*. Paris, 1865.

Dangeau, Marquis de. *Memoires*. Paris, 1917.

Elizabeth-Charlotte of Bavaria. *The Letters of Madame*. Translated by Gertrude S. Stevenson. New York: D. Appleton & Co., 1924.

Saint-Simon, Louis Duc de. *Memoires*. A. M. De Boislisle, editor. Paris 1918–26.

GENERAL

Angell, Norman. *The Story of Money*. New York: Frederick A. Stokes Company, 1929.

Anonymous. *Law et Les Chemins de Fer*. Paris, 1845.

Baldick, Robert. *The Duel: A History of Duelling*. New York: Clarkson N. Potter, Inc., 1966.

Baring-Gould, S. *Family Names and Their Story*. London, 1910. (Reprint of 1910 ed. by Genealogical Publishing Co., Baltimore, Md., 1968, and by Gale Research Co., Detroit, Michigan, 1969.)

Beljame, Alexandre. *La Prononciation du Nom de Jean Law le Financier*. Paris, 1891.

Blanc, Louis. *Histoire de la Révolution Française*. Paris, 1847.

Boulenger, Jacques. *The Seventeenth Century in France*. Gloucester, Mass.: Peter Smith, Publisher, Inc., 1963.

Carriera, Rosalba. *Journal de Rosalba Carriera Pendant son Séjour à Paris.* Paris, 1865.

Carswell, John. *The South Sea Bubble.* Palo Alto: Stanford Univ. Press, 1960.

Defoe, Daniel. *An Essay Upon Projects.* London, 1697.

————. *The True-Born Englishman.* London, 1703.

Engel, Claire-Eliane. *Le Régent.* Paris, 1969.

Fairley, John A. *Lauriston Castle.* Edinburgh, 1925.

Flynn, John T. *Men of Wealth.* New York: Simon & Schuster, Inc., 1941.

Ford, Franklin L. *Robe & Sword.* New York: Harper & Row, Inc., 1965, Torchbook.

Fortbonnais, François Veron de. *Recherches et Considérations sur les Finances de France, 1595–1721.* Paris, 1758.

Gaffarel, Paul, and M. de Duranty. *La Peste de 1720.* Paris, 1911.

Gardel, Henri. *La Monnaie et Le Change.* Paris, 1947.

Gayarre, Charles. *History of Louisiana.* New York, 1866. (There is a reprint of original edition by AMS Press, Inc., New York and by Claitors Pub. Div., Baton Rouge, La.)

Gilbert, Felix., ed. *The Norton History of Modern Europe.* New York: W. W. Norton & Co., 1971.

Gravier, Henri. *La Colonisation de la Louisiane.* Paris, 1904.

Hanotaux, Gabriel, and Alfred Martineau. *Histoire des Colonies Françaises.* Paris, n.d.

Harsin, Paul. *Les Doctrines Monétaires et Financières en France du XVI aut XVIII Siecle.* Paris, 1928.

Hatton, Ragnhild N. *Europe in the Age of Louis XIV.* New York: Harcourt, Brace, Jovanovich, Inc., 1969.

Hautchamp, Marmont du. *Histoire du System.* Paris, 1739.

Heinrich, Pierre. *La Louisiane sous La Compagnie des Indes, 1717–31.* Paris, 1907.

Hill, Christopher. *The Century of Revolution, 1603–1714.* New York: W. W. Norton & Co., 1966. Norton Lib. paperback.

Joliez, M. Alphonse. *Une Preface au Socialisme ou Le Système de Law et la Classe aux Capitalistes.* Paris, 1848.

Keynes, John Maynard. A Treatise on Money. Vol. 5 (pt. I) & vol. 6 (pt. II) in *The Collected Writings.* New York: St. Martin's Press, Inc., 1972.

Kunstler, Charles. *La Vie Quotidienne sous la Régence.* Paris, 1960.

Leclercq, Dom. *Histoire de la Régence.* Paris, 1921.

LeMontey, P. E. *Histoire de la Régence.* Paris, 1832.

Letwin, William. *The Origins of Scientific Economics.* New York: Doubleday & Co., Inc., 1965.

Levasseur, E. *Recherches Historiques sur le Systeme de Law*. Paris, 1854.

Lewis, W. H. *The Splendid Century*. New York: William Morrow & Co., 1971, paper.

——. *The Sunset of the Splendid Century*. New York, 1965.

Luthy, Herbert. *La Banque Protestante en France*. Paris, 1959.

Mackay, Charles. *Extraordinary Popular Delusions and the Madness of Crowds*. Wells, Vermont, 1932.

Michelet, Jules. *Histoire de France*, vol. XIV. Paris, 1887.

Montague, Lady Mary Wortley. *Complete Letters*. 3 vols. Robert Halsbrand, ed. New York: Oxford Univ. Press, 1965–1967.

Montesquieu, Le Baron Albert de. *Voyages de Montesquieu*. Paris, 1894.

Oudard, Georges. *Vieille Amérique: La Louisiane au Temps des Français*. Paris, 1931.

Palmer, R. R. *The World of the French Revolution*. New York: Harper & Row, Inc., 1972, Torchbook.

Perkins, J. P. *France Under the Regency*. Boston: Houghton Mifflin Company, 1901.

Prebble, John. *The Lion in the North*. New York: International Pubns. Service, 1971.

Prévost, L'Abbé. *Manon Lescaut*. New York: E. P. Dutton & Co., 1966, Everyman's Lib.

Rist, Charles. *Histoires des Doctrines Relatives au Credit a la Monnaie*. Paris, 1938.

Rochegude, Marquis de., and Jean-Paul Clebert. *Les Rues de Paris*. Paris, 1958.

Sedillot, René. *Histoire des Colonisations*. Paris, 1958.

Smith, Adam. *The Wealth of Nations*, London, 1776. Reprinted in many editions in the years since, with the most readily available for the general reader being the Everyman, Penguin and Modern Library editions.

Thompson, J. M. *European History 1484–1789*. New York: Harper & Row, Inc., 1969, Torchbook.

Tocqueville, Alexis de. *L'Ancien Régime et la Révolution Française*. Vol. 1. Paris, 1856. Available in paperback as a Doubleday Anchor book.

Trevelyan, G. M. *Illustrated English Social History*. New York: David McKay Co., 1949–1952.

Trintzius, René. *John Law et la Naissance du Dirigisme*. Paris, 1950.

Vauban, Marquis de (Sebastien Le Prestre). *Dîme Royale*. Paris, 1707.

Winsor, Justin. *Mississippi Basin: The Struggle in America Between England and France, 1697–1763*. Boston: Houghton Mifflin Co., 1895.

Index